Zane Grey

Revised Edition

Twayne's United States Authors Series

Kenneth E. Eble, Editor

University of Utah

TUSAS 218

ZANE GREY
(1872–1939)
Photograph courtesy of Dr. Loren Grey.

Zane Grey

Revised Edition

By Carlton Jackson

Western Kentucky University

Twayne Publishers
A Division of G. K. Hall & Co. • *Boston*

Zane Grey, Revised Edition
Carlton Jackson

Copyright 1989 by G. K. Hall & Co.
All rights reserved.
Published by Twayne Publishers
A Division of G. K. Hall & Co.
70 Lincoln Street
Boston, Massachusetts 02111

Copyediting supervised by Barbara Sutton.
Book production by Janet Z. Reynolds.
Book design by Barbara Anderson.

Typeset in 11 pt. Garamond
by Compset, Inc., Beverly, Massachusetts.

Printed on permanent/durable acid-free paper
and bound in the United States of America

Library of Congress Cataloging-in-Publication Data

Jackson, Carlton.
    Zane Grey.

    (Twayne's United States authors series ; TUSAS 218)
    Bibliography: p.
    Includes index.
    1. Grey, Zane, 1872–1939—Criticism and interpreta-
tion.   2. Western stories—History and criticism.
I. Title.   II. Series.
PS3513.R6545Z69   1989   813'.52   88-35777
ISBN 0-8057-7543-9

For Pat

Contents

About the Author

A native Alabaman, Carlton Jackson has been a professor of history at Western Kentucky University since 1961. He has had three senior Fulbright lecturing awards to India, Pakistan, and Bangladesh. He has lectured for the U.S. Information Agency in a dozen countries in Europe, Asia, and South America. In 1981 he was a visiting professor at the University of Graz, in Austria.

Professor Jackson is the author or co-author of eleven other books, and he has contributed some two dozen articles and short stories to various journals. Since 1982 he has been the book review editor of the Bowling Green *Park City Daily News*. Before going into teaching in 1957, he was a photojournalist for the Birmingham, Alabama *Post-Herald*.

Professor Jackson attended New Mexico Western University, University of Maryland, and Exeter College. He obtained his B.A. and M.A. degrees from Birmingham-Southern College and his Ph.D. from the University of Georgia.

Preface

When the first edition of *Zane Grey* was published in 1973 I was positive that everything—academically at least—had been said about the author that needed to be said. The ensuing fifteen years, however, have shown me how wrong I was in that supposition. Interest in Zane Grey—academic and otherwise—seems to be an undying phenomenon, and enough activity has taken place in the past decade and a half to warrant yet another look at the writer who at one time was the third best-seller in American literary history.

Perhaps the most significant development is that teachers of English literature seem to have a new interest in Zane Grey. Generally in the past, English teachers have treated the western novelist with disdain, denying him any consideration as a serious member of the literati. However, Grey seems to accommodate the nostalgic moods to which Americans seem prone, moods recalling times deemed to be simpler, more romantic, and less complicated than the present. Since a few English teachers at least believe their curriculum should, to some extent, reflect the times in which they live and the interests they embody, Zane Grey's works have begun to receive more academic attention than in the past. If the interest of high school teachers and university professors in Grey during the past fifteen years is any kind of index (and I believe it is), Zane Grey's sales in the bookstores may continue to dwindle, but his works will receive increased scholarly attention.

Throughout his life, Zane Grey was known primarily as a writer of romantic novels of the American West. His characters often were stereotyped, and his prose was sometimes forced and stilted. Still, his eighty-five books have sold over forty million copies in twenty different languages. He had so many unpublished book manuscripts (some had appeared in serial form in magazines) at the time of his death in 1939 that his publisher, Harper's decided to publish one a year until the supply was exhausted. The last one, *Boulder Dam,* appeared in 1953.

Grey regarded romanticism as tantamount to love. The Great West encouraged "love affairs" with nature, especially the wild beauty of open spaces, and with rugged individualism. Grey wrote about the West in the way that non-Westerners wanted him to. He developed a

western mythology that, along with the frontier theory of Frederick
Jackson Turner, helped to turn the West into the most romanticized
area of the United States. The West, to Grey, was as much an idea as
it was a geographical region. Perhaps the West did not offer the charm
with which Grey, Owen Wister, and others endowed it, but that was
not the most important point. The significant thing was that Americans *thought* the West had all those qualities.

Images that people have of an area often constitute its reality, and
in "image-making," Grey excelled. It would be incorrect to claim that
Grey built *only* a western mythology. His characterizations constitute
the weakest aspect of his writing. He exercised the novelist's license of
creating his own characters and of giving them the traits he wanted
them to have. Thus, many of his characters were not true to life; they
had superhuman qualities that few real people could approach.

Despite this weakness in characterization, Grey's descriptions of the
West were accurate, and most of the major events he talked about were
historically authentic. Thus Grey chronicled an entire era of American
history, and it is this aspect of his work that is most important. In *The
U.P. Trail,* for example, he wrote knowingly about the corrupt mach-
inations of the Credit Mobilier, and in *The Desert of Wheat* and *The Call
of the Canyon,* he described the swiftly changing social scene in America
and the shabby treatment given to veterans of World War I. In ad-
dressing himself to historical and contemporary problems, Grey was
much more than a "writer of westerns."

Grey's career led almost automatically to the question: can an author
be excellent and popular at the same time? Many people felt that the
two qualities were mutually exclusive—that only time could produce
popularity for an excellent writer. In respect to Grey, his novels from
1915 through the mid-1920s were on the best-selling lists, with only
the Bible and McGuffey's Readers outselling them. This fact certainly
attests to his contemporary popularity. If the mark of excellence de-
pends on time, Grey's books in the 1960s were still selling over a
million copies a year. They continue to serve as models for many movie
and television shows, and popular abridgments of his works sell rapidly
in England and the Commonwealth countries.

Perhaps the continuing fascination with Grey is generated by the
lure of escapism—fiction that does not attempt to do anything but
entertain. The Grey abridgments omit many descriptive passages included in the early editions, leaving mostly the action, and this magnified action may have kept Grey popular. The abridgments, partially

eliminating historical settings and descriptions, and stressing action, did not represent attempts to edit out inferior parts of his work but were merely an adjustment to changing reading habits.

It could also be Grey's treatment of a minority group that partially causes his readership to flourish. In our own era, much stress has been placed on equal and humanitarian treatment of minorities. Grey advocated this for the American Indian long before the concept became fashionable. Grey cared about the things he described in his pages, and his sincerity came across to the reader, and still does.

This study attempts to explain how and why Grey became a writer of western novels and to show the significance of his writing to American literature. No full-scale biography of Grey is attempted; his personal life is discussed only as it relates to his publishing record. The novels have been categorized, and representative novels of each category are discussed in some detail, while others are mentioned only to show thematic development and points of view. An effort has been made to give a critical assessment of Grey's works and to establish a rationale in which his contributions to literature may be evaluated.

I have not included in this study the novel by Grey that is still unpublished, *George Washington, Frontiersman.* Nor have I dealt with Helen Cody Westmore and Zane Grey, *Last of the Great Scouts,* for Grey wrote only the foreword and the conclusion of this book. Grey also wrote a chapter in *The Woman Accused,* and there is talk among Grey fans of a "lost" novel, *Heart of the Desert.* I have made no effort to treat these books here.

The major revision I have made in this edition of *Zane Grey* is the addition of a new chapter—chapter 9—to show what has happened to Zane Grey studies since 1973. Provided the opportunity to improve the old, I have also added and deleted wherever I thought appropriate. Maybe by the time the third edition comes around in another fifteen years, I'll get things just right!

I am still most grateful to those people and institutions that helped me with the 1973 book. They include Mary Clarke, Eleanora Evans, Joseph Slade, J. Crawford Crowe, Betty Mount, Sylvia Bowman, Sharon Buchanan, and Norris Schneider, as well as the staffs at the Library of Congress, University of Texas, New York Public Library, *Markham Review,* and Bowling Green, Kentucky, Public Library.

Many people helped me in the revised edition, and I wish to extend my thanks to them. My friend and colleague, Professor Lowell Harrison, read the original manuscript in 1973, and so I asked him to favor me again with chapter 9. Susan Tucker and her staff at the Interlibrary Loan Department at Western Kentucky University were indispensable to my work. My student assistant, Charles Borders, performed dozens of tasks for which I am grateful.

Other people I wish to thank are Dr. Loren Grey, Zane's son and president of Zane Grey, Inc., and Betty Zane Grosso, Zane's daughter. Both Loren and Betty have been courteous and helpful to me in my work on their father, and I am appreciative. My old friend, G. M. Farley, of Hagerstown, Maryland, came through, as he always does, with excitement and enthusiasm whenever the subject turns to Zane Grey. Joe Wheeler, Charles Pfeiffer, Cena Richeson, and James Vickers helped in this revision.

I must say a final word in this revision about my family. When *Zane Grey* came out in 1973, my daughter Hilary was not yet born. To her and the other children, Beverly, Daniel, and Matthew; and to the grandchildren, Colleen, Megan, Katie, Travis, Patrick, and Austin; and to Pat, I give my love and thanks.

Western Kentucky University   Carlton Jackson

Chronology

1872   Pearl Zane Gray born 31 January in Zanesville, Ohio, to Lewis and Josephine Gray. Later in life drops first name and changes surname spelling to "Grey."

1888–1892   Acquires informal knowledge of dentistry, learned from his father; plays baseball. Offered a baseball scholarship at the University of Pennsylvania.

1896   Graduates from the University of Pennsylvania.

1896–1903   Establishes dental practice in New York City.

1902   Meets Lina (Dolly) Roth, his future wife.

1902   "A Day on the Delaware," in *Recreation*, is his first published article.

1903   *Betty Zane* is first published book.

1905   Marries Lina Roth.

1907   Goes west with C. J. "Buffalo" Jones.

1910   *The Heritage of the Desert* is his first major success in the field of literature.

1912   *Riders of the Purple Sage*.

1907–1917   Travels extensively through Arizona, New Mexico, Cuba, and Mexico gathering material for his novels.

1917   *Wildfire*.

1918   Sets up a permanent homestead in California.

1918   *The U.P. Trail*.

1919   Crosses Death Valley for the first time.

1919   Writes first major fishing book, *Tales of Fishes*.

1921   Returns to hometown of Zanesville, Ohio, as a celebrated author.

1922   *To the Last Man*.

1924   Fishes extensively in Nova Scotia. Buys first boat, *Fisherman I*.

1925   *The Vanishing American*—the book Grey said he wanted to be remembered by—is published.

1926   *Under the Tonto Rim.*

1926–1929   Pays periodic visits to New Zealand and the South Seas.

1930   Twentieth anniversary of Grey's affiliation with Harper's Publishing Co.; is hailed as the most sought-after writer in America.

1930   *Shepherd of Guadaloupe.*

1931   Buys *Fisherman II.*

1937   Suffers stroke while fishing on North Umpqua River, Oregon.

1938   Undertakes fishing trip to Australia.

1939   *Western Union* is the last of Grey's novels published in his lifetime.

1939   Dies of a heart attack at his home in Altadena, California, 23 October.

Chapter One
Genesis of a Writer

Spectacular success for Zane Grey was probably the last thing that any citizen of Zanesville, Ohio, in the 1870s and 80s would have predicted. By all accounts Grey was a precocious lad who pulled up neighbors' tulips, picked on smaller boys, and dipped girls' pigtails into his inkwell at school. Early in life, he developed into a more avid fisherman than scholar. Grey often remarked that the best place in the world was Dillon's Falls on the Licking River. After Dillon's Falls, Grey was fond of the "Y" bridge in Zanesville, which spans the junction of the Muskingum and Licking rivers. Fishing to Grey was an obsession; he found peace and comfort in the solitude that the habit gave him. In later life, he held many world fishing records.

Early Literary Influences

The thrills of fishing produced in Grey an undying love for the out-of-doors. He roamed with gangs of boys to the fishing spots, to the baseball practice fields, and to a special place—a cave where he and his cohorts cooked, ate, told stories, and wrote. To carry on this clandestine life, cooking utensils were necessary, so the "Terror of the Terrace," as Grey was called by neighbors, took pots and pans and other items from the Gray household on Convers Avenue. It was while patronizing the cave that Grey wrote his first story, at the age of fourteen. Understandably enough, it was called "Jim of the Cave," and it was about a group of misunderstood boys who were trying to win the favor of a "light-haired" girl.

His first literary effort, however, was doomed. Grey's father, Dr. Lewis Gray, had wondered for some time about the disappearance of his kitchen paraphernalia. When he discovered that his own son had taken the equipment, he burst into the cave, tanned Zane's hide, and burned the manuscript of "Jim of the Cave." After this incident, Zane restricted his writings mostly to English assignments in school, a task he did not relish. There had been some instances of Grey writing poetry. When he was thirteen, he penned this advice to Anna Oldham:

> Friend Anna
> Remember this and bear in mind
> A good beau is hard to find.
> But if you find one gentle and gay
> Hang to his coat tail night and day
> But if your hands should choose to slip
> Catch another and let him rip.
> > Yours truly
> > Pearl Gray[1]

Later in Grey's life, he dropped his first name "Pearl" (given to him by his mother, probably in honor of England's Queen Victoria, who was fond of wearing clothes colored pearl gray) because readers always thought he was a woman, and started using his middle name, "Zane." At the same time, he substituted an "e" for the "a" in his last name. Grey was named for his great-grandfather, Ebenezer Zane, whose wife, Elizabeth, was half Indian. From this marriage Grey claimed his inheritance of Indian blood. Colonel Zane defended Fort Henry (present-day Wheeling, West Virginia) during the American Revolution, and for his services he received several "military warrants," enabling him to select plots of land for himself. One such tract was Zanesville, an area later incorporated into the state of Ohio. It was in that city on 31 January, 1872 that the Colonel's great-grandson, Zane Grey, was born. In several books, Grey listed the year of his birth as 1875, but records indicate that 1872 was the correct date. (See chapter 9 for a possible explanation of why Grey put his birth year at 1875 instead of 1872.)

Although Grey's ardor for literary production was cooled by the cave incident, he began reading a great deal. His favorite books were Daniel Defoe's *Robinson Crusoe,* James Fenimore Cooper's *The Last of the Mohicans,* and a book that Grey said he knew by heart, Charles McKnight's *Our Western Border,* published in 1876.[2] Grey was also intrigued by the publishing ideas of a man from Brooklyn, Erastus Beadle. In 1858 Beadle started writing short novels about the Revolution and the Mexican War. These ten-cent novelettes were melodramatic accounts of soldiers at war that sold quickly to the young generation. The "dime novel" became one of the major literary expressions in the country. As time went on, Beadle contracted with several authors to write stories for him. Two such writers interesting to Grey were Prentiss Eingrahm and Edward L. Wheeler, who wrote about Indians and border warfare, among other things.

Popular writing of a historical nature was the literature Grey enjoyed most as a boy. This enthusiasm was not sufficient to please his teachers, so Grey had only a mediocre record as a student. Later in life, his wife taught him the finer points of English grammar and also an appreciation of authors like Victor Hugo, Edgar Allan Poe, Rudyard Kipling, John Ruskin, Charles Darwin, Alfred Tennyson, and Matthew Arnold. But when Grey was a student at Moore School in Zanesville, sophisticated literature was the last thing on his mind. He dreamed of Dillon's Falls and big fish, home runs and shut-outs, the freedom of wide open spaces, and "light-haired" girls. These diversions helped Grey later, but they drove his mathematics and music teachers to distraction.

Grey's music teacher suddenly stopped the chorus during a session one day and told Grey to be quiet. Grey, who retorted that he had a good singing voice, demanded to know why the teacher had not taught him to use it. The teacher replied that he had attempted to teach Grey how to sing. Responding to this claim, Grey averred that the teacher certainly had given special lessons to some of the girls in the class. Grey climaxed the incident by closing his music book, slamming it against a wall, and swearing that he would never study music again.[3]

Such impertinence in the statement of opinion served Grey well in his future career, but it produced some uncomfortable moments for him as a teenager. Perhaps it was audacity of one kind or another that caused Grey's father to treat him sometimes in a punitive fashion. For example, his father, who liked to take afternoon naps, often required Zane to fan his face to keep off the flies. Frequently, Zane fanned until his father was sound asleep, then put a newspaper over the man's face and slipped off. Sometimes this ruse did not work, to Zane's keen disappointment. The father, a great lover of snow, eagerly looked forward to the first blasts of winter. When snow fell, one of Zane's duties was to go out with a bucket and collect the white stuff so his father could eat it. If the snow was not fresh enough, Zane had to make several trips to satisfy his father.

Dentistry and Baseball

Grey's father was determined that his son become a dentist. Hence, Zane spent much time working on vulcanized teeth—removing plaster of paris from them and polishing them on a lathe. When the family moved to Columbus, Ohio, Zane started an informal dentistry practice in the little town of Frazeysburg. Apparently the work was not completely abhorrent, for Grey recorded in his autobiography, "The Living Past," "I had all the young girls in the country coming for dental work whether they needed it or not." In due time the Ohio Dental Association became interested in Grey's activities of pulling, filling, and cleaning teeth—especially since Grey was still a minor and not a graduate of any dental school. A state dental inspector studied Grey's career, chased him out of the business, but predicted a brilliant future for him—in dentistry.

Grey's dental work helped to keep his right arm strong, the same arm that made him a baseball pitcher of professional caliber. Zane and his brother, Romer, were always fond of the game, but they did not play in earnest until the family moved to Columbus. In the town of Baltimore, Ohio, which Grey visited on dental business, he pitched a game for the local team whose opponents that day were from Jacktown, Ohio. Baltimore got several runs, and Grey's superb pitching kept the Jacktown team scoreless. Suddenly the umpire, who had been brought to the game by Jacktown, shouted: "Game called! Nine to nothing! Favor Jacktown! Baltimore pitcher uses a crooked ball!" Grey was, of course, delivering his curve ball, which he had perfected. The pitcher for Jacktown, however, apparently had never heard of a curve ball, for he went after Grey in a fashion that caused Zane to leave the playing field in haste. After the Jacktown incident, Grey played for the Town Street Club in Columbus and also for the Capitol team. Many of these games formed the basis for Grey's later stories about baseball such as *The Young Pitcher* and *The Red Headed Outfield*. While Grey was playing for an amateur league, a baseball scout offered him a scholarship to the University of Pennsylvania. This offer led Grey to make an important decision, one that affected his careers as a dentist and a writer.

When Grey matriculated at the University of Pennsylvania, he discovered that he had to pass freshman tests with an average of sixty before he would be eligible to play baseball. At this point, Grey undoubtedly regretted the nonchalance with which he had treated his high school subjects, for every test he took was returned with a grade below sixty. So it was a disheartened Grey who walked into Professor Robert Formad's class in histology to take the final examination. He had probably "crammed" for this test since he knew it was his last chance. To Grey's great amazement and pleasure, he scored ninety-nine on the histology test. The professor told him his good grade was in large part attributable to his drawing ability—an ability that served Grey later when he illustrated some of his books. Grey, in his unpublished autobiography, said of the histology test: "That 99 mark brought my average up beyond passing, and it was responsible for my baseball career, my finding myself in the East, and surely led to my literary career."

As a student at Pennsylvania, Grey was restless. He recorded in his autobiography that he could not concentrate on lectures: "My thoughts wandered afar, if not in green fields and quiet woods, then to dreams of what might come true. In truth, I was a poor student." Grey's prowess on the baseball field rather than his academic record got him through the University of Pennsylvania. A reason, perhaps, why he disliked the academic side of the university was the dental curriculum into which his father forced him. In 1896 Grey graduated from Pennsylvania, but he expressed doubts that he had truly earned a diploma. Shortly after his college days ended, Grey established dental practice in New York City.

One may wonder why Grey, the great lover of the outdoors that he was, chose New York as a place to practice his profession. One possible explanation was that he yearned for financial independence, and New York could give it to him quicker than other places. He wanted the leisure to follow his own interests, and money was essential. Dentistry, therefore, must always have been treated by Grey as a stopgap occupation, one that would suffice until he could return to his beloved fishing grounds. He made several important contacts in New York; some made him popular, and others helped launch him on a literary career. For example, he played baseball with an Orange, New Jersey, team. His fans attended the games, not just to see him hit home runs, but to get their teeth attended to on the playing field. Also, Grey joined a campfire club in New York, an organization devoted to big-game hunting. Through this affiliation, he managed to get his short article "A Day on the Delaware" (1902) printed in *Recreation* magazine. This small success whetted his appetite for writing, and he became ever more entranced with its possibilities.

Grey's stay in New York from 1896 to 1903 was one of the most significant periods in his life. He could not refrain from comparing the sidewalk jungles with the pristine natural scenes he remembered from his youth. Homesickness tended to magnify the beauty of the woodlands and streams of Zanesville and Lackawaxen, Pennsylvania, to which most of his family had moved after its sojourn in Columbus.

Throughout his writings were constant contrasts between the effete East and the manly West. These contrasts were developed in Grey's mind long before he headed for the western regions.

Quite frequently, Dr. Grey felt the call of the open spaces so intensely that he locked up his office and headed for the family home at Lackawaxen. On such an outing in 1902 Grey met his future wife. He and some friends were canoeing on the Delaware River near Lackawaxen when they saw some girls sitting around a cabin on the bank and flirted with the young ladies. One of them was Lina Roth of New York City, whom Grey called Dolly. During their courtship prior to their marriage in 1905, Dolly taught Grey to appreciate the subtle beauty of the English language.

The Ohio River Trilogy

His friendship with Dolly may have caused Grey to venture into writing his first book in 1902. He had wished long enough, he had studied sufficiently, and he had the moral support of Dolly, so he yielded to his writing instinct. During the day he labored half-heartedly over teeth; at night he worked exuberantly on his book. He wrote his first novel "in a dingy flat, on a kitchen table under a flickering light. All of one winter I labored over it, suffered, and hoped, was lifted up, and again plunged into despair." Under conditions such as these, only his writer's faith and belief in ultimate success sustained him. Grey *had* to write; had he not he would have been miserably unhappy for the rest of his life. Even if that first book had never been published, the writing of it gave him the miserable joy of being a writer and helped him to escape the drudgery of dentistry.

Grey's "masterpiece" of 1903 was *Betty Zane,* the first book of his Ohio River trilogy. Grey set *Betty Zane* in the American Revolution, and its ultimate success caused Grey to be compared with James Fenimore Cooper as a recorder of historical events. Grey had heard stories all his life about how his great-grandfather Ebenezer Zane had defended Fort Henry against Indian attacks. Colonel Zane, a native Virginian, took "tomahawk possession" of the place in 1769 by blazing a few trees with a tomahawk to show ownership. Grey stated in a preface to *Betty Zane* that he had derived his story from an old diary of the Colonel that had been hidden away in a picture frame. The diary was, however, as fictitious as some of the characters in the story. Even if the diary had existed, it is doubtful that it could have been hidden successfully in a picture frame.

Betty Zane, however, is mostly about real places, real events, and real people. Colonel Zane actually existed, as did Betty, Lewis Wetzel, the Girty brothers, and several Wyandotte, Shawnee, and Seneca Indians such as Pipe, Wingenund, and Cornplanter. *Betty Zane* is an example of a good historical novel for the time and place, and the main events are authentic. Grey used his dramatic license on occasion to make his story more exciting than it was. Its effect was to make readers aware of their heritage and show them how one incident of the Revolution helped produce a nationalistic experience.

The story opens with Colonel Zane's return from a hunting trip. At supper that night, Captain Boggs and his daughter Lydia are guests, and Boggs states his fears of an impending Indian attack. While the two men converse about this grave subject, Lydia and the Colonel's sister Betty indulge in girlish talk about the arrival in the neighborhood of a young man, a Southerner named Alfred Clarke. Early in the novel, Grey lets the reader know that Betty and Clarke will have a romance, though their initial meeting does not indicate such. Clarke shows sincerity in defending patriot land from the British by leaving a comfortable home in Virginia and coming to the untamed border to fight for the American side. The Colonel gives him an important position in protecting the fort, and in carrying out his duties, he runs afoul of Betty's desires to wander wherever she wishes.

Isaac Zane, the Colonel and Betty's brother, shows up at the fort, having escaped from several years' captivity by the Wyandottes. Through Isaac's contact with various Indians, and through his betrothal to an Indian princess, Myeerah, he knows that the British are planning a union with the Hurons, Delawares, Shawnees, and other tribes. Despite this news, the Zane household is celebrating Isaac's return. Lurking in the background of this and other events at the Zane house is the mysterious figure of Lewis Wetzel, who has been given many names by the Indians. To the Delawares he is "Deathwind"; to the Shawnees, "Longknife"; and to the Hurons, "Destroyer." Wetzel's family has been slaughtered in an Indian raid, and he has vowed undying vengeance by becoming a professional Indian hunter. When he stalks an Indian, legend has it that a low moaning wind sweeps through the forest just before he strikes. Lewis loves Betty but knows that his "occupation" will forever prevent him from winning her hand.

The joy of the Zanes over Isaac's return is short-lived, for he is again taken by the Indians. Confronting his fiancée, Myeerah, Isaac begs her to return to Fort Henry with him. She refuses, so "White Eagle," as Isaac is called, decides to abandon immediate escape attempts and gather information of possible use to the citizens of Fort Henry. Grey used Isaac's captivity to discuss the American Indian, his thesis being that the Indians were not barbarians until the white man made them so. He wrote of the several betrayals of Indians by white men that turned the native American into a hostile force. Grey may have made Wetzel the personification of glory, but his sympathy was with the Indians.

Isaac escapes again, only to lose himself hopelessly in the forest. He is finally found by Cornplanter, the Seneca chief, at whose camp plans are made to torture and kill Isaac. It is here that Isaac first meets the notorious white renegade, Simon Girty. The traitor takes a perverse pleasure in telling Isaac that nothing can save him, and he embellishes his opinion by relating the awful end that has come recently to Colonel William Crawford and his soldiers at the hands of the Indians. At the crucial moment, however, Myeerah appears with a group of Indians and saves Isaac. Then Isaac, in gratitude, offers to return to the Indian camp as Myeerah's husband. But the maiden, who wants only to please her lover, travels to Fort Henry with Isaac, where the two are married.

At the fort, celebrations are again in order, but an overhanging dread persists in the reports of an impending attack. The novel reaches its climax when a concerted British-Indian onslaught is launched against Fort Henry. During the fight, the defenders of the fort run out of gunpowder. Betty Zane runs from the fort to Colonel Zane's cabin to get a supply of the precious material, which she carries in an apron slung over her shoulder. Both to and from the cabin, Betty runs through a hail of bullets and arrows, and her heroic dash—historically accurate—saves the fort.

After the fort is saved Alfred and Betty are married, which was not the case historically. Peace with the Indians results largely from the union between Isaac and Myeerah. Colonel Zane, who receives a land patent from the government for his services, becomes an important landowner. Only the Indian, as Grey notes, is neglected in the postrevolutionary progress: "The Indian is almost forgotten; he is in the shadow; his songs are sung; no more will he sing to his dusky bride; his deeds are done; no more will he boast of his all-conquering arm or of his speed like the Northwind; no more will his heart bound at the whistle of the stag, for he sleeps in the shade of the oaks, under the moss and ferns."[4]

Betty Zane is a product of family stories and sense of history. The novel lays the groundwork for two more books about Ohio River country—indeed, one novel inspiring another becomes a Grey trademark, for many of his western novels, the ones for which he is best remembered, were written as sequels. However, Grey learned after he had completed *Betty Zane* the difference between writing a book and getting it published. He wearily carried his manuscript from one publisher to another, only to be turned down. Finally—and this was where Grey's dental practice paid off—he borrowed money from a patient and had the novel published at his own expense.[5] The title page read: "Betty Zane by P. Zane Grey. Cover design, letters and illustrations by the author."

Although *Betty Zane* was not an immediate financial success, its publication led Grey to a number of decisions, the first of which was to abandon dentistry. The second was to return to Zanesville to receive the acclaim of his friends and neighbors. On this visit in April 1904 he announced that henceforth his life was to be devoted "exclusively to literature," and he promised two more books about Wetzel. The third thing that *Betty Zane* did to Grey was to lead him to the altar. In November 1905 he and Dolly were married in New York and they established residence on the banks of the Delaware River in Lackawaxen, Pennsylvania. There Dolly continued to teach Zane the uses of verbs and nouns; there he also toiled day and night over two more books and several short pieces. That he was making little money on *Betty Zane* did not bother him. He was now an author, and though he had to borrow money to buy groceries, he had faith that all would be well.

Because of *Betty Zane,* Grey came into contact with Daniel Murphy, agent for the United Literary Press. The association between Grey and Murphy was a long and fruitful one. Murphy liked Grey from the first: "You are so complex, so multi-sided, so sensitive that I never attempt to judge you by my simple standards."[6]

Betty Zane also caused dozen of citizens to write to Grey or his publisher. R. B. Brown of the *Zanesville Courier* told the Francis Press: ". . . I confess to great satisfaction at the distinct literary ability he has displayed."[7] Fannie Burns wrote to Grey's father extolling *Betty Zane.* A glimpse into Grey's relationship with her was seen as she signed herself as Grey's "former teacher and present friend."[8] Inevitably, Grey received letters disputing the geographical facts of *Betty Zane.* Grey was informed that one does not go "down" the river from Fort Henry to Fort Pitt; one goes "Up!"[9] Regardless of whether the letters about *Betty Zane* were friendly or not, Grey gloried in all the interest he had caused by his literary creation.

In 1906 A. L. Burt accepted *Spirit of the Border,* the second novel of the Ohio River trilogy, which continued the story of Lewis Wetzel, who now had a partner, Jonathan Zane, brother of Betty and Ebenezer. He also had two more names given him by the Indians: *Le vent de la Mort* and *Atelang.* Wetzel and Jonathan conducted their relentless war against the Indians, but Ebenezer had compassion for the Native American: "Seldom had the rights of the Redman been thought of. The settler pushed onward, plodding, as it were, behind his plow with a rifle. He regarded the Indian as little better than a beast; he was easier to kill than to tame. How little the settler knew the proud independence, the wisdom, the stainless chastity of honor, which belonged to many Indian Chiefs!"[10]

The center of action in the novel is a Moravian mission called the Village of Peace. In their efforts to convert the Indians, the ministers antagonize the chief villain of the story, Jim Girty, brother of Simon. Wetzel urges the head missionary, Mr. Wells, to abandon the mission; if he does not, he will jeopardize the lives of all the people in it. Wells is grateful for Wetzel's help, but since he still regards him only as an "Indian-killer," he will not move. At this point Wetzel gives an explanation of practical Christianity: "No, I ain't a Christian, an' I am a killer of Injuns. . . . I don't know nothin' much 'cept the woods an' fields, an' if there's a God fer me He's out thar under the trees an' grass. . . . I advised you to go back to Fort Henry, because if you don't go now the chances are aginst your ever goin'. Christianity or no Christianity, such men as you hev no bisness in these woods" (179). Many times in his future novels, Grey was to expound on and enlarge this pragmatic view of Christianity.

Wells, anxious to stay at the mission, entreats Captain David Williamson to protect him. Williamson argues that the Indians and missionaries want to sacrifice themselves, so he will not offer any help. Besides, of Williamson's men, only eighteen say they will fight for the Christian Indians. A most fearful massacre of the Village of Peace is then conducted by Jim Girty and his Indian allies, who set upon the Christian Indians as they pray and sing hymns in the chapel. This historically accurate event leaves sixty-two Indian adults and thirty-four Indian children dead. Only two boys escape the cruel blow.[11]

The climax of the story occurs when Wetzel confronts the evil Girty at Beautiful Spring, nails him to a tree with his knife, and leaves Girty in agony to spill out his life's blood. As soon as Wetzel's deed is done, he turns around and sees his old enemy Wingenund in the shadows. Wingenund has been converted to Christianity, and his daughter has married a white man. Wetzel finally gives in to the urgings of white companions and spares Wingenund. Thus, the story ends. Some critics have objected to the excessive violence of *The Spirit of the Border*. Grey, however, would not apologize for the book's brutality; for brutality was the mark of the border.[12]

In the final book of the trilogy, *The Last Trail*, the Indian problem has been solved, and white rustlers, led by Bing Leggitt and Simon Girty, cause most of the trouble. Wetzel's and Jonathan Zane's last mission is to clear out the horse thieves before the border can be truly civilized. Reminiscenses of the events in the first two books are scattered in *The Last Trail:* Betty Zane's dash for the gunpowder is now legendary, and Captain Williamson's failure to protect the Christian Indians is related at one hearth after another; indeed, it is told that Williamson and his men carried out the massacre themselves. This account is the true one.

Grey uses more descriptions in this book than he did in its two predecessors. He describes the inner conflict that comes to a borderman when he falls in love. Jonathan meets Helen Sheppard, and loving her seems unavoidable: "He realized that men had always turned, at some time in their lives, to women even as the cypress leans toward the sun. The weakening of the sterner stuff in him; this softening of his heart, and especially the inquietitude, lack of joy and harmony in his old pursuit of the forest trails bewildered him, and troubled him some. Thousands of times his borderman's trail had been crossed, yet never to his sorrow until now when it had been crossed by a woman."[13] It is, of course, most convenient for Jonathan to start thinking of love and marriage as his work in clearing up the border slowed to a stop. The story ends with the destruction of the horse thieves and with all of the principal characters getting married except Wetzel, for whom marriage is completely out of harmony with his nature.

The western Virginia border has gone through all of its stages—wilderness, Indians, white rustlers, civilization—and all of its characters have passed into history. Grey could now turn his attention elsewhere.

Grey's reliance on James Fenimore Cooper is evident in the Ohio River trilogy, for he believed, like Cooper, that the truths of history could be taught in a work of fiction as well as in a history book. Likely, too, was the influence of Grey's favorite book as a youth, *Our Western Border*. The trilogy was a test of Grey's fortitude. He fought odds in writing it that would have been considered insurmountable by many

other writers. He was so confident of his future as a writer when the
reading public became familiar with his work that he paid the publishing expenses himself for his first novel and practically gave away
the next two.

By 1905 Grey had drawn up a list of "rules for my literary work."
He filled a diary with procedures to read ("Study the felicity of words"),
to observe ("in everything there is always something undiscovered.
Find it"), to think ("train the mind to think earnestly"), and to describe ("the object of description is not so much to tell the truth as to
give an impression of truth").[14] He constantly studied the technical
aspects of writing, depending primarily in this respect on the works of
Clayton Hamilton and J. H. Gardiner. Grey had the desire to write
and, he believed, the ability. All he needed was the opportunity.

The opportunity came one day in 1907 when Grey made the ac-
quaintance of a man some of his friends had mentioned to him. That
man was Charles Jesse "Buffalo" Jones, a well-known Westerner who
was in New York to show films of the wildlife in Yellowstone Park.
Grey suggested that he go with Jones to Arizona on a hunting trip and
write about the experiences. Before giving his consent, Jones needed
evidence that Grey could write, so Grey gave Jones a copy of *Betty
Zane*. As soon as Jones completed reading the book, he cordially invited Grey to accompany him to the West. This invitation opened a
new world for Zane Grey.

Chapter Two
The Desert Novels

Grey was thrilled at the chance to explore the West with Buffalo Jones. He had some misgivings, however, because he did not want to leave Dolly alone. She, believing this was Grey's great opportunity to secure firsthand knowledge of the West that would make his writings accepted by the reading public, insisted that he go.

The Last of the Plainsmen

The book that Grey wrote about his adventures with Jones was *The Last of the Plainsmen* (1908). A foundation work, it inspired many of Grey's later settings and events in his western novels. Jones, an intriguing character who was originally from Illinois, had hunted and killed buffalo for years before concluding that the great bison herds were becoming extinct. Jones laid down his rifle and spent the rest of his life trying to preserve the buffalo. One great hope in his life was to cross-breed the buffalo with black Galloway cattle. The partial success of this experiment was the famous "cattalo,"[1] said to be stronger and tastier than either a buffalo or a steer. Jones, adopting literally the biblical injunction that man have dominion over all the beasts of the earth, had a way with wild animals. He showed his belief in this role by capturing single-handedly some Yellowstone Park bears, stringing them up by their feet on a tree branch, and spanking them with a pole until they were subordinate to his wishes.[2] Because people in the East scoffed at reports of such exploits, Grey proposed to take photographs and write descriptions of Jones's deeds.

The trip with Jones introduced Grey to many of the major landmarks in the West, particularly in Arizona. Mormons guided Grey, Jones, and several other men as they crossed the Painted Desert, traversed the Big and Little Colorado rivers, climbed Buckskin Mountain, fought wildcats, and endured sandstorms and floods. Grey did not long remain a novice in this wild setting: when a Mormon gave him a too-

spirited horse, Grey remained in the saddle and won the unqualified
approval of his associates. Another time Grey shot a cougar while on a
hunt; he had either to shoot the animal or be injured or possibly killed
by it. Becoming an expert horseman and marksman in a short time,
he participated in a chase for wild horses and marveled at the dexterity
of Jones, then sixty-three years old, in trying to capture them.

Grey was enthralled by the Painted Desert. It was not like his previous mental images of it: "Imagination had pictured the desert for me
as a vast, sandy plain, flat and monotonous. Reality showed me desolate mountains gleaming bare in the sun, long lines of red bluffs, white
sand dunes, and hills of blue clay, areas of level ground—in all, a
many-hued, boundless world in itself, wonderful and beautiful, fading
all around into the purple haze of deceiving distance."[3] A desert sunrise
led him to ecstasy: "A stream of opal flowed out of the sun, to touch
each peak, mesa, dome, parapet, temple and tower, cliff and cleft into
the new-born life of another day" (245). When the day was done,
"night intervened, and a moving, changing, silent chaos pulsated under the bright stars. How infinite all this is! How impossible to understand! I exclaimed" (251).

The magical qualities of the desert and its sunrises and sunsets fascinated Grey throughout his life. His preoccupation with such scenes
was reflected in his novels, where characterization was always subordinate to setting. Man could never enchant him as the Grand Canyon
could: "Man was nothing, so let him be humble. This cataclysm of the
earth, this playground of a river was not inscrutable; it was only inevitable—as inevitable as nature herself. Millions of years in the by-
gone ages it had lain serene under a live moon; it would bask silent
under a rayless sun, in the onward edge of time.—It spoke simply,
though its words were grand: 'My spirit is the Spirit of Time, of Eternity, of God. Man is little, vain, vaunting. Listen. Tomorrow he shall
be gone' " (252).

After his travels with Jones, Grey returned to Lackawaxen to spend
several months writing *The Last of the Plainsmen*. It had some good
touches in it, as when Grey described one of Jones's earlier adventures
into the Arctic regions where he tried to capture a musk ox. Much of
the book, however, was written in a reminiscent, "campfire" style, one
not likely to attract a wide audience. Moreover, at the time Grey tried
to publish the book, President Theodore Roosevelt was on a highly
publicized trip to the West. Naturally, more people were interested in

Roosevelt in 1907 and 1908 than in some obscure dentist who was trying to write novels about the American West.

The lack of sales possibilities did not restrain Grey's enthusiasm in writing *The Last of the Plainsmen*. Shortly after he had finished the book, Jones appeared, and together they went to Harper's where Jones had a friend, Ripley Hitchcock. Grey, assured through this contact that his book would receive careful consideration, was heartened by the prospect of an acceptance. Several days later Grey was invited back to Harper's, where Hitchcock said of *The Last of the Plainsmen:* "I don't see anything in this to convince me you can write either narrative or fiction."[4]

Grey was, of course, plunged into despair over Hitchcock's decision. But from this chastening came a miraculous transformation in Grey as he recorded in an essay, "My Own Life," printed in a 1928 book by Harper's, *Zane Grey, The Man and His Work:* "Suddenly, something marvelous happened to me, in my mind, to my eyesight, to my breast. That moment should logically have been the end of my literary aspirations! From every point of view I seemed lost. But someone inside me cried out: 'He does not know! *They* are all wrong!' "[5] Years later, when Grey was a famous author, this experience must have prompted him to rescue one dejected character after another in his novels and lift him to the heights. Grey knew that such individual catharsis was possible—that victory could be gained from adversity. His critics may have disbelieved such dramatic turns of fate, saying they were unrealistic, but nonetheless such victories fascinated over forty million people.

As usual, Grey found greatest comfort in Dolly: "Let no man ever doubt the faith and spirit and love of a woman!"[6] She encouraged him to submit *The Last of the Plainsmen* to other publishers. While the manuscript made its rounds, Grey worked busily on another novel about the great American desert. Ultimately, *The Last of the Plainsmen* was accepted by the Outing Publishing Company in New York. A highlight in Grey's career occurred when Buffalo Jones attended an autograph dinner party and happily signed the book as "the last of the plainsmen." Grey described the event to his friend and agent, Daniel Murphy: "He [Jones] was simply great that night, and the crowd went wild. When my book was delivered each table got up with a roar. . . . Jones . . . talked about the book, and [said] it was the most thrilling and beautiful story ever written about a sporting event. When my turn came the roar that greeted me stunned me. I got up somehow, with nausea, chromatic aberration, diffuse sweating, prolapsis [*sic*] of the intestines, paralysis of the centers of equilibrium, and what might be called balmastatic globulation of the oracular function."[7]

Grey reported later that something of Jones always appeared in the great fictional characters that Grey created.[8] Jones held a commanding position in Grey's later novel, *The Raiders of Spanish Peaks,* for example, and in several articles and stories for boys. *Roping Lions in the Grand Canyon* was essentially a revised shorter version of *The Last of the Plainsmen,* and *The Young Forester* and *The Young Lion Hunter* were variants of the same basic work. Grey's descriptions of his western tour with Jones pulsated from the vast panorama of the book to the vivid closeups of the articles and stories, but what was often described hurriedly in the book was carefully scrutinized in the short articles and stories. "Lassoing Lions in the Siwash," in *Everybody's Magazine* of June 1908, was the first of several articles extracted from *The Last of the Plainsmen.* As late as 1922, in *Tales of Lonely Trails,* Grey was still explaining Buffalo Jones to the world.

Despite the tremendous value of Buffalo Jones to Grey's development as a writer of western novels, it was another man—Jim Emett— who most influenced Grey. Jim Emett, born in a covered wagon crossing the plains, spent his entire life on the desert; five nights out of every seven, Emett slept outdoors. Emett was in trouble in Flagstaff, Arizona, when Grey first met him in 1907: one Saunders had accused Emett of cattle rustling, and there was also bad blood between Emett and a man named Dimmick. When Emett and Dimmick ultimately pulled guns on each other, Grey—either bravely or naively—stepped between them and stopped the fight. The incident furnished Grey with much material for his stories.[9]

Emett, over six feet tall, had ponderous shoulders, a great "shaggy" head, and a white beard, and he "gave the impression of tremendous virility and dignity." He had a strange gift of revelation: "[H]e divined what the desert would come to mean to me. He . . . [saw] all it was to bring to me."[10] Emett, a Mormon, loved and cared for all creatures, including children—he had eighteen by two different wives. "Rustlers and horsethieves, outlaws from the notorious Hole in the Wall—All were welcomed by Jim Emett. He had no fear of any man. He feared only his God.[11] The greatest talent from Emett to Grey was the habit of silent watching: "Surely, of all the gifts that have come to me from contact with the West, this one of sheer love of wilderness beauty, color, grandeur, has been the greatest, the most significant for my work."[12]

The First Major Success

It was predictable, in view of his western tour with Jones, that Grey's first major success was a novel about the desert. *The Heritage of the Desert* set the theme of the romantic novels for which Grey became famous: having the West ultimately build individual character by transforming weaklings into strong men. When he completed the book in 1910, he returned to Harper's and presented the manuscript to Hitchcock. Days later he was called back to the publishing house, where a smiling Hitchcock pushed one of Harper's famous blue contracts at him—a contract that immediately became a treasured heirloom.

The main character of *The Heritage of the Desert* is twenty-four-year-old John Hare, an Easterner who comes to the West in the 1870s to regain his health and to restore some meaning to his life. In Salt Lake City he is mistaken for a cattleman's spy by outlaws and becomes a hunted man. Before the chief outlaw, a former Kentuckian named Dene, can find him, Hare is rescued by some Mormons headed by August Naab. One Mormon, Martin Cole, has doubts about playing Good Samaritan to Hare because Cole does not want to antagonize Dene. When Naab prevails, Hare stays with the group. Naab's blessing supper one night causes Hare's early religious thoughts to return. In Connecticut, he was flippant about religion, but Naab's piety touches him. The incident launches the novel's leading theme: the gentle callings of religion cannot destroy evil by a continual policy of appeasement toward bad men. This hard lesson August Naab ultimately comes to accept.

In the group of Mormons is Mescal, the young daughter of a Navajo Indian mother and a Spanish father. She has been reared and educated by the polygamous Mormons and is regarded by them as a future wife for Naab's son, Snap.[13] The son, however, is a surly, hard-drinking troublemaker, who proves that good people can sire rotten children. Snap's first wife hates Mescal because of the anticipated marriage, and Snap hates Hare because of the infatuation between the latter and Mescal, which grows with each page of the novel.

The antagonisms are brought together in the little settlement of White Sage, which Naab and Hare visit one day for supplies. While the two men are in town, these things happen: Mormon Bishop Caldwell "lays hands" on Hare, indicating a proselytizing effort; Martin Cole pronounces a malediction on a rancher named Holderness (who wants to marry Mescal) for cutting off the water supply to desert farmers; Snap wins a shoot-out with Jeff Larson over a horse-trading deal; and Naab disarms Dene for terrorizing Hare but refuses additional violence because of his religion. All of this fast-paced action occurs within the short space of one afternoon. The remainder of the novel is spent, for the most part, in settling all the personal conflicts inspired by that one trip to town.

At Naab's ranch, the Blue-Star, from which the roar of the mighty Colorado can be heard, the relationship between Naab and Hare draws close. The relationship is, in one instance, man to man because Naab gives Hare important responsibilities to show that he has faith in Hare's masculinity. It is also father to son, as Naab sees Snap slowly reject the old traditions and become a gunman. Naab begins to transfer to Hare the affection he once held for his oldest son. Hare's ingratiation of himself to Naab and Mescal produces for him a mortal enemy in Snap Naab. Because of this enmity, Naab assigns Hare to work in the sheep camp, high in the mountains. The strange thing about this assignment is that Mescal accompanies Hare, and Naab apparently sees no threat as a result to the planned marriage of Snap and Mescal.

In the high areas, many adventures befall Hare. He slowly learns to breathe comfortably in the juniper and black-sage infested grounds, he becomes expert at driving sheep, he forages a friendship with the two Indian workers at the camp, he spots a wild horse—Silvermane—and helps to capture and break it,[14] and he kills a bear just a step short of Mescal who is transfixed in horror. He regains his health. He falls in love with Mescal.

Mescal returns Hare's love, but she avoids him because of her Mormon upbringing and her obligation to marry Snap. Hare, infuriated, swears that the marriage with Snap will never take place; and he vents his anger by slipping away one day to White Sage where he shoots two outlaws, slaps Holderness, and runs down Dene on Silvermane. Despite Hare's escapades, the marriage plans continue. At Christmas time, the sheep camp is abandoned and the crew returns to Blue-Star. On the wedding eve, Mescal slips away with her horse, Black Bolly, her dog, Wolf, and her faithful Indian servant. She goes to a place where she does not expect to be found: the Painted Desert!

Searching for Mescal, Naab and Hare employ the services of Eschtah, the "wise old chief of all the desert Indians," who is Mescal's grandfather. The Indian orders some braves to look for Mescal, the "desert flower," but he admits the hopelessness of the situation. Mescal has been called back to the desert by the primitive instincts of her forefathers. As Hare gazes over the desert, seeing in it a deep and majestic nature, eternal and unchangeable, "it was only through Eschtah's eyes that he saw its parched slopes, its terrifying desolateness, its sleeping death."[15]

In the period following Mescal's flight and after Snap becomes foreman at the Holderness Ranch, Snap creeps behind Hare one day and shoots his unarmed adversary. Snap thinks he has killed Hare, but Naab nurses the young Easterner back to health. Snap's dastardly deed leads Naab to disown him, for Naab now is beginning to realize that it will take more than Christian prayers and supplications to stop the domineering tactics of Dene, Holderness, and Snap. Also, Naab absolves Mescal, if she ever can be found, of any duties, matrimonial or otherwise, to Snap.

On the first anniversary of Mescal's departure, Hare is awakened by imagined voices. Arising, he tells Naab he is going into the desert. He mounts Silvermane and finds Wolf—Mescal's dog—waiting for him on the bank of the river. When he enters the desert, beset by sandstorms and lack of water, Hare must put himself at the mercy of his horse and Mescal's dog. At the crucial moment—just when Hare is about to succumb to the elements—he finds Mescal. The maiden tells him she lived comfortably until her Indian servant died and food supplies were exhausted. Together, the lovers head back to Blue-Star.

A few days after Mescal's and Hare's return, outlaws appear under the leadership of Holderness, who is now a sheriff. In the shoot-out that follows, one of Naab's younger sons, Dave, is killed, and three outlaws, including Dene, are slain. Mescal escapes on Silvermane, with Holderness in pursuit. Thus, a showdown of all the contradicting forces is rapidly approaching. That the showdown is certain is indicated by Naab's conversion from an appeaser of outlaws to their sworn foe. He summons Eschtah and his braves, intending to go after the outlaws the next morning. During the night, however, Hare slips away on Black Bolly, Mescal's horse, to do Naab's job for him.

When Hare arrives in the Silver Cup camp, he, to his consternation, finds Silvermane tethered outside a cabin. Mescal is inside, a prisoner of Holderness and Snap. The two outlaws quarrel, and Holderness shoots Snap through the heart. Plainly, Holderness intends to have Mescal and use her for his own evil purposes. In his secret hiding place, Hare ponders what to do to save Mescal. Into the night he maintains his vigil. Then, an outlaw named Nebraska and a masked man untie Mescal and set her free. Mescal rides swiftly to White Sage where she is placed in the protective custody of Bishop Caldwell. Hare arrives there just a few minutes ahead of Holderness; the two men draw, Holderness loses.

By this time, a group of irate citizens has gathered, determined to hang every man in the outlaw group. Hare saves Nebraska from this fate by telling of the latter's part in helping Mescal escape. Hare also saves the masked rider but not before someone pulls off his mask. He is none other than Paul Caldwell, the eldest son of the Mormon bishop. At this point, Naab, the Old Lion, roars into White Sage, infuriated that Hare has robbed him of his vengeance against Holderness and the outlaws. It takes great force to keep Naab from hanging the Bishop's son despite the mitigating circumstances. When Naab's anger passes, he gives his blessings to the planned marriage of Hare and Mescal.

The book ends with a grand wedding. Mescal and Hare are married by Naab at Blue-Star under the shade of a cottonwood grove. Eschtah and his Indians, resplendent in their robes, are present. Hare and Mescal return to the old sheep camp high in the mountains where they once discovered their love for each other. This happy ending is the first of almost a hundred that Grey fashioned in his career as a writer of romantic novels of the American West.

The Heritage of the Desert is certainly melodramatic in its execution. There are too many coincidences in it, as when Hare hears the call of the desert on the exact anniversary of Mescal's flight from unhappiness, and when Hare conveniently finds Mescal being held captive by Holderness and Snap. The novel's themes, however, are universal in their application. There is, for example, the Good Samaritan theme, for only love for mankind causes Naab to rescue Hare on the White Sage Trail and keep him from the clutches of Dene. Naab does not know what manner of man Hare is; for all he knows, Hare might have deserved ill treatment from Dene. But to Naab, Hare is a human being, and "suffering is suffering."

Included in the religious aspects of the novel is the almost imperceptible change affecting Mormonism in the 1870s along the Utah-Arizona border. At first, Naab wants to convert Hare to the Mormon faith; it is his duty, as he sees it, to do so for his church. Naab also believes that passive goodwill ultimately reigns supreme over evil forces, but the desert teaches survival of the fittest for all the creatures who live on it—and man is not exempt from this requirement and must adjust to conditions. Naab also personifies Mormonism in its altering forms in other respects; he relinquishes his efforts to convert Hare but keeps him as a son; he comes to believe in doctoring bodily injuries; and he becomes convinced that prayers must sometimes be supplemented by hot lead if law and order were to prevail in the Western regions. This was not the only novel in which Grey wrote about the personal and institutional changes wrought by lawless days in the West. The theme recurs especially in two of his mountain novels, *The Riders of the Purple Sage* and *The Rainbow Trail.* In his treatment of changing Mormonism, Grey put the stamp of historical research on his novels, and he contributed to an understanding of that period in American history.

On the desert, the animal was superior to the human. In his search for Mescal, Hare would not have survived except for the enduring qualities and homing instincts of his horse and Mescal's dog. He puts himself at their mercy, and they bring him through successfully. Very little could have been accomplished in the West without burros, dogs, and good horseflesh. Grey came to love the four-footed beasts, even the wild ones, and he imparted this affection to his readers.

The novel also depicts the healing and Edenic qualities of the West. While Hare lived in the East, he was sickly with a bad lung. The rarefied atmosphere of the West soon corrects the problem. Also, out West, Hare is expected to be a man, to forget the "soft" life he led in the East. More important, when the West offers the opportunity to be a man, Hare rises to the challenge, meets it in a splendid manner, and receives manifold rewards for his efforts. He is just one Grey character out of hundreds who experience this kind of rejuvenation. This theme, perhaps more than any other, caused Grey to become known in some circles as a western image builder. If there was a Garden of Eden in this country, Grey let his readers know that it was West of the Mississippi River.

The Heritage of the Desert put Grey on a fairly solid literary footing. He was quite active immediately after the book's publication—so much so that in June 1910 he had to decline an invitation from Boy

Scout director, Daniel Beard, to visit Forest Lake near Redding, Connecticut. He said he was working on a juvenile book (probably *The Young Forester*) that had to be completed by the end of summer. His improved financial condition was apparent when he wrote, "I am interested in places where I might buy property and locate permanently."[16] Grey, however, was not yet firmly fixed as an author, despite these positive signs. His best known book, *Riders of the Purple Sage* (1912) was at first rejected by Harper's, although *The Heritage of the Desert* earned a comfortable income. Grey said in 1928, at the height of his career, that his publication troubles had never ended.[17]

Wanderer of the Wasteland

By 1910 Grey was earning enough money with his writings to travel whenever he wished and spent about half his time in Arizona, California, and New Mexico. He took extensive notes on these trips, which he used for articles, short stories, and novels. The desert continued to fascinate him. He crossed the Painted Desert again, as he had done with Buffalo Jones in 1907; he became familiar with the Sonora Desert along the Mexico-Arizona border; and in 1919, with a Norwegian, Sievert Nielson, he crossed Death Valley in the Mojave Desert. He observed that the desert brought out primitive instincts of man that could be used for purposes of either good or evil.[18] The desert focused on a peculiar trait a man might have and magnified it a dozenfold. To tell the effect of the desert on man was Grey's objective in a 1923 novel *Wanderer of the Wasteland*. He was from January to May 1919 writing this novel. In manuscript it was 170,000 words and 838 pages. "I do not know what it is that I have written. But I have never worked so hard on any book, never suffered so much or so long. . . . The only agony I feel now is the agony of dread. Have I written what I yearned to write?"[19]

Wanderer of the Wasteland employs a Cain and Abel conflict as its major dramatic problem: Adam Larey and his older brother Guerd quarrel over a woman. In the fight that ensues, Adam shoots Guerd. Thinking he has slain his brother, Adam flees into the desert to spend many years purging his soul of the guilt that fills it.

On the desert, Adam loses eighty pounds in one day. He is near death when a prospector, Dismukes, finds him. Later, however, when Adam is again on his own, his burro steals away with all his food. Thus, survival, the most primitive of man's instincts, becomes uppermost in his mind. While he endures this trial, Adam learns many secrets of nature; and one is that all animals live on one another. Adam knows that he, like all other creatures, will have to kill to survive; and he ruthlessly stalks partridges, rats, and snakes for food. When Adam does eat, he finds that a small amount of food stimulates sharp hunger pangs that themselves are almost fatal, whereas without food at all, there is no pain. He concludes that starving to death is an easy and painless way to die. Just before this happens to Adam, he is rescued again, this time by a band of Indians.

In time Adam comes to be called "Wansfell the Wanderer." In this role he is a knight in shining armor who rescues fair damsels from the clutches of evil villains. He kills a man named Baldy McKue who abducted and despoiled another man's wife, and he tries, vainly, to save the life of Magdelena Virey. Magdelena and her husband Elliott live in Death Valley in the path of an avalanche. Magdelena wronged Elliott in the past, so her travail in Death Valley is one of purgation. She, like Adam Larey, comes to the desert to atone for her manifold sins. She is resigned to her fate, for she does nothing as Elliott, while trying to activate the avalanche, rolls rocks toward their cabin each night. Wansfell begs Magdelena to leave, but she refuses; she seems to welcome the death that is sure to come. One night Elliott is able to start the avalanche, and before the terrible ordeal ends, both he and his wife are dead. Adam leaves the scene, taking a small picture of Magdelena's daughter, Ruth.

On the trail again, Adam thinks about God. Dismukes, the prospector, tells Adam that he will find God on the desert, but Adam doubts the prediction: "You're wrong. . . . I have no religion, no belief. I can't find any hope out there in the desert. Nature is pitiless, indifferent. The desert is but one of her playgrounds. Man has no right there."[20] But Adam's role as benefactor to helpless people causes him ultimately to view things differently. For example, he rescues Genie Linwood from kidnapers and takes her home to a mother dying of consumption. Just before her death, Mrs. Linwood tells Adam that he was the answer to her prayers. "What do you call this strength of yours that fulfilled my faith . . . that will be the salvation of my child?" (314). Adam's conclusion is pantheistic: "Could God be Nature—that thing, that terrible force, light, fire, water, pulse—that quickening of plant, flesh, stone, that dying of all only to renew . . . ?" (335). This reconciliation of God and nature, which up to Mrs. Linwood's death Adam denies, shows that Adam's spiritual powers have kept pace with

the physical; he has not reverted (as most men on the desert do) "to
mere unthinking instinct." His positive qualities come from God; their
magnification, from the desert. Thus God and nature come to be one
in Adam Larey's thinking.

Adam and Genie Linwood live and wander together for years, and
he fights hard to keep from falling in love with her. To love a woman
is out of the question for Adam Larey, "Wansfell the Wanderer" (very
much like Lewis Wetzel of the Ohio River trilogy), because he is his
brother's slayer and therefore must spend his life in contrition. Finally,
when the two visit the little settlement of San Ysabel, Genie meets a
young man, Gene Blair, and it is evident that they are meant for each
other. When Adam meets Ruth Virey, daughter of Magdelena, he does
not permit himself to love her; he leaves San Ysabel in terrible personal
conflict over whether to return to the desert or go back to Picacho (the
scene of strife with his brother) and take his legal punishment: "[T]he
I of Adam's soul was arraigned in pitiless strife with the Me of his
body. Like a wild and hunted creature he roamed the mountain top . . .
there to sit like a stone, to lie on his face, to writhe and fight and cry
in his torment" (408). Adam stands resolute in the end and returns to
Picacho. There he meets an old prospector, Merryvale, who tells him
that Guerd Larey had been only slightly injured in the fracas fourteen
years before. Thus for nought had Adam Larey become "Wansfell the
Wanderer." The twist of fate, the strange note of irony on which the
book ends, and the unresolved conflicts such as Adam's love for Ruth
Virey and his continuous search for God, suggest a sequel to *Wanderer
of the Wasteland*. When Grey wrote the sequel, he called it *Stairs of
Sand*.[21]

Wanderer of the Wasteland received much attention from readers in
this country, and prepublication sales amounting to over one hundred
thousand copies, but by 1923, such events were common for a Grey
work. The chief criticism of the novel came from Burton Rascoe of the
New York Tribune, who faulted Grey for allowing Adam Larey to inter-
fere so much in other people's affairs: "The moral ideas implicit in this
book and urged upon the readers are, in my opinion, decidedly
askew."[22] Rascoe asked: "Do Mr. Grey's readers believe in the existence
of such people as Mr. Grey depicts; do they accept the code of conduct
implicit in Mr. Grey's novels?" Professor Thomas K. Whipple, who
was annoyed that Grey's critics compared Grey with authors like Henry
James, Jane Austen, George Eliot, and Laurence Stern, answered Ras-

coe in an essay for the *New York Saturday Review of Literature:*

I no more believe in the existence of such people as Mr. Grey's than I believe in the existence of the shepherds of Theocritus; I no more accept the code of conduct implicit in Mr. Grey's novels than I do the conduct implicit in Congreve's comedies. There is no reason for comparing him with anyone, unless with the competitors in his own genre. . . . If he must be classified, however, let it be with the authors of "Beowulf" and of the Icelandic sagas. Mr. Grey's work [in its totality] is a primitive epic, and has the characteristics of other primitive epics. [23]

The sequel to *Wanderer of the Wasteland* continued the major themes inspired in Grey by the desert. *Stairs of Sand* was an appropriate title, for the book implied that life itself is roughly comparable to "stairs of sand" that shift, change, and threaten peril. The time for *Stairs of Sand* was approximately eighteen years later than the setting in *Wanderer of the Wasteland*. Ruth Virey, a major character in *Stairs of Sand,* is Guerd Larey's wife; she married because of pressure from her grandfather, Caleb Hunt, for he was a business partner with none other than Guerd. The unhappy marriage has produced in Ruth a tendency toward self-pity; indeed, Adam Larey, who finds Ruth after four years of searching, urges her to let the desert have its way with her, so she might "live to love what makes you suffer most." [24] To endure the desert, says Adam, would make a real woman of Ruth, and allowing the desert to develop Ruth's true womanhood becomes the novel's major objective: "The paradox of Ruth's life was that the desert had given her many of its attributes—its changeableness, its fiery depth, its mystery and moods and passion, and its beauty, and withheld its freedom, its strength, its indifference" (253).

Stairs of Sand again asserts that the desert "seizes upon any characteristic peculiar to person or plant or animal and develops it with an appalling intensity" (23–24). At the beginning, Ruth's "peculiar" but not quite dominant characteristic is self-pity; but because the desert teaches and intensifies survival instincts, the denouement occurs when Ruth realizes that she can kill Guerd Larey to prevent him from ruining several lives. This realization starts Ruth on a new track; her old petulant, egotistic self vanishes; she is reborn into self-reliance, and her true womanhood begins to develop. Adam Larey's love for her and the desert setting teach her these things.

A subplot of the novel deals with Guerd Larey's cruelty to his wife and with his plans to betray his business partner to capitalize on newly developing railroad wealth. Adam Larey is positive that Guerd's activities dictate against his living a long life, but who is to end it? Adam already has spent fourteen years as a wanderer of the desert, expurgating his soul for a crime he did not commit. Adam is willing to kill his brother and sets out to do so, but Merryvale, the prospector, and now Adam's partner, makes it unnecessary. At the novel's end Merryvale shoots Guerd twice, erasing from the desert at least one baneful influence. Adam and Ruth now can marry and live happily ever after.

The Changing Desert

The desert novels discussed so far are set in the late nineteenth century. The scene for *Heritage of the Desert* is Arizona's Painted Desert; for *Wanderer of the Wasteland* and *Stairs of Sand,* the Mojave Desert of California. Implicit in the novels is a pessimistic, original-sin view of mankind. Man usually enters the desert because of some ill-fated love affair, the remembrance of which causes the desert to magnify man's baser points. If he goes to find gold, he usually fails, so he spends his life on the desert brooding over his misfortunes. The desert quickly activates evil instincts in most men doomed to travel over it; and only a few people, like Adam Larey and Ruth Virey, can rise above the doleful effects of the desert.

In time, however, the desert became more habitable for the people on it. An old idea in America was that "God had hidden the New World until men were equal to its promise."[25] This concept may have motivated Grey when he wrote several novels depicting the desert as man's savior from the squalor of the East. A quickening technology—particularly in the form of the automobile—and World War I and its aftermath allowed Grey to write about a different desert than the one inhabited by Dismukes, Merryvale, and "Wansfell the Wanderer." This "new" desert had all the good and bad qualities of the "old," but the humans on it had attained a technological and sociological frame of mind. Grey abhorred not only the growth of materialism caused by technology but also American involvement in world affairs. The desert, for Grey, was the great leveler; it was made livable by technology, but it taught men lessons against pervading materialism. The desert novels in this category were set in the period from 1911 to 1932, and the first one was *Desert Gold* (1913).

Border Strife

The setting for *Desert Gold* is the Sonora Desert along the Mexico-Arizona border, in two different time periods. The narrative begins in the late nineteenth century when two men—Cameron and Warren—encounter each other in the desert. Cameron (whose real name is Burton) is in the desert to lament the loss of his wife and to punish himself by remembering her; Warren, to forget his loving daughter who has disappeared and is now presumed dead. The desert is to help one man to remember and another man to forget. In true Zane Grey style, the two men unknowingly are father-in-law and son-in-law to each other, for the missing woman turns out to be young Cameron's lost wife and the aged Warren's lost daughter. The two men become lost in the desert. Warren soon dies, but before Cameron expires, he finds a fabulous treasure of gold. He marks the place for someone's future reference and with the certificate proving his marriage to Nell Warren.

Desert Gold then shifts to the early part of the twentieth century, about the year 1911. A revolution is raging in Mexico, producing trouble for American settlements in the vicinity. Some of the Mexican riders are not revolutionists at all, but bandits who cross the international border at will. One such person was Rojas, the kidnaper of a beautiful maiden, Mercedes Castaneda. Mercedes's lover, George Thorpe, enlists the aid of Richard Gale (a rich Easterner in the West to prove his manhood) to wrest Mercedes from Rojas' grasp. Richard causes a commotion to divert Rojas' attention and during the turmoil escapes with Mercedes. He receives help in this endeavor from two cowboys, Ladd and Lash, who guide the fugitives to the ranch of Belding, United States Inspector of Immigration. Belding has a stepdaughter named Nell Burton.

At Belding's ranch, Richard gets a job patrolling the border to prevent illegal entry. On patrol one day Richard comes to a waterhole. Mexican bandits are encamped there, so Richard watches them from a safe distance. Two Indians happen on the scene—one a Papago, the other a Yaqui.[26] The Mexicans kill the Papago and then try to stamp the Yaqui to death with their horses. At this point, Richard drives off the Mexicans and rescues the Indian. Soon afterward Richard learns of the irrepressible hatred between Mexicans and Yaquis. The Mexicans have enslaved the Yaquis (Mountain Aztecs) and set them to work in the henequin fields of the Yucatan Peninsula. The Yaqui who survived becomes Richard's teacher: "[A]lways before him was an example that made him despair of a white man's equality. Color, race, blood, breeding—what were these in the wilderness?"[27] Through Yaqui, the desert teaches Richard the tenaciousness of life, stoicism, and endurance of strength: a far cry from the free-wheeling life he had pursued in the East.

Rojas appears at the ranch to recapture Mercedes. To escape him, Richard, Thorpe, Mercedes, and the two cowboys, Ladd and Lash, started a long trip to Yuma across the treacherous lava beds. Without the survival skills of Yaqui, the group would have perished. Rojas follows but is tricked by Yaqui and plunges down a cliff to his death. The group remains in the lava fields for several weeks while Ladd recuperates from bullet wounds and from having a cholla (Grey spelled it "choya") cactus blade driven into his face while fighting Rojas.

When the group returns to Belding's ranch, many changes have transpired. A land promoter, Ben Chase, has all but cheated Belding out of his holdings, and his son, Radford, has become another "Rojas" in relation to Nell. Also, Richard's parents, who have come from the East to visit their prodigal son, are amazed to hear of his exploits and astounded that their son, who comes from a wealthy family, works for forty dollars a month. It does not take long for Richard Gale to set things right after his return: he badly beats Radford Chase and forces Bern Chase to stop harassing Belding. This revenge does not bring back Belding's property, however, nor does it erase the fact that Chase has staked legitimate claims to most of the remaining land in the area.

At this dark point, Yaqui bids Richard to follow him into the No-Name Mountains. Going to the source of the Forlorn River, they find the gold that Burton (Cameron) had left many years before. They also discover a twenty-one-year-old certificate that records the marriage of Burton and Nell Warren, the present Mrs. Belding. This proves that Nell Burton is not illegitimate and destroys the last obstacle to her marriage to Richard. On the day of the wedding, Yaqui goes home— to the lava beds. His work is done, for he has fashioned Richard Gale into a powerful force.

Grey uses the same basic themes in *Desert Gold* as he had in his other novels: individualism, the Edenic and healing qualities of the West, and the transforming power of the desert. The author, however, develops two new themes in *Desert Gold,* and one of these is the role of the heroine. Rojas constantly tells Mercedes that he will reform if she will love him. When she refuses, Rojas becomes meaner than ever, and he blames Mercedes for the deterioration. Radford Chase plays the same game with Nell Burton: if Nell will return his love, he will become a model citizen. If she will not, says Radford, she will cause him to do things, the responsibility for which he could not accept. Grey presents this dilemma to many of his heroines. In one novel he allows the heroine to give the love that the bad man wants, but it is to no avail, indicating that appeasement of evil-doers is a mistake.

The second new development in *Desert Gold* is antiracism, for Grey portrays the tragic aspects of racial hatred. Not only in *Desert Gold*, but in a short story titled "Yaqui," Grey wrote of the internecine strife between the Mexicans and the Yaquis. The Yaquis had lived for centuries in the Sierra Madres, and like the United States Indians, they were unsettled by gold prospectors. They moved from the mountains into the desert and finally went to the lava beds from which could be seen in the distance the Gulf of California. Even in this forlorn place, the Yaquis were not safe, for each winter the goldseekers came from the South. The animosities generated between the Yaquis and Mexicans amounted to a war of extermination in which time dictated against the Indians. Grey's sympathy for American Indians who were mistreated by white settlers was well known, and his support of the Yaquis against the Mexicans harmonized perfectly with his views.

The continuing strife along the Mexican border prompted another desert novel, *The Light of Western Stars* (1914). When Madeline ("Majesty") Hammond, a New York society girl, buys a ranch in Southern Arizona, she becomes involved in the struggle between Mexican leaders Francisco Madero and Victoriano Huerta. Majesty's favorite cowboy, Gene Stewart (called El Capitan), joins the Madero faction and fights against Don Carlos, a wealthy Mexican supporter of Huerta. The belligerency between these two moves the novel's events along at a rapid pace.

A highlight in the novel is "cowboy golf." President William Howard Taft popularized golf in the United States, so it was natural for Grey to feature the game in one of his books. The cowboys are entranced by golf, begging off work to practice. When some of Majesty's eastern friends visit the ranch, a golf "tournament" is arranged. The event proceeds nicely until Monty Price disagrees with the umpire, an Englishman named Castleton, about the lay of the ball. Monty discusses the matter with his hand on his six-shooter, a fact that considerably tempers Castleton's rebuttal. The "tournament" ends amid merrymaking from the spectators.

In addition to golf, the automobile is a feature in *The Light of Western*

Stars. The old-time cowboys distrust the car, saying it will never take the place of the horse and buggy. Even Link Stevens, the "chauffeur," thinks he is breaking a bronc when he drives the vehicle. He can travel sixty-three miles in an hour and fifteen minutes. Understandably, other occupants of the car are usually reluctant passengers.

In fact, Gene Stewart avoids execution by the Mexican revolutionists because of the automobile. Captured by them, he is sentenced to death, but Majesty uses her wealth and power to contact prominent senators in Washington who intercede on Stewart's behalf and get him pardoned. Although Stewart is pardoned, the site of the execution is Mezquital, well over a hundred miles from Majesty's ranch and cut off from telegraphic facilities. The only way to get word to the officials in time to stop the killing is a wild automobile ride in which Stevens makes record time despite several blow-outs caused by cholla. Because the party goes to Mezquital just in time to save Gene, he and Majesty like automobiles for the rest of their lives.

In time, after their marriage, Majesty bears Stewart a child. They name her Madge and call her "Majesty." Her career as a young college lady is followed in Grey's sequel to *The Light of Western Stars,* the novel *Majesty's Rancho.*

As Grey's novels appeared more and more rapidly, the story spread that he never revised after he finished writing. Several reviews and essays reported that after he gave his manuscript to Dolly, he never looked at it again until it was in print. Grey did, however, edit *The Light of Western Stars* and some of his other novels. He wrote to Murphy in July 1912:

Dear Dan,

Dolly agrees with you about the detached nature of several of these chapters. I "sit" on myself too much to please Mr. H[arper?] and a lot of critics.

I must go back, cut out, condense, change a little, and write in more story & action.

My idea is to bring forth Pat Hawe [a sheriff in the novel who was badge happy] & Don Carlos, and make a strong scene *before* the cowboy golf chapter.

Then I'll improve that. I'll write in some more action, etc. just after that chapter. Then I'll cut the "Mountain Trail," the "Crags," a little to help along with the idea.

What do you think of this?

The succeeding chapters according to Dolly are *splendid.*

Got my statement from Harpers. 2000 copies of Riders [of the Purple Sage]
sold before the last edition. Isn't that fine?
Let me have a line from you.

> Sincerely
> Zane[28]

By the time Grey wrote *Majesty's Rancho* (1937) the internal com-
bustion engine was in ill-repute with many lovers of old fashioned
ways. The plot is set in the mid-1930s. Gene Stewart, now an aging
man and doting father, is bothered by cattle rustling. He and his men
cannot understand why the cattle tracks end at the state highway until
the book's hero, Lance Sidway, deduces correctly that the stolen cattle
are hauled away in trucks. Rustling has become a mechanical art, and
the gangster elements, led by "Honey Bee" Uhl, invade the territory
with their big gaudy cars and their slick methods of operation. "Progress" in the form of motorized vehicles exacts a high price from society
in the lives it changes.

Majesty, now a college student, typifies much of the changed thinking about young people. As she tells her mother: "For young people
[the] modern thing seems to be to break all the laws—speed laws,
booze laws! There is no such thing as modesty, as I remember you
taught it to me. Pagans, I fear! I haven't opened a Bible since my
religion course during my sophomore year."[29] Majesty finally sees the
light and changes her ways because of Lance Sidway's love and because
of the deep influence of the desert around her. But Grey talks about
the thousands of other young people who do not change in a novel
called *The Call of the Canyon.*

The Lure of the Desert

In *The Call of the Canyon* (1924) Carley Burke goes to the West to
find Glenn Kilbourne, her fiancé, who left the East to recuperate from
wounds received in World War I. She finds him, but he will not return
to New York with her; he prefers the life of a hog farmer to that of a
businessman. Finally, Carley leaves without him, but not before buying land in the Arizona desert. Returned to New York City, Carley
compares life in the East and West and frequently finds herself defending the West. Her friend Eleanor states the modernist's viewpoint:
"The preachers and reformers and bishops and rabbis make me sick.

They rave about jazz. Jazz—the discordant note of our decadence.—
The idiots! If they could be women for a while they would realize the
errors of their ways. But they will never, never abolish jazz—*never*, for
it is the grandest, the most wonderful, the most absolutely necessary
thing for women in this terrible age of smotheration."[30] Finally, Carley
can sustain no more of such talk, so she utters a dreadful malediction
on her associates and their way of life. What is wrong with this country? Carley Burke tells them.

The role of women is especially despicable to Carley: women got the
vote, only to stay away from the polls; women mock prohibition laws;
and they allow their children to go to dance halls and movie theaters.
Young girls ape the women by wearing short skirts, using lipstick, and
plucking their eyebrows. Women actually stand on street corners distributing pamphlets urging birth control. Women cannot stand child-
birth; or if they give birth, they will not nurse their babies themselves.
Carley closes her tirade with these words: "You doll women, you par-
asites, you toys of men, you silken-wrapped geisha girls, you painted,
idle, purring cats, you parody of the females of your species—find
brains enough if you can to see the doom hanging over you and revolt
before it is too late!" (247). In rejecting urban life, Carley hastens back
to her canyons to marry Glenn Kilbourne.

For anyone who ever has wondered about the source of Grey's popularity, Carley's condemnation of urban life and values gives the answer. Grey's audience, the middle and lower-middle classes, had values
that were essentially rural, and they applauded when someone spoke as
harshly about the city element as Carley Burke did. Most of Grey's
work was serialized in magazines appealing to middle-class moral standards. *Call of the Canyon,* for example, appeared in *Ladies' Home Journal*
in several installments in 1921 and 1922, and other magazines such as
The Country Gentleman and *Collier's Weekly* frequently serialized Grey's
novels.

L. H. Robbins, reviewing the book in the *New York Times,* credited
Grey's appeal in part to the cleanness and freshness of his stories. "Is
it possible that even now [1924] the majority of readers like their
fiction decent? Is it possible that the Sophisticates, with all their bal-
lyhooing for this candid novel or that pathologic play, have not yet
prevailed against the standards of respectability that seem to them so
deplorable?[31] Robbins complimented *The Call of the Canyon* for its understanding of sex and presumably for its treatment of sex in an inof-
fensive manner: "Mr. Grey demonstrates that one may touch Freud

without being defiled." The scenery in the novel "does more than fill space. Potent in its influence upon the people of the story, it is a character in itself; the leading character indeed. The wild, lonely, fearfully beautiful Arizona desert has never been better done."[32]

Grey's attacks against post–World War I moral standards were so appealing that he continued writing novels, articles, and short stories on the subject. One of his most cutting assaults on the "new morality" came in *The Day of the Beast,* an eastern novel. Not dealing with the desert, it maintained, nevertheless, the theme of lamentation over the condition to which America had degenerated. The book was serialized in 1922 in *The Country Gentleman.*[33] Other books emphasizing this theme and using the desert as a cure for evil were *Captives of the Desert,* serialized as *Desert Bound* in 1925 by *McCall's,* and *The Lost Pueblo.* The latter was published in 1927 by *Collier's Weekly* under the title *The Water-Hole.*

Grey believed that the novelist has "an appalling responsibility in these modern days of materialism to dare to foster idealism and love of nature, chivalry in men and chastity in women."[34] In fulfilling his role as a social force, Grey became highly moralistic. A book like *The Call of the Canyon* may have struck reviewer Robbins as "clean and fresh" due, in part, to the absence of violent death in its pages, and such an absence is a rarity since only a few of Grey's books avoid violence. Most are replete with sudden, awful death; the casualty rate climbs sometimes into the hundreds within the space of three hundred or so pages. These somber events occur in a setting that is both beautiful and deadly: the desert. If a man's good qualities are ascendant, the desert develops them; if his bad qualities are predominant (as in the case of most people), the desert promotes them and makes their possessor little short of a beast. Grey illustrates this point endlessly in such novels as *Wanderer of the Wasteland, Stairs of Sand,* and *Black Mesa* (published in 1955).

When one considered these possibilities of the desert in developing man's good or bad traits, the picture of the urban East became forlorn indeed—enough so to cause millions of readers to yearn for Western parts. Since most people were unable to go West, they went vicariously with Zane Grey. He was their guide, and in the process, he became much more influential than historian Frederick Jackson Turner in interpreting the value of the West—both historically and contemporarily—to the American public. The desert caused Grey to explore the themes of survival of the fittest and to contrast new trends with old.

In pursuing this course, many of his novels in this category were alike, with Grey adopting a "preaching" stance. The criticism was sometimes made that Grey wrote only one novel and that everything else was just a variant. This criticism was valid only in part for categories of Grey's writing, such as deserts, mountains, and cowboys and was not valid at all for his works as a whole.

The desert was first in Grey's affections for places because it brought out the "ineradicable and unconscious wildness of savage nature in man"[35] and tested him in respect to character and fortitude. He used the desert to show men away from civilization pitted against nature in much the same way as Joseph Conrad used the sea. It was to the barren wastelands that a man must go to transcend mere existence, to find his soul, and to grasp the idea of what Charles Darwin called natural selection. After the desert, the mountains intrigued Grey; they complemented the desert by showing that nature was larger than human life, causing the thoughtful man to ponder his origins and his fate. Within this reflective framework came the knowledge of evolution of all living things and the significance of the balance of nature. Grey thoroughly explored these themes in his work categorized as "mountain novels."

Chapter Three
The Mountain Novels

A deep love of nature inspired Zane Grey to write, and the fields and streams of Zanesville and Lackawaxen first taught him this love. His trip west with Buffalo Jones in 1907 nurtured it, and his note-taking excursions into the deserts and mountains matured it. After 1910 he was increasingly absent from his home in Lackawaxen and from the residence he maintained in Middlebury, New York. He spent his time in the Western regions, practicing the art of "silent watching." At the same time, Grey became enamored of evolutionary theories of Charles Darwin. These influences on Grey within a mountain setting added to what Jim Emett had already taught him and helped Grey to write some of his most memorable novels.

His sense of history was enlarged by coming into contact with several Mormons in mountainous surroundings. He became much interested in Mormonism—what it had been and what it was becoming. In his opinion, Mormons mistreated women and were religious fanatics.[1] Grey's disdain toward Mormonism as an institution was implied in *The Heritage of the Desert* (1910). Two years later, when *Riders of the Purple Sage* was printed, his anti-Mormonism was complete. In this book, generally acknowledged as his most popular, Grey elaborates on the price one must pay to retain personal beliefs, and he shows how tragedy can disrupt lives when a group refuses to believe that "good" and "bad" are relative terms.

Riders of the Purple Sage

Mormonism in its least appealing form was delineated in *Riders of the Purple Sage* (1912). Jane Withersteen, heiress of a fortune left by her Mormon father, befriends Berne Venters, a non-Mormon. Mormon Elder Tull and his associates, who take exception to this friendship, prepare to whip Venters, but at the critical moment, Lassiter, a well-known gunman, arrives and rescues Venters. The hatred that Lassiter feels for the Mormons has been fueled by an eighteen-year search for his sister, Millie Erne, who was lured away from her husband by Mormons. In retaliation for Lassiter's rescue of Venters, the Mormons blind Lassiter's horse by roping it and holding hot irons near its eyes. They swear to kill Lassiter, but because the former Texan is a "fast-draw" with his six-shooters, the Mormons are wary. When Lassiter discovers that Millie is dead, he sets out to find the Mormon who ruined her life. The theme of revenge is thus firmly established at the novel's beginning. Jane Withersteen tries to dissuade Lassiter, telling him that vengeance does not belong to man but to God. Jane's trial, then, is to keep Lassiter from killing again (because it is implicit, although not stated, that she loves him) and to reconcile herself to harassment for befriending non-Mormons while retaining her Mormonism.

The Mormons of Cottonwood, the village where Jane lives in 1871, do not exactly pursue a "reign of terror" against non-Mormons or those Mormons who cooperate with non-Mormons. But Elder Tull (who wants Jane as one of his wives), Bishop Dyer, and their followers make life uncomfortable for anyone who departs from the rigid codes of obedience inculcated by the Mormon Church. They stampede Jane's cattle by waving white flags, by using a mirror to deflect the rays of the sun into the cattle's faces, and by setting a coyote's tail afire and turning the animal loose amid the herd. The Mormon leaders are especially incensed when Jane takes in a non-Mormon girl whose mother dies; and little Fay Larkin becomes a central figure in Grey's later book, *The Rainbow Trail*.

As time passes, Jane's dilemma worsens. She hires Lassiter to ride for her, yet wants him to throw away his guns. Lassiter hotly refuses: "Gun-packing in the West since the Civil War has growed into a kind of moral law."[2] Although the Mormon leadership intensifies its drive by turning Jane's house servants against her and by stealing her prize horses, she still will not renounce the faith in which she was reared. Lassiter simply cannot understand Jane's position: "Among many thousands of women you're one who has bucked against your churchmen. They tried you out, an' failed of persuasion, an' finally of threats—you meet now the cold steel of a will as far from Christlike as the universe is wide. What do they care for your soul?" (174).

While Jane and Lassiter confront the Mormons of Cottonwood, Venters, riding for Jane, has an adventure of his own when he is accosted by an outlaw, Oldring, and a "masked rider." Venters shoots both people, but Oldring escapes and Venters apprehends the "masked rider," only to discover that "he" is a girl named Bess. For several weeks Venters nurses the gunshot victim, fervently praying that she will not die. When she is well enough to move, Venters heads back for Cottonwood; but on the way he finds a secluded valley, the entrance of which is guarded by a great balancing rock, put there no doubt by ancient peoples to ward off enemy attacks. If the rock ever rolls, Surprise Valley, as Venters calls his and Bess's paradise, will be isolated from the world.

Long after Bess's complete recovery, the two make no effort to leave: they find numerous signs of a primitive life that once flourished in the valley; they find food supplies; they find gold, and, naturally, they find their love for each other. The valley causes the two lovers to ponder the meaning of existence: Bess asks, "Did the people who lived here once have the same feelings as we have? What was the good of their living at all? They're gone! What's the meaning of it all—of us?" Venters replies, "Maybe we're higher in the scale of human beings—in intelligence. But who knows? We can't be any higher in the things for which life is lived at all."

> What are they?
> Why—I suppose relationship, friendship, love.
> Love!
> Yes, love of man for woman—love of woman for man. That's the nature, the meaning, the best of life itself. (181–182)

Thus, love between one man and one woman was the noblest function of mankind. This thought came close to being the major theme not only in *Riders of the Purple Sage* but in several other Grey novels.

Venters occasionally leaves his valley for grain and vegetables, neither of which is in great supply. On one such trip, Lassiter secretly trails Venters, learns of Surprise Valley, but does not tell Jane of his discovery. Events rapidly come to a head at Cottonwood as Lassiter, positive that it is Bishop Dyer who led his sister Millie Erne astray, swears to kill Dyer for all the misery he has caused. Jane entreats Lassiter to forget any ideas of revenge, but not even Jane's admission that it was her own father who defiled Lassiter's sister alters his decision. Lassiter—telling Jane that "It's for you!" (288, 292)—exterminates Dyer by first shooting him in the arms and then methodically pumping bullets into his body. After the deed, Lassiter and Jane flee from an enraged Mormon citizenry.

Lassiter heads for Surprise Valley, in the vicinity of which he meets Venters and Bess, who are leaving for Venters' old home in Quincy,

Illinois. When Jane learns that Venters and Bess lived together in Surprise Valley for several weeks, she is infuriated. Despite her Mormonism, which, as she often said, nullifies the possibility of any amorous
attachment to Venters or to any other non-Mormon, Jane feels slighted
and jealous. She expresses her feelings, although she and Lassiter are
being pursued by Elder Tull and the Mormons. All becomes well, however, when Lassiter tells Bess's story as he heard it from the outlaw
Oldring: Bess was really Elizabeth Erne, daughter of Millie. Bishop
Dyer stole Elizabeth from Millie when Elizabeth was three years old
and gave her to Oldring to be raised as an outlaw, an action undertaken
to destroy any chance that Elizabeth's real parents would regain her.
Although an outlaw, Oldring has loved Bess as a daughter and developed her character in positive, humanitarian ways. Lassiter's revelation
mollifies Jane, and she gives Venters and Bess her two favorite horses,
Night and Black Star, to facilitate their flight from Utah.

On the trail again, Lassiter, Jane, and the young girl Fay Larkin
manage to reach the opening of Surprise Valley. While Lassiter fights
off the Mormon pursuers, "phases of the history of the world flashed
through [Jane's] mind—Greek and Roman wars, dark, mediaeval
times, the crimes in the name of religion. Greed, power, oppression,
fanaticism, love, hate, revenge, justice, freedom—for these, men
killed one another" (273). Just before Tull and his men surround the
besieged couple and child, Lassiter rolls the balancing rock, closing the
outlet to Surprise Valley. He wavers at the start, but Jane shouts her
love to him above the din of gunfire, and he heaves the rock into place.
They marry and remain in Surprise Valley for many years until a young
preacher from Illinois, disheartened by the narrow beliefs of his Prot-
estant congregation, comes west at the bidding of Venters and Bess
and finds them. The minister's name is John Shefford, and Grey tells
Shefford's story in *The Rainbow Trail,* the sequel to *Riders of the Purple
Sage.*

In *Riders of the Purple Sage,* Grey develops two traditionally western
themes and one that was universal in application. The role of the frontier woman was the first, the necessity of the "fast-draw" artist to the
growth of the West was another, and third was the strong appeal for
relativism in matters of moral judgment.

Jane Withersteen could have led a very comfortable life, honored by
her fellow churchmen. Because she chooses, however, to help people
other than Mormons, she is harassed and even terrorized. Jane person-

ifies the frontier woman: courageous, determined, changeable, indispensable. Grey does not say why Jane's views of religion differ so much from those of her father and other Mormon officials. Apparently Jane does not believe she has betrayed Mormonism—she makes references to retaining her religion—but she feels Mormonism has forsaken her. She does not approve of intolerant treatment of her fellows. She sees the necessity for change to which other Mormons are blind. Thus, like August Naab in Grey's earlier novel, Jane Withersteen is symbolic of a changing institution, the Mormon Church.

Sharply different from Jane's ways—which in themselves were vital to Western development—are those of the gunman. Throughout the book Grey draws contrasts between the gentle callings of Jane and the violent missions of Lassiter, but at the book's end he makes it quite clear that both conditions were of equal importance in settling the West. Not only in *Riders of the Purple Sage,* but in dozens of other novels, Grey writes of the gunman. Generally a gunman is a cowboy wronged by either a woman or the law. He usually does not like to kill—Grey's fast-drawer is sickened each time he shoots a man—but once he has established a reputation, he has to protect it in every little town he visits. Luckily, the inclinations of most gunmen were toward law and order. Without their help, ordinary men simply could not have coped with the lawless elements. Grey is thus complimentary about most of the gunmen he discusses in the thousands of pages he wrote.

The third major theme in *Riders* is the relativism of moral persuasions: there is much evil in Bishop Dyer, a man who presents to the world a visage of benevolence; but there is much good in Oldring, known to the outside world as a vicious outlaw. The Christian ethic can be stated in different ways by different people, and still be legitimate: a man's calling or religion are not necessarily an index to his ideas of humanity. (Grey demonstrates this especially well in some of his Indian novels). In this connection, Grey shows that of all the fanaticisms, religious fanaticism is the worst because it strips its victims of any self-pride or identification. Religious intolerance also causes a great deal of unnecessary conflict and bloodshed. Grey applies the dictum, "You must change to stay where you are," to Mormonism. Failure to reform and fanaticism hastened the radical changes that ultimately affected the Mormon Church.

That the reading public enthusiastically accepted *Riders of the Purple Sage* was indicated by huge sales of the book and by favorable reviews.

The *Review of Reviews* liked *Riders of the Purple Sage* because it was not servile to any European model but was pure Americana, though exaggerated fiction: "The ruthlessness of Mormonism in that period of Western development is laid bare with great accuracy and the literary artistry of the book is superior to that of many that have been praised above it."[3] *The Nation* computed the mortality rate in the book at well over a hundred, caused primarily by Lassiter and Venters in their efforts to escape the revenge of Mormondom. The story contained all the emotional elements, said the *Nation,* that had ever been dreamed of or invented.[4] Even *The New York Times* was kind to Grey on this occasion; its reviewer lauded *Riders of the Purple Sage* as superior to Grey's earlier book, *The Heritage of the Desert. Riders* was closer knit in construction, better balanced in component elements, and more poignant in its emotional qualities.[5] Further evidence of the book's popularity was the proposal by a Mr. Van Brunt in 1913 that he dramatize the story for stage production—a suggestion never fulfilled, though some of Grey's later works were turned into plays.[6] As late as 1950, the U.S. State Department wanted to translate *Riders* into Annamese for propaganda purposes in Indo-China, but this plan did not materialize.[7]

The Rainbow Trail

Even before *Riders* was published, Grey was busily working on another novel about the American West, *The Rainbow Trail* (1915), which dealt with the Reverend John Shefford, who goes west from Quincy, Illinois, in part to forget the quarrels with his congregation, and also to find Cottonwood, where Jane Withersteen, Lassiter, and Fay Larkin once lived. Cottonwood, however, is now abandoned, and in its place is a "sealed-wife" village, where Mormons hide their wives to escape prosecution by the federal government for practicing polygamy. In a small community known as Stonebridge, Shefford attends a Mormon service; and he concludes that both Mormon and other religions suffer from the same weakness: they exist only to uphold the founders of a church. He asks, "is there no religion divorced from power?"

In Stonebridge is a mysterious woman named Mary, called the Sago Lily, and Shefford wonders if Mary is one of the sealed wives. He begins meeting her frequently and learns in due time that the Sago Lily is none other than Fay Larkin. (Grey never explains how or when Fay left Surprise Valley.) She is not a sealed wife or even a Mormon, although the Mormon community exerts great pressure on her to join them. In a way, she relives the experiences of Jane Withersteen of an earlier age. Finally, in desperation, Fay and Shefford flee from Stonebridge to escape the Mormons who are tormenting her and the glare of publicity caused by government investigations into the sealed-wife villages.

The two head for Surprise Valley by the path Fay has memorized. There they find Jane Withersteen and Jim Lassiter, who have lived for many years in the secluded Paradise. When the group leaves and heads for Nonnezoshe, "the Rainbow Bridge,"[8] it is guided by a Navajo, Nas Ta Bega, and followed by an Indian renegade, Shadd. They finally reach a trading post and make plans to go to Illinois, where Berne and Bess Venters are waiting to see them.

The Rainbow Trail was serialized as *The Desert Crucible* in 1915 by *Argosy*. The book's main thrust is the continuing change in Mormonism in the last quarter of the nineteenth century, for a young generation of Mormons was more willing to change than its elders had been. Its historical themes deal with sealed-wife villages and the conflict between the government and long-established religious habits. Themes of religious prejudice, with the intent of showing that there was little difference between Mormon and non-Mormon narrowness, run throughout the book. Finally, Grey continues a theme that he emphasized in previous books: the mistreatment of Indians by the white man. Both Nas Ta Bega (who actually existed) and Shadd are wronged, but each reacts differently: Nas Ta Bega uses his powers for good; Shadd, for evil.

Grey was pleased with *The Rainbow Trail,* and well he might have been. Mary Roberts Rinehart wrote a glowing review of it, former skeptic Ripley Hitchcock sent a warm letter of congratulations, and Dolly Grey spoke of it as one of her husband's "thinking novels."[9] Before too many more years passed, Grey was publicly heralded as the writer most in demand by publishers; and Harper's offered first a five- and then a ten-year contract, with varying rates of royalty that were always higher than standard (in one instance, he received 20 percent royalties for some of his collected short stories). In the midst of his growing popularity as a literary author, Grey tried to keep things in perspective: to write every day (although he did not always to this), to fish whenever possible, and to avoid morbid spells of depression. History, cowboys, and horseflesh continued to fascinate him; but he always turned to the mountains for the real lessons of nature.

Darwinian Influences

Grey's 1920 novel, *Man of the Forest,* shows more clearly than most of his books how mountainous settings inspired thoughts of evolution; but the story itself is typical of Grey. Milt Dale is regarded by the citizens of Pine, Arizona, as lazy and shiftless because he will not take a job on a ranch. Milt is gifted as a mechanic, however, so the people of Pine are always happy to see him. When Helen Rayner and her sister Bo come to Pine from the East to oversee their ailing uncle's ranch, Grey gives a preview of the novel's theme as Milt tells Helen that actually to know the value of life, one must do five things at one time or another: go hungry, be away from home, face death, desire to kill someone, and be madly in love. The book's plot involves Helen's apprenticeship as a rancher, evil men trying to take her property, and Milt's foiling their designs. The love affair between Milt and Helen is easily predictable.

The novel is replete with passages about the evolution of man from a state of barbarism to that of civilization. Such statements indicate that man is but a part of a grand, inscrutable design in which the trials of life such as the five Milt mentions are necessary to all living things. Thoughts of "natural selection" or "survival of the fittest," underlie these passages. Charles Darwin says in *The Descent of Man*: "Natural selection follows from the struggle for existence; and this from a rapid rate of increase."[10] Zane Grey says in *Man of the Forest*: "If you're quick to see, you'll learn that the nature here in the wilds is the same as that of men—trees fight to live—birds fight—animals fight—men fight. They all live off one another."[11]

When Darwinists made these points in the early part of the twentieth century, the rural and small-town middle classes usually charged them with error about human nature or with atheism. Yet when Zane Grey said the same things in less formal language, the middle classes regarded him as a man of great common sense and insight. Thus, Grey unwittingly became an acceptable interpreter of Darwinism to a great mass of America's citizens, and the impact was significant. It was not only in *Man of the Forest* that these thoughts were evident but also in several other novels.

Lucy Watson, for example, in *Under the Tonto Rim* (1926), thinks: "In ages back all the wandering tribes of men had to hunt to live, and their problems were few. . . . Through the long ages, these savages had progressed mentally and spiritually. Lucy saw that as a law of life."[12] This novel concerns a female social worker who goes into the wild Tonto country of central Arizona to work with the settlers. At first Lucy believes she symbolizes the advanced culture of her day: "These backwoods people were many generations behind city people in their development" (80). At the end of the book, however, Lucy Watson, social worker, marries Edd Denmeade, hunter of wild bees and a resident of the Tonto. Grey was a close student of Darwin, so evolutionary beliefs in his novels are to be expected. Moreover, Grey wrote most of the books dealing with this subject in a remote mountain fastness in the shadow of the Tonto Rim where he had an excellent chance to study nature firsthand, to read Darwin, and to incorporate these points into his written work. *Under the Tonto Rim* first appeared in 1925 in the pages of *Ladies' Home Journal*.[13] Its original title was *The Bee Hunter*, but it was changed, partly, because Gene Stratton Porter's new novel, *Keeper of the Bees*, could conceivably cause confusion among readers.[14] *Man of the Forest* was serialized in 1917 by *The Country Gentleman*. Although Grey found it difficult to concentrate on revising the novel for book publication, it proved to be one of his most popular efforts. Related in principle to *Man of the Forest* was *The Deer Stalker*, a 1925 serialization in *The Country Gentleman*, which was published in book form in 1949. In it, the deer population on Buckskin Mountain in northern Arizona has increased because of unrestrained slaughter of cougars. When the deer multiply so fast that there are not enough grazes and forages for them, they face starvation. The balance of nature has been broken, says one of the characters in the book: "Herds of deer, running free, will never thrive whar' the cougars have been killed off. The price of healthy life in the open is eternal vigilance—eternal watch an' struggle against death by violence. Man cain't remove the balance an' expect Nature to correct it. These heah ain't had nothin' to chek their overbreedin' and inbreedin'. They jest doubled and trebled."[15]

The government's "solution" to the problems causes anguish among the forest rangers of Buckskin Mountain, for unhampered hunting designed to destroy twenty-five thousand deer is decided on. Thad Eberne, the chief ranger, is ultimately dismissed from the forestry service for objecting to the invasion of the area by hundreds of unskilled hunters who in many instances do not kill the deer but inflict painful injuries on them. Rangers spend days following the path of hunters to find the results of their amateurism and to kill the wounded, crippled deer. The whole gory situation illustrates to Grey the baneful effects of man's meddling with nature.

This preoccupation with nature—its balance, its beauty, and its evolution—dominated the Grey novels about the wild, mountainous regions of the Tonto country. One such novel, *Stranger from the Tonto* (1956), was a contrived story. Its hero, Kent Wingfield, makes most of his decisions about love and action before he ever meets the other characters. His mountain heritage, though, is the most significant thing about Wingfield; as in so many of his novels, Grey makes setting and description more important than characterization.

When Wingfield sets out to rescue a girl, Lucy Bonesteel, from Southern Utah's notorious Hole in the Wall Gang, he develops his instincts for survival, and his sense of nature matures in doing so. In Utah, Wingfield stands in awe of the canyon country: "He felt the awful solemnity of the eons that had produced this phenomenon, the august reign of a spirit to which time, life, death, were nothing, the invisible proof of eternity."[16] Wingfield not only saves Lucy but also rehabilitates her father, Avid Bonesteel, the leader of the Hole in the Wall Gang. This effort succeeds because of Wingfield's superior background. Grey once more endows a character with superhuman qualities, thereby causing critics to doubt his sense of realism.

A similar thing occurs in another of Grey's mountain novels, *The Mysterious Rider*, serialized in *The Country Gentleman*, published as a book in 1921, and turned into a play in 1923 called *Hell-Bent Wade*. Set in the late nineteenth century in Colorado, the novel concerns the love of a man for his spoiled son. Bill Belllounds simply cannot grasp what everybody else sees—that his son Jack is a thoroughly rotten person. Bill even expects Columbine, whom he has reared after rescuing her from Indians, to become Jack's bride. Columbine's lot, as well as that of her cowboy sweetheart, Wilson Moore, is desperate until the arrival of a mysterious rider known as Hell-Bent Wade because of the bad luck that always seems to follow him.

Wade wrongly accused his wife of infidelity eighteen years before, and as a result, she left his house, taking their young daughter with her. Indians killed the mother and apparently kidnapped the daughter. So Hell-Bent becomes a wanderer, doomed to a life of self-punishment because of his base deed. As does Adam Larey in *Wanderer of the Wasteland*, Wade deliberately seeks situations in which he can be of service to his fellow human beings, for through good works, he believes he can atone for his past sins. It is natural, then, for Wade to be interested in a doting father who is trying to marry his horrible son to his lovely adopted daughter. Wade takes employment at the Belllounds' ranch and is soon in the midst of events. He makes efforts to reform Jack Belllounds, but in vain. Finally, when Wade discovers that Jack is rustling his own father's cattle and laying the deed to Wilson Moore, he decides to rid the world of a problem. He and Jack shoot it out and both become casualties. While this occurs, Columbine discovers that Wade is her father. The story ends with Columbine and Wilson planning their marriage.

The Mysterious Rider is a study of the loner, so familiar to students of western history. There is a direct line between "Wansfell the Wanderer" and Hell-Bent Wade. Each, in his own way, fights the elements, but mostly himself. In the process, each contributes greatly to the betterment of the human race; and they are proof that through suffering and struggle, there is "survival of the fittest." There are many loners in Grey's treatment of the West, but these two are the most typical. Grey was eminently qualified to write about loners, for he was largely one himself, at least concerning literature, and disliked most of the literary forms of his day. He once visited a publisher and was given an advertisement of a national, best-selling novel as an example of what his own writing should be. Grey hated the novel in question and said that "it is as far from literature as the world is wide." Grey told the publisher that he would be ashamed to have his name on such a book.[17] Thus, as Grey very definitely set himself apart from most literature of the time, several of his novels deal with individuals who run counter to prevailing trends.

The play produced from *The Mysterious Rider* contains four acts and was done in collaboration with a New York dramatist, Frank McGlynn.[18] Although the play tends to be even more melodramatic than the novel, it stresses the nature of life, its brevity, and its cruelty. A major weakness of the play is that a main incident—one involving Jack's fight with Wilson and one that inspires much of the subsequent action—takes place completely off stage. Thus, the audience (if there ever was one, for there is no evidence that this play was performed) had to guess many of the play's motivating factors. In the book, Wade and Jack kill each other; in the play, however, Bill Belllounds finally learns the truth about his son and banishes him. At that same time, Hell-Bent Wade departs to continue his life's mission of helping people. The curtain falls as Columbine rushes to Wade calling him "Father!"

Happily for his supporters and for the literary world at large, Grey did not try to write many plays. His great strength was in novels and short stories and to these he committed himself. His mountain novels continued to emphasize the themes of evolution, survival of the fittest, the beauty of nature, and the loner. *Sunset Pass* (1931), set in New Mexico, and *Robber's Roost* (1932), in the mountains of Southern Utah, present additional discussions of the loner. In *Sunset Pass* Trueman Rock seeks to bring a rustling family to justice. Rock's chief dilemma is that he falls in love with the culprit's daughter. As in so many other of Grey's novels, the hero not only wins the hand of the maiden but reforms through love and example the erring parents. *Robber's Roost* is about outlaws who capture a beautiful woman, sister of a rich English rancher, ostensibly for ransom money; but there was another purpose. Grey wrote in a letter: "It never occurred to me that the motive [in *Robber's Roost*] was really rape. Most of all the present day novels are worse than rape. But I'm glad to get a chance to correct the blunder. . . . I'll gladly correct and do what's important" [to remove obvious suggestions of rape].[19] Even the hint of employing themes used extensively by current literature displeased Grey.

Gold Fever

The discovery of gold in the Saw-Tooth Mountains of Idaho inspired two mountain novels:[20] *The Border Legion* (1916) and *Thunder Mountain* (1935). *The Border Legion* was developed from an idea given to Grey by a friend, Robert Hobart Davis. Grey, who believed the story would make a play and a strong photodrama, asserted that "I am absolutely sure that it will be one of my stories that are read at one sitting."[21] *The Border Legion* concerns the gold rush of the 1860s in Idaho. Joan Randle, originally from Missouri, quarrels with her sweetheart, Jim Cleve, causing Cleve to join outlaws headed by the notorious Jack Kells. In anguish over her deed, Joan sets out to find Cleve and make amends, but on her way she is kidnapped by Kells. In Kells's camp, Joan, who wears a mask and masculine attire to keep her sex from being known, is nicknamed "Dandy Dale."

Joan plays an ironic role in the novel. Her deeds almost turn a good man bad (Cleve) and a bad man good (Kells). When Cleve discovers who Dandy Dale is, his first thought is to kill her and then himself. But when Joan convinces him that she has not been sexually violated, the two make up and even slip a parson into camp one night to marry them. Cleve and Joan, as husband and wife, try to escape from Kells and his men in the midst of a gold rush. Grey graphically describes men gone mad over gold: "It was a time in which the worst of men's nature stalked forth, hydra-headed and dead, roaring for gold, spitting fire, and shedding blood. It was a time when gold and fire and blood were one. . . . It was a time, for all it enriched the world with yellow treasure, when might was right, when men were hopeless, when death stalked rampant. The sun rose gold and it set red. It was the hour of Gold!"[22] Lust for gold in many men is stronger than that for a woman, so Kells's greed causes his destruction. At the novel's end, Kells and his gang shoot it out with one another, and only Jim Cleve and his wife, Joan, escape to live happily in their love for each other.

The theme of what lust for gold does to men was continued by Grey in his novel, *Thunder Mountain* (1935). At the novel's beginning, Thunder Mountain in Idaho is in a pure state of nature. First, the beavers abound, then the Indian. While at Thunder Mountain, the Indian finds gold, presaging the white man and evil days: "No voice, no warning, no spirit, no God could drive him [the white man] away."[23] At the end of the novel, Thunder Mountain is crumbling away: "As if in mockery of the littleness of man, Nature pealed out the doom which the wise old beaver and the savage chief had foreseen— For ages its foundations had groaned warnings. And now the hour of descent had come" (382). Nature, in the fierce setting of a mountain, shows that ultimately it will prevail over the wishes of man.

The chief character is Lee (Kalispel) Emerson, one of the first white men to see gold as well as a quartz lode on Thunder Mountain. He wants to sell the quartz lode, so he leaves to find a buyer. On his return, news of the gold supply has spread, and Thunder Mountain has grown in population, "as if by magic" (145). Lee's own claim has been preempted. During the course of the book, Lee not only discovers a gold thief who plagues the area, but also marries a dance-hall girl. The book ends with Parson Weeks at the marriage ceremony paying a ringing tribute to western womanhood: "It is a hard country, this glorious West of ours. It takes big women to stand it. . . . They are making the West. Who shall remember in threescore years, when the broad land will be prosperous with cities and ranches, that the grandmothers of that generation, ever were, let us say, dance-hall girls? And if it were remembered, who could bring calumny against the strong-souled mothers of the West?" (298–99).

The Western Woman

Grey told the story of a strong-souled mother of the West in his mountain novel set in the Tonto, initially called *Frontier Wife,* but changed to *30,000 on the Hoof* (1940). This novel is one of only two mountain novels that deal extensively with modern times—World War I and its aftermath. Actually, the novel is a saga, for it tells the story of a man and his trials from the last days of Indian warfare under General George Crook to the landing of troops in France under General John Pershing. Logan Huett stays in Arizona after his discharge from the army in the 1880s and telegraphs his proposal that Lucinda Baker in Missouri join him and become his wife. They settle in Sycamore Canyon in Arizona's Tonto Country, where Logan's great dream is to raise a herd of thirty-thousand head of cattle. He fights droughts, blizzards, grasshoppers, rustlers, and swindlers to achieve this goal. Through his ordeals, his one mainstay is his beloved wife, Lucinda. She bears him three sons, George, Abraham (see, however, chapter 9 for a different explanation for Abe), and Grant. She and Logan also rear a girl named Barbara who they found lost in the Tonto and who ultimately marries the second son, Abe.

By the time of World War I, Logan is nearing his long-sought dream of a thirty-thousand head herd. When he finally sells to the government and wants cash rather than a check, the government man fills a box full of newspapers and tinfoil and gives it to Logan; and not until some time later does Logan discover that he has been cheated out of nearly a million dollars. At about the time the government agent swindles Logan, his sons are called away to war "to make the world safe for democracy." Logan is not too apprehensive about his sons' chances until he sees a newsreel at a movie: "All these scenes purported to have actually been filmed at the front made Logan sick and dazed. 'So that's war?' he muttered, jostling through the noisy crowd emerging into the street. 'And I sent my sons into that. . . . Good God! I reckoned they'd have a chance. Man to man, with rifles, behind trees and rocks, where the sharp eye and crack shot would prove who was best! But *that*—God Almighty—what would you call that?"[24] Lucinda thought of the war: "Men had always, from the remote aboriginal days, loved to fight. But it was the women who bore sons and therefore the brunt of war. . . . She had to face her soul now, and perhaps some day the final sacrifice of a mother, and she needed God" (236). The hateful news finally comes about her sons: George and Grant have been killed in action, and Abe is missing. Lucinda and Huett suddenly realize that the loss of their money to the government agent is nothing compared to the loss of their sons. The trials of Job continue to stalk the Huett family as Barbara (Abe's wife) loses her mind. One day, however, Abe shows up without any warning, and things begin to reverse for the Logan household.

The United States government comes very close to being the villain in this book. Its agent cheats Logan out of his cattle money, and when Logan goes to Washington to protest, he is further mistreated. As if this is not bad enough, he has to sacrifice his sons to a war whose necessity for American involvement was seriously doubted by many people. The book also contains themes traditional to the mountains of the West: the growth of manhood, perseverance, and trustworthiness. The novel develops forcefully the theme of womanhood. Logan may be the strong, pioneer type, but he never would have succeeded without Lucinda's love and moral support. Grey wanted very much to put this point into the story when he rewrote it to enlarge the woman's perspective.[25] Dolly was quite complimentary of *30,000 on the Hoof*, calling it a "very interesting and well written story," though it moved a bit slowly for serialization;[26] and Grey was delighted with his efforts. He wrote to Harper's requesting an early publication of *30,000 on the Hoof*, "for which I selected a better title, *The Frontier Wife*. This is perhaps my most powerful novel and it has a tremendous climax built around the world war and which showed what that catastrophe did to many of our frontier people."[27]

The themes treated, the poignancy, and the style of writing made *30,000 on the Hoof* one of Grey's best literary efforts. He had hunted in the Tonto country, which is the novel's setting, and had found the old trail used by General Crook and also the abandoned ranch of a man named Jones who had once dreamed about a herd of thirty-thousand cattle and who raised three sons and an adopted daughter, only to have the joys of life dashed by a horrible war.[28] Thus, the novel is about real people, real events, and real emotions.

Grey's Popularity

Grey commented further on governmental indifference to the suffering of citizens (especially veterans) caused by World War I in his other

mountain novel treating modern times. *The Shepherd of Guadaloupe*
(1930), in which Clifton Forrest, just home from the war, is shattered
in body and spirit. Doctors give him only one month to live; but it is
not long before he, like other Grey characters, begins improving in the
New Mexico setting: "He felt, he heard, he saw, he smelled the physical objects of Nature about him."[29] Clifton finds on his return from
war that his house and land have been taken by his father's old enemy,
Jed Lundeen. When Lundeen's daughter, Virginia, tells her father that
his treatment of the Forrests is immoral, his answer is an index to
the times: "Not in this day and age" (68). Ultimately, however, right
and true love won: Clifton gets back his property and wins Virginia's
hand, putting an end to the "Forrest-Lundeen" feud that raged for
years.

Publication of *The Shepherd of Guadaloupe* in 1930 marked the twentieth anniversary of Grey's affiliation with Harper's Publishing Company. When the book's dust jacket offered a free photograph of Grey
to any interested reader, hundreds of glowing tributes came from people all over the globe about Grey's power as a writer. One reader closed
her letter with what was actually a compliment: "Hoping your next
story is better than all the rest."[30] Another reader said, "*The Shepherd
of Guadaloupe* shows that this isn't an entirely Synthetic Age [1930]—
that it doesn't, in literature, take a lover and a boudoir to complete a
picture of married life and that true courage isn't born of the potency
of your neighbor's gin."[31] Sophisticated reviewers may have scorned
Zane Grey, but the world was clearly not listening to them.

Grey's mountain novels covered a range of themes from survival of
the fittest to social commentary about the government and modern
times. He was at the height of his power when many of these books
were written, and this influence was apparent as he wrote in his diary
in 1920 (the year *Man of the Forest* was published), "I seem to find
myself a name to reckon with in the world of publishers. I have two
offers, three perhaps, that are larger than any ever offered to an American writer. . . . I believe my long sought-for goal is in sight. And I
shall work as never before."[32] He continued writing novels at a feverish
pace throughout the 1920s. At his home in Altadena, California, he
used an old Morris chair with a lapboard over it to compose his stories,
writing his manuscripts in pencil on legal pad paper. He also traveled
extensively, but he always wrote, although sometimes sporadically,
even while away from home. Some of his very popular books were

written in places like Long Key, Florida; New Zealand; Central American jungles; and Australia. As Grey's fame grew, so did his confidence, but he still suffered frequently from spells of depression. His enormous output of novels in the 1920s was due, in part, to a turning point that had occurred in his career in 1918—one caused by the publication of a historical novel.

Chapter Four
The Historical Novels

In a very real sense, most of Zane Grey's works were historical novels because he gave, on the whole, accurate reconstructions of the periods he wrote about. He usually took copious notes on visits to the places he described, and he profited from associations with "old timers" who actually had seen what Grey put into his novels. These firsthand accounts were often passed to Grey in distorted form, but combined with his own experiences, observations, and reading, they helped him to produce a fairly authentic picture of the Old West. For example, Grey often heard from his friend and guide, Al Doyle, stories about the building of the Union Pacific Railroad, which became the foundation for Grey's novel, *The U.P. Trail*.[1] The stories of Buffalo Jones, Jim Emett, John Wetherill, and many other Westerners were stored in Grey's memory, sometimes for years, and then used in his novels, short stories, and articles.[2] Grey's history depicted the epic sweep of events. Even the novels that dealt with wretched feuds implied that the reader's life was somehow better because of all the bloodshed. Grey wanted his readers to appreciate their ancestors; thus, many of his historical novels became studies in patriotism.

Grey's historical novels were based on specific historical incidents. Building the Union Pacific Railroad, Boulder Dam, and Western Union are landmarks in the history of this country. The frequent lack of humanity toward Indians, the widespread activity of the International Workers of the World both during and after World War I, the occurrence of range wars, the passing of the buffalo, and the fight against predatory economic interests are also well documented. Through his research, Grey discusses these points in most of his other novels, but in the historical novels, they become the central focal point—the moving force of the novels themselves.

The History of a Railroad

In *The U.P. Trail* (1918), Grey's first historical novel dealing with the West, he depicts the building of the Union Pacific Railroad as a

52

"work of giants," and he desired that his novel embrace "all that could be possible during that wild time and colossal enterprise."[3] In the course of the railroad's construction, it comes to mean different things to different people: to Warren Neale, engineer, it is a dream; to several railroad commissioners, like Allison Lee, it is a source of profit; to Slingerland the trapper, it is the end of America's great wilderness;[4] and to the Indian, it is the death-knell of his way of life.

The main character, Warren Neale, an Easterner, is young and idealistic; he believes he is participating in an event of worldwide significance, and he cannot understand why some men think differently: "Why could not all men be right-minded about a noble cause and work unselfishly for the development of the West and the future generations?"[5] Neale spends much time thwarting the purposes of profiteers and lamenting the underhanded tactics of the construction companies—primarily the Credit Mobilier—which has contracted to build the railroad. On the surface, building the Union Pacific Railroad appears to be one of the most adventurous and romantic episodes in American history, but underneath all the show is a grasping bureaucracy mired in corruption. One of the greatest despoilers is Commissioner Lee; ironically, Neale loves his daughter, Allie.

Neale and his sidekick, Larry Red King (who turns out to be the brother of the notorious Texas gunman, Kingfisher), find Allie after an Indian attack in which she is the only survivor. Just before Allie's mother dies in the Indian raid she tells Allie the truth about her father—that she is the daughter of Commissioner Lee. Neale and Larry Red King nurse Allie back to health; both fall in love with her, but Allie prefers Neale. Later, Allie is kidnapped by gambler Durade, her mother's second husband, and forcibly kept at his gambling saloon at the head of the railroad, a wild place named Benton, where life is cheap indeed. Before Allie is rescued from the gambling saloon, several men are killed, including Larry Red King. When Allie is safe and reunited with her father, all should be well for Allie and Neale, but nothing is further from the truth. Her father doubts Neale's morals since Neale publicly befriends Beauty Stanton, operator of a local saloon, and fights Allison over operations of the Union Pacific Railroad. Allie is sent to Omaha where she stays for months yearning for her lover. Finally, she can bear it no longer, so she leaves her father for Warren Neale.

Allie finds Neale at Promontory Point, Utah, where the last spikes of the transcontinental railroad are about to be driven. Arizona donates a spike of gold, silver and iron for the occasion; Nevada, one of silver; and California, one of pure gold. Thousands of people, including the

famed Irish builders, gather to witness the historic event. The driving
of the last spike is to be heard all over the country by telegraphic
facilities, after which the vast audience shouts "Done!" to a waiting
world. Neale's heart is full as he watches these proceedings; to him,
the scene is "great, beautiful, final." He has a tremendous sense of
fulfillment, and the only thing missing is his beloved Allie. But in the
middle of the ceremonies, Neale feels a small hand in his; he looks
around and sees Allie. His triumph is complete.

A Turning Point in Grey's Career

The U.P. Trail represented a personal triumph for Grey, because it
marked an important turning point in his career. Before 1918 Grey
had regarded his western novels and short stories as "stepping stones
to a higher plane of literature." His "apprenticeship" in the western
field was preparation for the Great American Novel, in which the psychological aspects of youth would be fully explored. The success of *The
U.P. Trail,* however, and the personal exuberance that its thrust gave
to Grey led to his decision to stay solely in westerns and adventure
stories: "My power and my study and passion shall be directed to that
which already I have written best—the beauty and color and mystery
of great spaces, of the open, of Nature in her wild moods. This decision
has been a relief."[6]
    Not only did Grey put these thoughts about *The U.P. Trail* into his
diary, he also wrote essentially the same things to Hitchcock at Harper's: "Much good has come to me, in the way of significant appreciation, since *The U.P. Trail* was published. It is like wine."[7] Grey's
decision was quickly applauded by Hitchcock and the other editors at
Harper's, who had no desire to lose their most popular writer. In still
another letter, Grey said in relation to *The U.P. Trail:* "All these years
my idea has been to win a public, and then write the powerful psychological novels of love, passion, and tragedy, that I am capable of writing. . . . For long I have been divided between this course, and of
throwing all my study and work, passion and nature, into what I really
do best—an interpretation of Nature."[8] Having made this important
decision about his writing, Grey wavered only once, in 1922, when he
allowed the nonwestern novel, *The Day of the Beast,* to be published.
Significantly, that book was one of the least successful he ever wrote.
    Grey apparently found 1918 the year to express the courage of his
convictions. Not only did he come to a basic decision regarding the
type of literature he would write, he also publicized his violent anti-

Germanism. World War I upset the world's equilibrium, and Grey blamed the Germans. In April 1917 he recorded in his diary: "We are on the eve of war with Germany and the soldiers have been sent all over the U.S. to guard bridges, water-powers, and public buildings. Meanwhile, there is hell in Washington, excitement all over the country. . . . I am perhaps as far as any man from wanting war. Yet I come from a family of fighters. . . . I am no pacifist—no peace at any price man. . . . I hate war more than I hate anything else. The agony to women and children I cannot forgive."[9] By the close of the following year, Grey's feelings against the Germans had grown to vitriolic proportions: "Right has prevailed over the Brute, but after effects are deadly. Famine stalks abroad. . . . Germans should not pay in gold— but in blood."[10] With these viewpoints toward the Germans, it was easily predictable that Grey would write a novel dealing with the World War, *The Desert of Wheat.*

Grey versus the "Wobblies"

Grey, accompanied by Dolly, visited the wheat-growing areas of Washington state in preparation for writing *The Desert of Wheat* (1919). While there, he read scientific articles about wheat diseases; and he also familiarized himself with the operations of the International Workmen of the World (IWW), clipping long newspaper passages about the "Wobblies" to his manuscript.[11] His trip and his studies were significant enough for several newspapers to write stories about them; thus, the American reading public was prepared for an anti-German novel from Zane Grey.

The novel's setting is the Bend country in Washington in 1917, just after the United States has entered the war against Germany. There are two dramatic conflicts in the book: first is Kurt Dorn's argument with his German-born father, who believes that the United States is being led astray by England; and this father-son confrontation causes Kurt to have guilt feelings about his German background. The second conflict occurs between the area's wheat farmers and the IWW, which wants to undermine the growth of agricultural products for use by the United States military forces.

Grey treats the Wobblies as a corrupt labor union at best, as spies for the Germans at worst. The organization intimidates farm workers, causing many to walk off their jobs; and it throws phosphorus cakes into wheat fields, which ignite through the hot rays of the sun. While fighting such a fire, Kurt's father dies of a heart attack. Just before he expires, he admits his errors in blindly supporting the German cause. The situation improves considerably after a group of concerned citizens decides to deal with the IWW in the "good old Western way": they hang the Wobbly leader and leave his body tied to a railroad trestle where everybody—friend and foe—can see it. The sight tempers activist plans by the IWW.

The war causes Kurt Dorn to suffer inner conflicts. The area's residents try to convince him that he can best serve his country by staying at home and raising wheat; but he cannot do that, despite its importance. The war has become a very personal thing to him; he has, it seems, a debt that he must pay for his German origins. When he joins the army, his reasons are mostly personal. Even the woman he loves, Lenore Anderson, cannot dissuade him from this course of action. In combat, Kurt does not experience the thrill from inflicting his first casualty that he imagined he would: "His life on earth, his spirit in the beyond, could never be now what they might have been. And he sobbed through grinding teeth as he felt the disintegrating, agonizing, irremediable forces at work on body, mind, and soul."[12] His fatalism causes him to become a hero in an advance against the Germans, but he is wounded so seriously that a specialist gives him only a short time to live. Kurt takes his discharge and returns home to Washington. There, trying to fathom life in general and his own in particular, Kurt thinks: "What were wounds, blood, mangled flesh, agony, and death to men—to those who went out for liberation of something unproven in themselves? Life was only a breath. The secret must lie in the beyond, for men could not act that way for nothing" (348).

When Lenore Anderson nurses Kurt back to health, she grows pensive about the role of womanhood in war. In the original manuscript of *The Desert of Wheat* Grey states (but later deleted) the problem that war presents to women: "They [women] were cursed with lesser bodies [than men] and blessed with higher souls. War was night, hell and devastation to women. . . . If materialistic war meant the survival of the fittest in the evolution of the race, sacrifices of mothers to that inscrutable design running through the ages was made to be only a monstrous lie, an animal function abhorrent and base."[13] In the published work, Grey gives women a solution to the problem of war: they should band together and refuse to have children. This denial to the male ego would cause a miraculous change in the occurrence of wars; thus, "would come an end to violence, to greed, to hate, to war, to the black and hideous imperfection of mankind" (353). Lenore fulfills the requirements of a Grey heroine by nursing Kurt back to health, marrying him, and then becoming his major source of strength.

The Desert of Wheat was lauded by reviewer Theodore Brooke in *Harper's Magazine*. He liked Grey's treatment of the hero, Kurt Dorn, who had to fight not only with "musket and muscles" but also with mind and soul. The heroine comes off better, in Brooke's opinion, than in Grey's previous novels.[14] The tribute to *The Desert of Wheat* that Grey liked best, however, was the one his native Zanesville paid it when he went home in 1921: "I was sought, praised, flattered, entertained as never before in my life. I belonged to Zanesville. I was a Zane, and these people, my old friends, and many new ones, are proud of me. The reception filled me with awe, wonder, sadness & gratitude."[15] As a special honor to Grey, the movie based on the novel was played in the town's cinema. Although Dolly had stated previously that the movie suffered from a marked departure from the book,[16] its showing while Grey was in Zanesville provided some poignant moments for him.

The most nostalgic moment for Grey, however, in that 1921 homecoming occurred as he walked down a street and saw this poem in a store window:

> Come along with me Mr. Gray[*sic*]
> We'll go fishing at Dillon's today,
> Forget "Betty Zane" and all the rest
> For a day of the sport you used to love best.
> For all the honors they've paid you, I ween
> You'd gladly exchange for one glimpse of that scene.
> The "Plains" and "The Rockies" bow low to your pen
> But the Muskingum and Licking are calling again
> There's "Cannon Hell" Putnam and old Cedar Rock
> And the Swimmin' hole! down by the old steam-boat lock.
> The "Diamond" up at the old White House ground,
> Say, boy, shall I stop or how does it sound?

The author, C. M. Shrider, a young storeclerk, had pieced together Grey's old haunts by talking to Grey's contemporaries.[17] Grey tenderly remembered the incident for the rest of his life.

Activity on the Rogue

Grey's preoccupation with World War I continued in *Rogue River Feud,* a novel that was serialized in 1929 by *Country Gentleman* under the title *Rustlers of Silver River.* The story's main character is Kevin Bell, a part of whose jaw has been shot away in combat. He faces a different kind of struggle when he becomes a civilian and fights a big canning company in Oregon for using illegally sized nets to catch salmon at the mouth of the Rogue River. Bell also hates the timber barons who indiscriminately destroy the redwood trees of California and the white cedars of Oregon. Although Bell is denied any help from the government for his war-sustained injuries, the government regularly votes advantages in the form of tax breaks, and even subsidies, to the predatory business interests in this country. Such a condition embitters people like Kevin Bell and his partner, Garry Lord.

As to be expected, the love of a good woman saves Kevin Bell, for Beryl Aard shows him the uselessness of brooding over past failures. Life is meant to be lived happily. Ultimately, through perseverance, Kevin gets the illegally operating canneries investigated and activities of corrupt law officials looked into. He concludes at the book's end that the "feud" has been mostly with himself. He is still embittered from the war and from his experiences thereafter, so much so that he says he will fight again only if the country were under direct physical invasion, but will continue to combat despoilers. He attains personal happiness through Beryl's love, showing that one must somehow find a balance between life as it is, and life as it is wished.

As in *30,000 on the Hoof,* the federal government is largely the villain of *Rogue River Feud.* Grey was not antigovernment, but he definitely questioned many of its procedures. Why allow grasping profiteers to destroy the beauty and the resources of the country—not only allow, but help—while thousands of war veterans went without? This action was a mark of great ingratitude, one that badly needed correcting. He wrote on this subject to Dolly: "The times are bad. The war left greed, selfishness, lawlessness, and crookedness paramount in the hearts of almost all men. I fear my patriotism has been dealt a blow from which it will never recover."[18] Grey's continued stance of social commentator dictated against his being merely a "writer of Western novels."

A Famous Feud

Grey achieved additional recognition as a historical novelist by writing about a feud different from the one involving government and big business. *To the Last Man* (1922), a copiously researched novel, delved deeply into the Graham-Tewksbury feud, which started in Texas and ended in the Tonto country of Arizona. [19] In Tonto history it was known as the Pleasant Valley War and as something of a "feud within a feud," for it involved personal hatred between two families in the context of a cattleman-sheepman war. Grey changed the name to the "Jorth-Isbel feud." During the Civil War, Gaston Isbel serves in the Confederate army, but in his absence, Lee Jorth courts and marries Isbel's sweetheart. Thus, the basis is laid for a feud that ultimately affects several generations.

The book's only heroic characters are women. Ellen Jorth wants to be true to her father's side in the feud, but she needs love as well. (Her mother died years earlier.) When she meets Jean Isbel she hates him—on the surface. But his presence causes her unconsciously to feel the need and desire of loving and of being loved: "It was new, sensorial life, elemental, primitive, a liberation of a million inherited instincts, quivering and physical, over which Ellen had no . . . control. [20]" Not understanding this sudden rush of sensations, Ellen wants to be hidden, "covered by green thicket, lost in the wildness of Nature, unconsciously seeking a Mother" (230). Theodore Brooke, reviewing *To the Last Man* for *Harper's Magazine,* tended to make Ellen's path to love with Jean Isbel the most important thing in the novel: "Grey reveals new powers which even his staunchest admirers could never dream he possessed. There is a delicacy of touch in his handling of Ellen which enables him to look deep into the heart of the Motherless girl men called a 'hussy.'" [21] Ellen is as close to nature as any character Grey ever created and symbolizes the primitivism of that wild country. Yet, love, man's paramount emotion, is the final victor.

Ellen and Jean, members of a younger generation of Jorths and Isbels, are caught—like Shakespeare's Romeo and Juliet—in a cruel dilemma. Logic tells them that the feud is wrong, but a sense of loyalty ties them to their families. They are forced to walk a tightrope of indecision until most of the warring factions are destroyed and they can freely express their love for each other. Unlike the couple in the most famous feud story of all time, Ellen and Jean are not "starcrossed": the combination of a Zane Grey romance and a country that could be called "the land of the happy ending" dictated against ultimate tragedy for the young lovers.

Grey uses a horrifying incident to extol the virtues and bravery of womanhood. When the Jorths one day besiege the Isbels, two of the Isbel faction are killed before they can take cover. While their bodies lie in a field, the Jorths turn loose a herd of hogs that head straight for the corpses. When the women in the beleaguered Isbel camp exhort the men to recover the bodies and all refuse, two women brave Jorth fire to put their men into shallow, temporary graves to keep them from being eaten by the swine. The deed is so brave that it causes a ceasefire by the feuders, who look on in awe. Base man is thus sharply contrasted with noble woman.

After the Jorth-Isbel feud passes into history when the last of the major participants is killed, Ellen and Jean find a common enemy—an outlaw named Colton who rides for the notorious Hash Knife Outfit and who uses the feud as a front for his evil deeds. He is finally killed by Jean Isbel, thus erasing the last barrier to Ellen and Jean's marriage.

To the Last Man is largely a psychological study of a feud mentality, where a struggle continues long after most people have forgotten the reason for it. Vanity is the disease that propels it; love, the quality that stops it. It may be that Grey's former wish to write a great psychological novel never quite left him despite his disavowals of it after *The U.P. Trail* was published. Perhaps *To the Last Man* was, in part, a tribute to that subconscious desire. If so, the psychological-historical combination within a Western setting produced a quite significant piece of work.

The Passing of the Buffalo

Feuds and range wars, frequent occurrences in the Old West, marked the violence of the time and place, and they ended the career of more than one illustrious person. Billy the Kid, for example, was slain as a result of New Mexico's Lincoln County War, which was alluded to but never fully treated in several of Grey's novels. Grey wanted to encompass the entire range of human experience in the West—to capture on paper man's splendor in one instance and his greed in another. Expressive of greed was a historical novel by Grey, *The Thundering Herd* (1925), that is not unlike *To the Last Man* in its extreme violence and in its delineation of man's less noble instincts. *The Thundering Herd* is the story of the buffalo and the tragedy of its passing. Grey, who had been interested in the historical aspects of the great buffalo slaughter ever since his association with Buffalo Jones, tells in his novel of the carnage and shows, in no uncertain terms, how man is debased by it.

Many professional hunters were convinced that they were serving civilization when they went by the thousands into the Staked Plains of Texas and New Mexico. They were opening the Southwest for farmers and cattlemen—a feat that not even the United States Army could accomplish. The Indian threat decreased in proportion to the number of buffalo killed, and more than 200,000 buffalo hides from the Southwest herd were shipped East in 1876. Later the bones were picked up and sold for fertilizer. Only the Indians regarded the buffalo as a major food supply—one reason the government made no effort to stop the wanton destruction of the bison herds. With their source of food exhausted, the Indians became dependent on, and subservient to, the federal government and were forced to accept reservation life.

In the novel, a woman, Millie Fayre, sees the horror of the buffalo slaughter, and she entreats her sweetheart, Tom Doan, to give up the business—indeed, she makes relinquishing it a condition of her marriage to him. Tom swears to comply with Millie's wishes as soon as he has earned enough money to buy a ranch. One day, however, Tom has to kill a motherless young buffalo: "This incident boded ill for Tom. It fixed his mind on this thing he was doing and left him no peace. Thousands and thousands of beautiful little buffalo calves were rendered motherless by the hide-hunters. That was to Tom the unforgivable brutality."[22] Tom ultimately concludes that buffalo hunters are degraded by the wholesale slaughter, for nature never meant for such fearful events to occur. Tom is in a distinct minority in forming these conclusions, but Millie Fayre hastens his decision to give up buffalo hunting.

Grey was personally dissatisfied with *The Thundering Herd* when he finished writing it: "I do not feel that I have done well in writing of this romance of the buffalo. Always I have that feeling at the end of work. I seemed to have failed of the great epic strife I set out to picture."[23] He wanted the book to be a social force, as he indicated when he wrote an account of it to the readers of *Boy's Magazine:* "I hope you boys, and all my readers, will be interested in the story, not only because I have tried to draw a true picture of the extermination of one of the most wonderful of our own American animals, but also that it may give you the impulse toward conservation of what wild life still exists in our great country."[24]

One reason that Grey was not too pleased with *The Thundering Herd* may have been that his editors wanted him to change the novel's ending to give greater depth to the characters.[25] Characterization did not come easily to Grey, and his attempted improvement of it in *The Thun-*

dering Herd was a failure. He continually told the editors that the book was a saga of the buffalo and that characterization therefore was deliberately minimized. A second problem with *The Thundering Herd* was that fiction in 1925 was in a weakened condition as general entertainment trends veered away from the literary world and radios, automobiles, and movies became the most popular diversions of the day. Publishing fiction became so competitive that an editor expressed the opinion that "even Zane Grey cannot afford to have a 'flivver.'"[26] At approximately the time that this dialogue took place about *The Thundering Herd,* another of Grey's books touched off a controversy, and this was the novel that Grey told a friend he would like to be remembered by, *The Vanishing American.*

Grey's Famous Indian Novel

Zane Grey as a social agitator never came off better than in *The Vanishing American* (1925). Long sympathetic to the Indian, Grey drew a poignant and stark portrait of the Native American, but in doing so, he gave offense to the Bureau of Indian Affairs as well as several religious groups in the United States.

The setting is the Nopah reservation[27] during the era of World War I. The chief character is Nophaie, who, when just a babe, is kidnapped by white men and then turned loose to wander in the wilderness. Some wealthy Easterners find him, rear him, and give him a white man's education. In college he is "Lo Blandy," a great scholar and athlete, and his sweetheart is Marian Warner, whom he calls "Benow di Cleash." After graduation, Marian visits the reservation, to which Nophaie returns, and there she witnesses tragic events.

The Indian reservation is a gallery of horrors. A man named Blucher, a German, is head of it. When America enters the war in 1917, Blucher, showing clearly his sympathy with the German cause, discourages Indians from volunteering. The head of the missionary force on the reservation is Morgan, a cruel and wicked man who hides his baseness behind the "Old Book" and commits crime after crime in its name. Behind these two people is a coterie of disreputable associates. Grey says of the Indian agents: "They were holding down an irksome job; they were out there because they had failed in the East or for poor health or because they had political influence enough to gain a job they were not equal to. . . . Some there were who had honestly tried hard to adopt themselves to this work, only to find it beyond them.[28] Of the missionaries, Grey wrote: "The sincere missionary, the man who left home and comfort and friends to go into a lonely hard country, burning with zeal to convey the blessings of Jesus Christ to those he considered heathen, had little conception of the true nature of his task, of the absurdity of converting Indians in a short time. . . . How little did the world outside a reservation know of this tremendous and staggering question! The good missionary's life was a martyrdom" (151).

Caught between the inept forces of the Indian Bureau on one hand and the misguided efforts of missionary boards on the other, the life of the reservation Indian is sad indeed. Few people listen to Nophaie's suggestions that people like Morgan be removed, that the Indian be given land to work, that the Indian send his children to school where he wishes, and that Indians move freely among whites. In the context of these forlorn conditions events occur of grotesque proportions. The Indians resist Morgan's rule that children attend church in his chapel and are harshly reprimanded for their opinions. In World War I, the Indian is subjected to further abuse by the "bunko game" of having to adopt some general into a tribe; such a deed, according to Grey, is usually a cheap political trick to keep some person in power. As if Indian agents and missionaries are not enough, the postwar influenza epidemics exact fearful tolls on the tribes, and over three thousand Nopahs, to say nothing of those from other tribes, die from influenza. Nophaie catches the dread disease but recovers.

Nophaie represents a threat to white authority on the reservation. He has been educated in a white man's college but ultimately rejects the white man's life. Usually a white-educated Indian does not pose such a problem, because once educated an Indian never can return to the old tribal beliefs and superstitions but never can win acceptance from the white community. The frustration resulting from such a condition usually turns the Indian into a nonentity. Nophaie does not follow this path. If anything, the white man's education enables him to draw a sharp contrast between the primitive, natural, pure life of his youth and the so-called progress of twentieth-century America. He rebels against the white ideal of progress and suffers as a result. Despite his rebellion, he loves a white woman. Marian Warner returns his love, but the accumulated tragedies affecting their lives bode ill for its fulfillment.

The book ends with Nophaie, having recovered from influenza, making a pilgrimage in gratitude to Naza, a sacred bridge that has been a symbol of the Indians' pantheistic religion for generations. The

trek to and from it is excruciating, but Nophaie gets there and finds
God—his God, not the white man's. (In the 1982 edition of *The Vanishing American,* however, Nophaie's God is the same "to all humanity.") When he returns to the reservation where Marian is waiting for
him, he is so weakened by his exhausting journey that he again falls
ill. This time he does not recover and is therefore a symbol of the
vanishing American. This novel was the only one that Grey ever wrote
with a Western setting that did not end on a happy note. (However,
see chapter 9 for a discussion of the novel as it was originally written
and finally published in 1982.) In style, balance, and emotions it
evokes, *The Vanishing American* is perhaps Grey's best book.

It took Grey from 5 May to 18 June 1922, to write *The Vanishing
American.* On the last stretch of its writing, he labored for fourteen
consecutive hours, but he did not suffer the usual negative reactions
when he had completed it—"I went the whole distance with this novel
without one day of depression, let alone bad spell."[29] Perhaps his sta-
bility was due to his decision to write and fish on alternate days. When
the book first appeared in 1922 as a serial in *Ladies' Home Journal,* it
came under attack from several religious sources. When plans were
announced for Harper's to publish the book and for a movie based on
it to be released simultaneously, some denominations feared a general
muckraking attack on missionaries. When the editor of *Ladies' Home
Journal* wrote to Harper's of the controversy caused by serializing *The
Vanishing American,* he expressed the opinion that adverse comments
were not sufficient to affect publication of the book.[30] Even so, Grey
endured a trying time relative to the planned appearances of the book
and movie.

The Harper's editor suggested a number of changes in *The Vanishing
American.* One related to the construction of the novel: Grey should
change the time of Nophaie's death to give the book a climax equal to
its opening,[31] and he complied with this request. As time passed, however, it became obvious, at least to Grey, that Harper's was reluctant
to publish the book for fear of offending church people. The hesitation
angered Grey, and he stated that he would withdraw his manuscript
but for the planned simultaneous appearances of the book and the
movie.[32] He was inclined to be a "little sore," he said, because this was
the first time he had "ever bucked up against the Church or religious
element. I begin to understand a little of the narrow controversy between modernists and fundamentalists."[33] Grey stated his position in
a long, often impassioned, letter to the publishing company.

He wrote just after his third revision of the manuscript: "I have studied the Navajo Indian for twelve years. I know their wrongs. The missionaries sent out there are almost everyone mean, vicious, weak, immoral, useless men," and then in a blaze of anticlimax, he added, "and some of them are crooks. They cheat and rob the Indian and more heinously they seduce every Indian girl they can get hold of. It is common knowledge on the reservation. And mind you this is only the Navajo Reservation. My purpose was to expose this terrible condition—to help the great public to understand the Indians' wrongs."[34] Grey expressed doubts in this letter that religious people read his books to any extent; even if they did, "I would want them to read what I wrote as the truth about missionaries and their wrongs to the Indian. If it offended them—no matter. If it aroused a controversy—well and good. But in any event it was my record of a certain phase of American Western history. Eventually, it was going to be believed. The *truth* always comes out."[35] Grey closed his letter by asserting that recent official disclosures about the Indian board and the current debate in religious circles on modernism and fundamentalism made 1925 the psychological time to publish *The Vanishing American.*

Grey ultimately got most of what he wanted in his book, but his troubles with it were not yet over. The movie producers gave him some bad moments. Grey complained during the filming that the book and the movie were too far apart from each other. He insisted that the action and spirit of his books be put on the screen and that the moviemakers "interpolate something of the poetry and legend of the Indian."[36] These and similar requests reduced to negligibility some critics' charges that Grey wrote only for the movies.

The West: Repository of Greatness

The last of Grey's works published during his lifetime was also a historical novel, *Western Union* (1939), which concerned the telegraph, another development that changed life, especially the Indian's. When Grey had attempted to dictate stories as early as 1918, he gave up the practice as impracticable, but much of *Western Union* was dictated because a stroke two years before had altered his writing habits. The infirmity did not keep Grey from thoroughly researching his subject, and the novel contains a solid account of the trials workers encountered while installing transcontinental telegraphic facilities. Grey wrote his book in the first person and dedicated it to a "single thread of wire" running across the country. Aside from characterization, which is often weak in Grey novels, *Western Union* is strong in organization, balance of events, and historical authenticity.

The story's narrator is Wayne Cameron, an idealistic young Easterner who, like Warren Neale of the Union Pacific Railroad of a later period, believes he is privileged to participate in spectacular events. In constructing the line in 1861, the crews encounter several problems; and one of these is Indian raids by the Cheyenne, Arapaho, and Utes. A stage driver named Hawkins gives the Indian's point of view: the idea of progress is good, he said, "but it doesn't do 'way with the fact that this was the red man's country, thet he was depraved by liquor, thet he has been robbed, an' will go on bein' robbed until what's left of him will be driven back into the waste places of the West. Jest how it is in the sight of God, I cain't reckon. But in mine it shore ain't a purty picture."[37] Hawkins may be the character in the book making the statement, but Zane Grey is speaking.

Another difficulty that the telegraph crews face is timber rustlers—people who claim that Western Union has illegally cut timber from their homesteads; and Cameron spends much time invalidating their charges. Buffalo stampedes threaten the men and their outfits. When, to protect newly installed poles from animals, the chief engineer, Edward Creighton, puts spikes around them, he does not anticipate buffalos coming along and scratching their backs on the spikes to get rid of the mud and vermin on them. More than twenty-five miles of poles are destroyed before the error is discovered. In addition to Indians, rustlers, and buffaloes, nature challenges the telegraph stringers, mostly in the form of floods and electrical storms. But the event is too big, too promising, for any force, individual or collective, to destroy it: "Its meaning was tremendous. Thousands of men and women from the South and East had become imbued with the hope of finding a better life in the West, and fired with this pioneer spirit they had pulled up their roots and started across the Plains. It was the beginning of a great empire in the West" (155).

Western Union has the usual number of Grey type characters in it who indulge in the now familiar melodrama of his novels. As in most instances, however, the thing with Grey in *Western Union* is the setting and the event, not the characters. The sweep of events, the whole of which is greater than the sum of its parts, motivated Grey, for he wanted people to experience a surge of nationalism when reading his historical novels. *Western Union* ends on a patriotic note when the first message transmitted is from California's chief justice, who pledges his state's loyalty to President Lincoln in the Civil War that has just started. The telegraph figured prominently in the ultimate Union victory, so Grey did not overlook its importance in holding the Union together. Indeed, the string of wire becomes a symbol of the great strength and fortitude of the United States.

Grey tended to make huge construction projects symbolic of America's progress in the world and to denote superhuman efforts in which ordinary men would find no place. The Union Pacific Railroad and Western Union were excellent examples of this aspect of Grey's thoughts. Another feat that required extraordinary men—not just in terms of building, but of idealism as well—was the construction of Hoover Dam on the Nevada-Arizona border. After its completion, its name was changed to Boulder Dam, and then several years later it reacquired its original name. When Grey wrote his novel, it was called Boulder Dam, the name he used for the title of his novel. Hoover Dam, the greatest water barrier in the world and one of history's great engineering accomplishments,[38] attracted worldwide attention as armies of engineers, drillers, dynamiters, and steam-shovelers converged on the scene to harness the powers of the Colorado River. The project turned Las Vegas, Nevada, into a boom town that overshadowed even the frenzied days of frontiers and gold rushes.

The book's hero, Lynn Weston, is not an Easterner like Warren Neale of the Union Pacific or Wayne Cameron of Western Union. Weston comes, however, from a wealthy California family that threatens his individuality. Thus, just as Boulder Dam personifies a nation's greatness, it symbolizes manhood for Lynn personally. Because he wants to run the entire gauntlet of experience at the dam, he is a sand and gravel man for a time, then a steam-shoveler, a cliff driller, a scaler, and finally, a supervisor. The work is invigorating, intriguing, and perilous.

The greatest threat to the dam, however, does not come from natural sources: Communists begin underhanded work to hamper, or even prevent, the dam's construction. Grey, always a conservative author, distrusted anything that hinted of a marked change in tradition; therefore, he fought against Communist infiltration, real or imagined. He wrote in a letter in 1934 of his belief that Communists inspired the labor strikes in San Francisco, and he thought the authorities should "deal summarily with that element."[39] In *Boulder Dam*, Grey summarizes his thoughts through the words of Lynn Weston: "These damn Reds! Had they gotten a foothold here in the greatest and best paid labor project ever conceived? What was the United States coming to?"[40] The book is full of hectic chases in which Lynn Weston fights both Communists and gangsters. In the end, a "reformed" gangster helps Lynn to rescue his girl, Anne Vandergrift, from Communist criminal elements.[41] Thus, the story ends on a happy note, with Grey musing about man's genius in building the dam.

Time, however, was on nature's side, so Grey wondered how long it would be before nature reclaimed what man had taken from her. Grey was awed by the magnitude of the undertaking and stood in reverence at this accomplishment of man, but he could not quite bring himself to the point of allowing man to get away with Boulder Dam. He sprinkled his narrative with references to the fact that the Colorado existed long before man and would probably outlast him. Even a mighty structure like Boulder Dam was only a transient thing in the grand scheme of eternity.

From the Union Pacific Railroad to Boulder Dam, Grey reveals the West as America's best repository for greatness. The West encourages manliness; it follows, then, that manly things be built and manly events take place. The West becomes the proving ground for the splendor of the nation and for the maturity of the individual. Grey overdraws this picture several times, but the total result of his work is acceptable historical and social comment. *The Vanishing American,* for example, is comparable to Helen Hunt Jackson's *Ramona* and is written in the same vein as Upton Sinclair's *The Jungle.* Perhaps *The Vanishing American* did not influence governmental policy as much as did *The Jungle,* but it made thousands of fair-minded people take notice of the Indian problem for the first time. *Rogue River Feud* undoubtedly had its effects, too, on those people whose job was to encourage fair business practices.

In respect to these questions of setting the social order straight, Grey's influence may have been greater than has been supposed. Grey believed, apparently, that history was at its best when it applied to contemporary problems, thus becoming a social force. History could never predict events, but it could offer a number of alternatives and indicate which one was likely to be best. Thus, Grey's historical novels, for all of their overwriting, made significant suggestions for the betterment of the human condition.

Chapter Five
Horses

When Christopher Columbus made a second voyage to the New World in 1493, he brought with him a number of stallions, mares, and mules. When Hernando Cortez invaded Mexico twenty-five years later, he took with him from Cuba the descendants of those animals and introduced horseflesh to the mainland of the North American continent. Several years after this occurrence, the Spanish explorer, Francisco Coronado, wandered throughout the country now known as the American Southwest, and during this expedition, he abandoned or lost many of his horses. These animals were the ancestors of the multitudes of horses that ultimately roamed the western regions. Without horseflesh, western development would have been much more difficult than it was, if not impossible: the horse was literally the difference sometimes between life and death for a person. It was not unusual for a horse to attain a high degree of intelligence—sometimes, apparently, even higher than that of its owner. A horse generally had great stamina, and it brought men through difficulties that alone they could not have overcome. Little wonder, then, that the westerner's love for his horse often surpassed any affection he had for gold or for women—or that one of the most serious crimes was to steal a man's horse.

Very early in Grey's career as a recorder of western history, he appreciated the value of a horse. In *The Last of the Plainsmen*, Grey sang the praises of horseflesh as he described the futile efforts of mere humans to capture "Silvermane," king of the wild horses. The great stallion was subdued only in the pages of *The Heritage of the Desert*, becoming, as it were, one of the book's leading characters. By 1912 Grey owned several horses, and his favorites Black Star and Night figured prominently in *Riders of the Purple Sage*. Blanco Diablo and Blanco Sol, two more of Grey's horses, were featured in *Desert Gold*. He became an astute observer of horses, writing into his notebook descriptions of their habits, of their fortitude, and of their nobility. Horses played an important role in the majority of Grey's novels, and the horse itself was the central character in two.

Wildfire

The first of Grey's "horse" novels was *Wildfire,* serialized by *Country Gentleman* in 1916 and published as a book the following year. Grey was becoming, in 1917, a celebrated man of letters; and *Wildfire* was enthusiastically received by readers—so much so that Hitchcock informed Grey that *Wildfire* had surpassed all of Harper's expectations.[1] The novel's setting is the canyon country of Northern Arizona, just south of the Utah border; and the time is the late nineteenth century, when the cattle industry made the horse such a valuable creature that most western states passed laws stipulating capital punishment for horse thieves.

A major part of the story deals with the Bostil-Creech feud, started because of a dispute over horses. Bostil, a sane man on everything but horses, robs, lies, and cheats to get a horse that he wants. At one time he and Creech were good friends, but a horse trade turns them into bitter enemies. Bostil can have no friends if any conversations revolve (as they usually do) around horses. Bostil even cuts the lines to the ferryboat one night to keep Creech's horses from being transported across the river to participate in a race. The deed is a hollow victory for Bostil, though, because the rains come, causing the river to flood and maroon the horses. Before the waters recede, Creech's horses starve to death, a turn of events that is disheartening to a lover of horseflesh.

Bostil is not the only, or even the most intense, horse lover in the novel, just the most malignant. His daughter Lucy torments Bostil by taunting him over the supposed superiority of his favorite horse, Sage King. Lucy encourages Slone, a trapper of wild horses, to run newly captured Wildfire in a race against Sage King. During the event, the two horses fight each other so much that no clearcut decision is established. As Lucy expects, Bostil covets Wildfire, causing animosities to develop between himself and Slone. To complicate matters, Slone and Lucy fall in love with each other. Bostil hints on numerous occasions that he is not beyond trading his beloved daughter for the magnificent horse.

Before Bostil is forced to make a choice, Lucy is kidnapped by Creech and his son Joel. On the trail, father and son quarrel over the treatment of their victim, and Joel shoots his father. Maddened, Joel strips Lucy naked, ties her to the back of Sage King, and sets the grass afire. At this point, Slone appears on the scene, and a terrific race ensues between Wildfire and Sage King. Wildfire wins, but by exerting himself so much that he dies of exhaustion. Slone's recovery of Lucy wins Bostil's gratitude, causing Bostil to reflect on his past selfishness and leading to his promise of better citizenship on the subject of horses.

Grey uses a horse in this novel to get at the peculiar characteristics of the human element, for he recognizes that a lucid person can be insane, or obsessed, about one particular thing. Bostil is of two personalities: one that deals with people and one that deals with horses. Grey read enough of Clayton Hamilton's *Manual of Fiction* to know that characters must always act within the laws of their imagined existence; that the rules of life, not the author's will, must decide the destinies of heroes and heroines; and that characters must be typical of the class to which they belong.[2] Under these conditions in a good work of fiction, the characters become as true as real life. Bostil is a case in point because he typifies the thoughts of so many Westerners about horses.

The horse, Wildfire, becomes a pivot point for the expression of several different feelings. The great steed inspires in Bostil an overpowering sense of competition through which he can gain power over men. Wildfire creates a challenge for Slone in that it takes him several months and near-fatal exertion to capture the horse, and Wildfire brings out Lucy's feelings of awe and respect. One horse—one object—translates many powerful and different emotions into reality, and this animal even makes the evil of an outlaw, Cordts, more felt than seen. Cordts appears only a few times in the book, and even then in an innocuous manner; but Cordts is a horse-thief, and readers know almost instinctively that, whereas Bostil probably would not kill for horseflesh, Cordts would. Thus Cordts becomes one of Grey's most unusual villains because of his prolonged absences in the pages of *Wildfire*. Ordinarily, to keep a major character in a novel subordinated to this extent is the mark of poor technique. When an author can succeed, however, as Grey does, in making a character's influence greater than his presence, the impact is significant.

Grey might not have intended the term "Wildfire" to signify anything in particular. Few authors deliberately write symbolism into their own stories. But for this novel, "wildfire" is a horse, a condition (Joel Creech's setting the grass afire turns the surroundings into an inferno), and a frame of mind. The sacrifice of Wildfire's life sets loose the positive events that have been impossible before: the gentle acts of Bostil and the fulfillment of true love between Lucy and Slone. Thus, sacrifice—on this occasion, a horse's—is made an important key to happiness.

Tappan's Burro

Grey continued to explore man's love of beast, and beast's love of man, in *Tappan's Burro*. This piece of writing, published in 1923 in *Ladies' Home Journal,* is actually a novelette, the main purpose of which was to "glorify the burro." Grey thought several times of enlarging the work to novel length, but he finally decided that its intensity required something shorter than a full-scale book.[3] This decision was a good one on Grey's part because *Ladies' Home Journal* offered him the highest price for the story he had "ever heard of."[4]

Tappan is more a naturalist than a prospector, but mostly he is a dreamer. When he cannot leave a newly born, sickly burro to die, he stays in camp near the Chocolate Mountains in California. During the two weeks he remains at the site, he discovers gold, so he concludes that the burro, whom he names Jenet, has brought him the good luck. As time passes, the man and the animal become inseparable companions. Jenet is Tappan's "ship of the desert," for without her, he could not wander through the wastelands. They camp in the Panamint Mountains on the northern slope of Death Valley, where Tappan again finds gold. Raiders appear, however, causing Tappan to strike out across Death Valley to elude them. Confronting the terrible furnace winds, Tappan passes into unconsciousness; when awakened, he finds that Jenet has brought him through the ordeal to an oasis. A grateful Tappan swears that he never will forget Jenet's deed, and together they head for Superstition Mountain in Arizona where Tappan wants to search for a gold mine known as The Lost Dutchman.

They do not quite make their destination because of a woman. Tappan and Jenet are camped in the Tonto country one night when Jake Beam and his sister, Madge, appear. In due time, Tappan and Madge fall in love with each other, and Madge begs Tappan to take her away from Jake. Tappan agrees, deciding, in the interest of mobility, to leave Jenet behind. On the trail out of the Tonto, Tappan's horses bolt and run away; while he is tracking them, Madge takes his money, and with Jake, who is actually her husband, absconds with it. Tappan spends the next year searching for the Beams. He has no resentment against Madge, just blind love. Then one day he thinks of Jenet, so he returns to the Tonto where he finds the burro patiently waiting for him. He promises that he never will leave her again. The months turned into years and Tappan begins to age. The companionship of Tappan and Jenet becomes indestructible—not even Madge Beam could have disturbed it.

But another danger threatens the closeness in the form of Jess Blade, who comes into Tappan's camp one night claiming that he had been robbed and is invited by Tappan to share his facilities. When winter arrives, the two men are marooned by a snow storm. Tappan will not leave without Jenet, for heavy snow is the only substance she cannot easily traverse. Blade, infuriated, starts to shoot Jenet, but Tappan stops him, and in the fight that follows, kills Blade. When Tappan attempts to get himself and Jenet out of the snow-bound wilderness, Jenet is dependent on Tappan, for the first time, not only for her well-being but for her very existence. Tappan puts Jenet on a folded tarpaulin and pulls her over the crust of the snow, as though on a sled. Far beyond the point where the food vanishes, Tappan labors to get out of the snow. He finally makes it. Jenet is safe. Tappan can now relax and get a good night's rest. He falls asleep, but he does not awaken the next morning. As a horse sacrificed his life in *Wildfire* for humans, the opposite is true in *Tappan's Burro*. In both instances, the emphasis is on sacrifice.

As in *Wildfire*, Grey probably had no thought of writing into *Tappan's Burro* any deep psychological insights. All he wanted to do was tell a good story in which the faithfulness of a burro to its master is demonstrated. In the process, however, Grey hit some universal themes, which showed the necessity for the emotion of love not only to receive from its object but to bestow itself on the object as well. Tappan has a need to express love toward some other living thing, not especially in a male-female context, but in the form of communion with a creature of nature. This need for love is the reason Tappan does not hate Madge Beam when she steals his money and leaves, for she is not that personal to him. Finally, Tappan remembers another object toward which his need to express a love for nature can be satisfied, and thus he returns to Jenet.

Another theme presented by *Tappan's Burro* is familiar to Grey's readers: Tappan wants to atone for guilt feelings occasioned by his long abandonment of Jenet. The effort to repay his debts and his need for an empathetic relationship with a creature of nature cause Tappan to save Jenet from Blade's rifle and then pull the burro over endless miles of snow. It is not love of horseflesh—but more a love for a creature of nature—that makes Tappan do these things. He certainly is not the fanatical admirer of horses that Bostil was. Whereas Bostil used horse-flesh to gain dominancy over man, Tappan employs it to discover nature itself. His association with Jenet helps him to know that he, too, is a product of nature and is as subject to its rules as any other creature on earth.

Tappan's Burro magnifies emotions that in longer works would not have been as intense. Perhaps this has accounted for the story's sustained popularity. Readers can get through it rather quickly and can easily recognize one or more of their own habits in Grey's descriptions and expostulations. This story and *Wildfire* were the only two "horse-flesh" works of Grey that had the animals themselves as the prime movers of the plot.[5] In all the others, the horse is central, but people propel the events.

For Love of a Horse

Two such novels are *Forlorn River* (1927) and its sequel *Nevada* (1928). The setting for the first book is Upper California's Lake Tule area in the late nineteenth century. The principal characters, Ben Ide and "Nevada," are hunters of wild horses and are regarded by many people in neighboring villages as thieves. Ben's one great obsession is to capture the grand wild horse, California Red, and his search for the horse produces a number of conflicts.

For one thing, Ben's father is a newly rich rancher who cannot understand Ben's "wild" ways of chasing horses. Ben's love is Ina Blaine, daughter of another member of the *nouveau riche*. Ina, who has been to college, is disdainful of the profiteering in land and cattle that she sees about her. Nevada loves Hettie Ide, Ben's sister; but because of Nevada's unknown background, Hettie's father forbids any romance. The story's villain is Lew Setter, who shrewdly works through the elder Ide and the elder Blaine to "frame" Ben and Nevada as horse thieves. Setter wants for himself all the land that the two young men have homesteaded, and in trying to get it, he uses the services of a real horse thief, Bill Hall.

Ben, Nevada, and an Indian helper named Modoc suspect Hall of stealing horses on Setter's orders. They track Hall one day, catch him with the incriminating evidence, and besiege Hall and his men for several weeks. When the outlaw gang has starved enough, it surrenders; and the whole group heads back for Tule Lake, where Hall promises to confess. On the way, however, Ben spots California Red on ice where he can get little footing so that he can be captured, but it requires skill to bring the great beast under the governance of a rope. When Ben offers to release Bill Hall and his gang if they will help capture California Red, Hall agrees, and the job is done. Thus another episode occurs in which love of horseflesh causes men's logic to go astray.

After catching California Red, Ben returns to his ranch where he is attacked by Setter and several cohorts. In the midst of the fracas, Nevada rides up and shoots the outlaws. Setter, before he expires, recognizes Nevada's true identity, but he is too weak to divulge it to anyone. Nevada leaves hurriedly, knowing that he cannot remain in the area, for he is really Jim Lacy, a gunman well known in Nevada. His heart breaks as he leaves his friend, Ben, and his true love, Hettie—but such is the doleful fate of a gunman.

Forlorn River, a 1926 serialization by *Ladies' Home Journal,* may be set in the late nineteenth century, but the materialistic, land-grabbing tactics of Setter, Blaine, and Ide are descriptive of the 1920s. This is a novel, then, in which events contemporary to Grey figure prominently in thematic development, and the novel presents the sharp contrast between old and young generations. The younger set generally condemns the new values of profiteering that are creeping into the age; but both the older men, who were poor most of their lives, are rendered irrational by sudden wealth. Grey makes it clear that they are guilty not of evil but of gullibility in letting sharpsters like Setter manipulate them. Nevada's shoot-out at the novel's end brings all the differing factions together, as Setter and his henchmen are at last seen in their true light. Ben and his father are reconciled with each other, and Ben and Ina are married. The only forlorn characters left are Nevada and Hettie, who long for each other, and California Red, who simply will not submit to training techniques and thus remains the wild creature he always has been. There are enough unresolved conflicts in *Forlorn River* to recommend a sequel; and one appeared as a serial in late 1926 in *American Magazine* and as a book two years later with the title *Nevada.*

Trouble, in this novel, seems automatically to follow Jim Lacy, or Nevada, who is also known now in local circles as "Texas Jack." After fleeing California, he is forced to shoot a man in Lineville, Nevada, an action that causes his hasty departure for Arizona. In that state he becomes involved with a group of rustlers, the Pine Tree Gang. Cattlemen of the area fear Lacy, but in reality he is a spy for the Cattleman's Association, his job being to uncover the leader of the outlaw gang.

While these events transpire, the Blaines arrive. They have moved to Arizona for its superior climate after Ben's father dies and his mother becomes ill. Once settled into the cattle-raising business, the Blaines hear stories about Texas Jack and listen to the legends of Jim Lacy. Nevada finally succeeds in destroying the head of the rustling outfit, a man who recently participated in New Mexico's Lincoln County War. Inevitably, Hettie finds Nevada and very quickly assumes that he is a bad man. All is well, however, when Judge Franklidge, a prominent member of the Cattlemen's Association, explains Nevada's connection with the outlaws. The judge gives eloquent testimony not only to Jim Lacy but to the western gunman in general: "I have met or seen many of the noted killers. . . . These men are not murderers. They are a product of the times. The West could never have been populated without them. They strike a balance between the hordes of ruffians, outlaws, strong evil characters . . . and the wild life of a wild era. It is the West as any Westerner knows it now. And as such we could not be pioneers, we could not progress without this violence. . . . The rub is that only iron-nerved youths like Billy the Kid, or Jim Lacy, can meet such men on their own ground."[6] Thus, as in *Riders of the Purple Sage,* Grey shows the significance of the gunman to western development. Next to his six-shooter, the gunman depended most for his well-being on his horse. The gunman and the horse were twin agents of progress in the West.

By the time *Nevada* was published in book form (1928), Grey's long popularity was declining. He had slipped off the best-selling lists in 1925 because, he believed, a new group of writers was getting an increasing amount of Harper's attention and because a continued slump in the book market was caused by radio and movies.[7] Grey felt that his work was not being sufficiently publicized: "In this day of advertizing, *any* author, *any* commodity, no matter how famous or good, must be continually boosted—certainly kept before the public."[8] This condition was somewhat ameliorated for Grey when *Nevada's* popularity got his name listed in the pages of *The Bookman.*[9]

Wild Horses

The book following *Nevada* continued Grey's fascination with horses. *Wild Horse Mesa,* set in the rugged canyons of Utah in the early 1870s, was published as a book in 1928 but had already been serialized in 1924 by *The Country Gentleman.* Grey wrote most of this book in Long Key, Florida, and he suffered frequent rounds of depression while writing it. When he neared the end of the manuscript of *Wild Horse Mesa,*[10] he worked extraordinarily long periods, writing a minimum of twelve and a maximum of twenty-seven pages a day during the last two weeks of labor.[11]

In this novel, Chayne Weymer, with his horse Brutus (one of Grey's horses in real life), hunts for a wild stallion, Panquitch. In doing so, he runs across the Melberne-Loughbridge group, which captures and sells wild horses. A sinister figure, Bent Mannerube (in reality, a horse thief), appears on the scene and becomes in due time foreman for Melberne and Loughbridge. He suggests building enclosures strung with barbed wire into which to drive the horses. This operation is a cruel one, for it kills some horses and injures many others. Loughbridge is interested only in profit, however, so he orders Mannerube to proceed with his plans, causing Melberne to break the partnership. Melberne's decision is helped considerably by the words and deeds of his daughter, Sue, who hates Mannerube and his brutality to horses.

Sue and Chayne dislike, too, Mannerube's treatment of Indians. He is a constant bother to Sosie, an Indian girl who has been educated in white schools and who is, as a result, powerless as a force for social and political advancement. Sosie sums up the problem of trying to return to tribal life after exposure to white customs: "We girls learn the white people's way of living. We learn to like clean bodies, clean clothes, clean food. When we try to correct our mothers and fathers we're accused of being too good for our own people. My father says to me: 'You're my blood. Why aren't my ways right for you?' Then when I tell him, he can't understand."[12] Ill-treatment of the Indian, so much a part of Zane Grey's literary canon, is a major consideration of *Wild Horse Mesa,* and horses also influence the action, for love of good horses brings together Chayne Weymer and Toddy Nokin, Sosie's father, and helps them ultimately to defeat the evil designs of Mannerube and his gang.

While chasing horses and protecting Indian rights, Chayne persists

in his search for the wild horse Panquitch. Accompanied by Sue,
Chayne spots the splendid beast one day, and when he trails him, the
horse leads them to a secluded area, full of wild horses, which Chayne
immediately names "Wild Horse Mesa." The structure stands as a
monument to eternity, and the wild horses on it are nature's handi-
work. Chayne exultantly says: "It may be long before another rider, or
an Indian, happens on this secret. Maybe never. Some distant day air-
ships might land on Wild Horse Mesa. But what if they do? An hour
of curiosity, an achievement to boast of—then gone! Wild Horse Mesa
rises even above the world of rock. It was meant for eagles, wild
horses—and for lonely souls like mine" (364). The book ends on a note
of unity: Melberne and Loughbridge come back together as partners;
the effort to capture Panquitch is abandoned, and he remains free to
roam his mesa, as much a part of nature as the mesa itself; and Chayne
and Sue are married.

The themes of *Wild Horse Mesa* repeat those of dozens of other books
Grey wrote. There are many instances in Grey's writings of a cowboy's
trailing a wild horse, sometimes for months, catching it, and then
turning it loose because of sudden feelings of nobility. When such
events occur, the cowboy seems to be happier than he would have been
had he kept the horse in captivity. By setting the horse free, the cowboy somehow senses the possessive attitude of nature toward its nobler
creatures. Although this situation does not occur in *Wild Horse Mesa,*
Chayne's decision to let Panquitch alone is akin to it.

Another thematic concern of *Wild Horse Mesa* is the Indian in relation to the white man. Grey's most famous Indian story is *The Vanishing
American,* but he also wrote several short pieces about Indians, including *Blue Feather* (1961) and *The Great Slave* (1920). In dozens of his
books, the Indian figures prominently at one point or another. Even
when an Indian is obviously wrong, Grey either hints or states outright
that it is still the white man's fault for bringing out the Indian's savage
instincts to begin with. *Wild Horse Mesa* is such a book. Grey's readers
expected frequent remarks from him about the ill treatment of the
Indian—not that they intended to do anything about it—and he rarely
disappointed them.

Horses offered a livelihood to many citizens of the West and a chance
to escape from an unhappy life. This is true for Panhandle Smith, and
several other people, in a Grey story serialized by *The Country Gentleman*
in 1927 as *Open Range,* and published in book form twenty years later

as *Valley of Wild Horses*. The story begins in the Texas Panhandle during the height of the cattle industry. Bill Smith calls his newborn son Panhandle, over the vigorous protests of his wife, Margaret. In the course of time, Panhandle hits the trail and is separated from his parents for several years. Then he decides one day that a recently developed restlessness is homesickness, quits his job as a cowpuncher, and heads home. When he gets there, he finds that his parents have departed. Bill Smith, who was cheated out of his property by Jard Hardman, has followed Hardman to New Mexico in hopes of recovering his fortune.

When Panhandle gets to Marco, New Mexico, he finds that his aged and somewhat infirm father has not recovered his losses from Hardman and has taken employment in a wagon shop. On hearing of his family's dire straits, Panhandle stops Jard Hardman's offensive behavior and also protects his love, Lucy Blake, from the advances of Jard's son, Dick. While this fastpaced action occurs, Panhandle discovers a valley full of horses; if they can be captured and sold, the Smith family can earn enough money to realize their dream of homesteading in Arizona. Panhandle and his father, assisted by several cowboys, set up a wild-horse camp. Unlike many other trappers of wild horses, Panhandle hates barbed wire and the practice of bending one of the horse's front legs and binding it with leather straps to make it easier to herd the animal.

In discussing the wild-horse camp, Grey gives a useful insight into the spirit of both the cowboy and the horse. "Cowboys were of an infinite variety of types, yet they all fell under two classes: Those who were brutal with horses and those who were gentle. The bronco, the outlaw, the wild horse had to be broken to be ridden. Many of them hated the saddle, the bit, the rider, and would not tolerate them except when mastered. These horses had to be hurt to be subdued. Then there were cowboys, great horsemen, who never wanted any kind of a horse save one that would kick, bite, pitch. It was a kind of cowboy vanity."[13]

The Smiths, overcoming the ordeals of adverse weather and bad men, finally gather enough horses, which they sell at ten dollars a head, enabling them to move to Arizona. Thus, horses offer an opportunity for independence and for the enjoyment of a place that Grey endows more than once with Edenic qualities: Arizona. He once stated that Arizona stars would be moons in any other state.[14] Arizona, first in Grey's ranking of states,[15] becomes the promised land in *Valley of*

Wild Horses, a place dreamed about and yearned for. Only the deserving, Grey makes it clear, can benefit permanently from what it has to offer.

Horses for Chicken Feed

For the last of his "horse" novels, Grey used a setting in Washington state, but *Horse Heaven Hill* is close to being the worst novel Zane Grey ever wrote. It was kept in manuscript form from the mid-1930s until 1959, when it was published as a book. Grey has little description and philosophy in this book, two attributes of all his other works. The dialogue was painful: "If you think I'm wonderful, and if I think you're wonderful, then it must all be wonderful."[16] There are several interesting episodes in the book, but, on the whole, it is not equal to the rest of Grey's output.[17]

The main activity of the novel is undertaken by Hurd Blanding, who gathers up wild horses at Horse Heaven Hill and sells them for three dollars each to manufacturers of chicken feed. Most of the settlers in the area approve of this gruesome practice because the horses eat grass reserved for cattle. The story's climax is better than the rest of the book foreshadows, for it gives a vivid description of what happens when men go mad for profit from horseflesh. If the horses are to be sold to chicken-feed manufacturers, there is no special need to keep them healthy. Thus, terrified horses are pushed into small enclosures where they break their legs and impale themselves on stakes driven into the fence. In one round-up, over three thousand horses are shoved into a small corral, where the killing and maiming reach horrendous proportions.

When Grey finished working on the book, he wrote that "Horse Heaven Hill intrigued me. The idea of killing wild horses for chicken-feed. I was sort of obsessed with the horror of it, to one who loved wild horses."[18] Unfortunately, the story was not convincing, regardless of how true it was. The motive for destroying the horses came at the wrong time; it was just not plausible to sell them for chicken-feed when their value was attested to every day. This misplacement of time and of motive causes many of the novel's events to be forced. Of course, Grey set other novels in an early period and then moved the plots along with incidents and attitudes that belonged to his own era; a case in point is *Forlorn River.* But in such books, Grey talks about motives that are uniform from the viewpoint of time and place. The failure to do that in *Horse Heaven Hill* produced a poor book.

Perhaps it was fitting that *Horse Heaven Hill* was the last of Grey's "horse" novels. His first one, *Wildfire,* in 1917, was about horses at the height of their splendor, and the mood and style of *Wildfire* match the conditions of horses it describes. *Horse Heaven Hill,* however, shows the once proud horse becoming superannuated, the melancholy fact of which may have affected Grey's writing. During much of the time he wrote the novel, he was traveling. In 1935, he went to Roseburg, Oregon, and in 1936, he visited Australia. On the journeys, he fished, wrote novels and short stories, and took notes for works of the future.[19]

By the early-1930s, Grey no longer feared reviewers. He had written ten years before an extensive "answer to the critics" and had ceased thereafter to let them disturb him. He chose, instead, to pursue the path suggested for him by one of his friends: "I have come to realize the sincerity of Zane Grey, and of his pen, and of the great message he has to deliver. A message of keen appreciation in those things of Nature that are true and clean and beautiful. A sturdy fighting purpose and a steady influence for better understanding of Americanism and of Pioneer days."[20] Above all, Grey wanted to be treated as the sincere author that he was; and he complained about the unfairness of critics in this respect: "I have never yet gotten the kind of criticism that I yearn for. My books do not receive serious reviews. Not one of these higher class critics takes me seriously, if he ever reads me at all. . . . Someday I shall drive past this barren cold coterie of arbiters."[21] He did—several times.

Regardless of Grey's occasional inferior output, he did more to explain the West than any other person contemporary to him. In the 1920s and 1930s, his name was synonymous with a rugged way of life (some journals called him the "high priest of the out-of-doors") and with western history. Although he no longer occupied the best-selling lists in the 1930s, thousands of readers still followed him faithfully as he explored the themes of unity in nature, greed *versus* benevolence, and the universal might of true love. They believed him when he spoke of the cowboy and his horse because he was an authority.

The subject of horses was, in a way, that of the West itself. It brought out the best and the worst in the people who responded to it. True cowboys loved horses and hated barbed wire. Entrepreneurs loved profit and used barbed wire liberally to get it. Between these two divergent types and views, much western history occurred. In the long run, the entrepreneur had his way, and the cowboy of the fabulous cattle industry days of the 1880s and 1890s faded into oblivion. Through his novels, however, Grey ensured that the cowboy and his faithful horse would not be forgotten. He often reached the heights of ecstasy in his descriptions and memorializations of the American cowboy.

Chapter Six
Cowboys and Indians

The open-range cattle industry flourished in the United States approximately between 1865 and 1890. New markets in the East, developed by improved rail facilities and refrigerated cars, largely accounted for the prosperity. Towns like Abilene and Dodge City, Kansas, became famous because of their location at the junction of a railroad and the "long drive." Thousands of cattle were driven from Texas over a path known usually as the Chisholm Trail, "regardless of where it ran."[1] The "long drive" was lengthy in distance and consuming in time, and its successful operation depended on many things: adequate finances, good weather, pacified Indians, and, most of all, the cowboy's skill. The American cowboy became the most romanticized figure in United States history. His image showed him as an expert marksman, a great lover, an imbiber of strong drink, a practical joker, a protector of womanhood, and a hundred other things. In true life, generally, the cowboy's lot was hard and monotonous, full of strenuous labor. There were enough high points in a cowboy's career, however, to cause writers of fiction to develop the western story as a distinct genre of literature. Owen Wister set the trend with *The Virginian,* and Zane Grey became its most famous practitioner.

Cowboys were inseparably connected with the open-range cattle industry. In herding cattle for long distances, they developed a jargon and a music peculiarly their own. The cowboys' slow drawl and their ballads (often composed and sung to soothe restless cattle) became famous. Cowboys usually were young and intense, and their long abstentions from gaiety while on the trail caused a number of overreactions, particularly from drinking "red liquor," once they got into a town. The dream of practically every cowboy was to have a "spread" of his own. He generally typified a statement made by Benjamin Franklin in the eighteenth century that, until land availability disappeared in America, few people would want to work for somebody else. Therefore, many cowboys yearned to become landlords themselves, and they worked assiduously toward that goal. The cattle industry was conducted by well-established ranchers with the assistance of young men on their way up. Often this arrangement encouraged cordial relationships between employers and workers, in which not only the virtue of private ownership of property was shown, but chivalric attitudes were demonstrated. Grey elaborates on both of these patterns in his 1939 novel, *Knights of the Range.*

Comradeship

Knights of the Range is set in eastern New Mexico in the mid-1870s when the territory has no law except that of the six-shooter. Colonel Lee Ripple, who came to the area in 1855, has established a huge ranching enterprise on the level of New Mexico's most famous rancher, Lucien Maxwell, of Taos. Ripple's daughter, Holly, who takes over the ranch after his death, manages its affairs during the most tumultuous time in New Mexico history: "This period saw the inception and development of the Lincoln County War, the bloodiest of all frontier wars [which Grey describes], in which three hundred men were killed. It saw the rise of Billy the Kid and Jesse Evans, mere youths in years, but who had not peers in cold nerve, or guncraft, or bloody deeds."[2]

The novel has the usual number of robbers, rustlers, and forlorn lovers. Its distinctive aspect, however, is the "Knights of the Round Table" theme that Grey adopts. Holly, the last of the Ripples, regards her cowboys not as mere employees but as members of her family. Her father referred to them as "Rowdies of the Saddle," but Holly changes the title to "Knights of the Range." Every cowboy in her employ loves her; it is clear that they would unhesitatingly die for her. In partial return for this gesture of chivalry toward her, Holly continues her father's tradition of holding an elaborate banquet each year.

At the event in 1874, Holly speaks feelingly to her cowboys, giving an impromptu history of the West and ending with the serious problems they face with the area's rustlers. Response to her address is given by Brazos Keene, a Texan, "the wildest, the most untamable, yet the most fascinating and lovable of all Holly's cowboys" (65). After faltering for a moment, Brazos urges his compatriots to ever greater exertions on behalf of their beloved mistress. He even foreswears racial discrimination as he singles out the group's only black cowboy, Rideem Jackson, and said: "I'm sinkin' race prejudice an' all thet other damn selfish rot. We've got a common cause, men" (151).

Brazos is hopelessly in love with Holly Ripple, but her affections are directed toward a gunman, Renn Frayne, a former Easterner. Frayne leads the attack against rustlers and other spoilsmen, while holding to the belief that the line between branding and stealing cattle is difficult to define. The cowboy is the most innocent figure in the matter of appropriating mavericks (unbranded calves roaming the range), yet, says Frayne, he usually gets most of the blame. The guilty parties generally are established businessmen who are crooked underneath all of their respectable appearances, and the "McCoy-Slaughter Combine" is an example. Sewall McCoy and Russ Slaughter, as it turns out, are behind the cattle rustling, although on the surface, they are respected ranchers. In the climax, when McCoy and Slaughter hire gunman Jeff Rankin to deal with the Knights of the Range, a general shoot-out occurs in which Frayne outdraws Rankin and then also kills McCoy and Slaughter. After this event, Holly and Frayne are married. In despair over losing Holly, Brazos Keene rides away to become a lonely wanderer.

Knights of the Range shows the qualities of loyalty, intemperateness, juvenility, and deadliness characteristic of the American cowboy. It also indicates that some of their mutual concerns were too important to be undermined by long-standing personal beliefs; thus, in the interest of protecting Holly Ripple's property, Brazos Keene gives up his race hatred. A corporate effort in defense of private property is a major idea that Grey develops in *Knights of the Range* and the welfare of the group is a fitting subject for a novel written during the depression of the 1930s. Yet Grey had difficulty in selling *Knights of the Range*: even an old standby of Grey's, *Collier's,* turned down the manuscript on grounds that it was too much of a panorama and not enough of story,[3] and *Cosmopolitan* was unable to work out a schedule for it.[4] These rejections showed that an author, no matter how famous he became, still had to convince editors of his work's merits. *Knights of the Range* was finally serialized in 1935 by the *Chicago Tribune,* and it was published in book form in 1939 by Harper's.

A sequel of sorts to *Knights of the Range* is Grey's novel *Twin Sombreros* (1941), which continues the story of Brazos Keene[5] (played by John Wayne in the movie version), the personification of the American cowboy. When the story begins, five years have passed since Brazos left Holly Ripple and Renn Frayne. He has not suffered unduly, however, for he is still very much interested in members of the opposite sex. If he was a tragic figure like "Hell-Bent Wade" in Grey's *The Mysterious Rider,* Brazos would reject womanhood from the viewpoint of personal love. But he is a young cowboy, and heartbreak in young cowboys, Grey demonstrates, is rarely permanent.

The theme of chivalry continues in *Twin Sombreros,* as well as the effort to defend private property from men of ill will. Wandering as he does, Brazos seems almost automatically to find trouble. He stops at a cabin one night, for example, and is awakened early the next morning by what he thinks is the sound of rain. He smells blood, however, and soon discovers a body in the cabin's loft. Naturally, Brazos is "framed" for killing the man, Allen Neece. He is arrested by a crooked deputy sheriff and immediately saved from hanging by a fellow Texan.

After exoneration for the Neece murder, Brazos decides to find out who the culprits are. He visits Abe Neece, Allen's father, and discovers that Neece was once the owner of a ranch called "Twin Sombreros," now in the hands of a dubious character, Raines Surface. Another discovery, more pleasant than the first, is identical twins, June and Janis, daughters of Abe Neece, and Brazos quickly falls in love with both girls. In due time, Brazos discovers that Surface is behind the Neece killing and that he has wrongly taken the elder Neece's ranch. After restoring the ranch to Neece, Brazos faces another difficulty: which twin does he want, and how can he tell them apart? One solution to the problem is that he marry both of them. Being fearful of polygamy, however, Brazos again hits the trail. He is followed and found in a Texas town by Janis Neece, and the two are wed.

Twin Sombreros, serialized in 1940 by the *New York News Syndicate* and published as a book the following year, emphasizes the doctrines of good works. Brazos Keene was only one of hundreds of men roaming the western regions, deliberately playing the role of the Good Samaritan—playing it, in the case of Brazos, to forget the supposed heartbreak of losing Holly Ripple. The book was not as realistic or as historically significant, in Grey's opinion, as several of his other productions, but he predicted success for it.[6] However, the magazine to which he first submitted it, *Collier's,* turned it down. In assessing his publishing problems in the mid-1930s, Dolly advised Grey to write "one of your old-time exciting stories."[7] She also urged him to readapt himself to present conditions. Dolly told him: "It is only age that cannot change, and you are not old. You have the youth and flexibility still to conquer, but you have fallen into ways of self-indulgence, into vanities of position." Dolly then gave a glimpse of the effects of the depression: "Believe me, no one is too proud to retrench in these days. It is those who do not when they ought to, who are looked down upon."[8] Such counsel from Dolly indicates that she was the strongest single force in Zane Grey's life.

Somewhat similar to *Knights of the Range* and *Twin Sombreros* in themes of chivalry, but not as fully executed, is Grey's novel *Raiders of Spanish Peaks* (1938), originally titled *The Three Range Riders*.[9] Three men, Laramie Nelson, Trace Williams, and Lonesome Mulhall, become famous throughout Kansas and a part of Colorado as shooters, trackers, and lovers. Their major objective is to save enough money to buy a ranch, so at the basis of all their escapades is the desire to own property. One day the trio rides into Garden City, Kansas, founded by Buffalo Jones, the man with whom Grey first went West. In the town, they meet Jones and a friend of his, John Lindsay of Sandusky, Ohio. Lindsay has bought a ranch in Colorado called "Spanish Peaks." He is such a tenderfoot that Jones easily talks Nelson, Mulhall, and Williams into accompanying Lindsay to Colorado and getting him started as a rancher. Lindsay's three beautiful daughters help the cowboys considerably in making their decisions. Thus the stage is set for what to Zane Grey readers was an ordinary western situation: strong, manly Westerners helping weak, effete Easterners get a new start in life. This assistance seemed to be the mission of those who had grown up in the West, and rarely did their goodwill, practiced in splendid settings, fail to transform the Easterner.

Rustling, claimed Grey, was the biggest problem of ranchers during the last quarter of the nineteenth century. Buffalo Jones tells Lindsay what is ahead of him:

We are now in the midst of what I might call the third great movement of early frontier history—the cattle movement. . . . For years now vast herds of cattle have been driven North an' West an' shipped East on cattle-trains. The cattle business is well on an' fortunes are bein' made. With endless range, fine grass an' water, nothin' else could be expected. . . . But rustlin' now is a business. The rustler has come into his own. He steals herds of cattle in a raid. Or he will be your neighbor rancher, brandin' all your calves. The demand for cattle is big. Ready money always. An' this rustlin is goin' to grow an' have its way for I don't know how long. Years, anyway.[10]

Jones's speech to Lindsay lays the framework for most of the story. The three cowboys fight off rustlers and other intruders while the Colorado air restores the elder Lindsay to health and the setting makes a man of his son. During this process, fully predictable love affairs blossom between the cowboys and the three Lindsay girls. The rustlers are routed or hanged, a Cattleman's Protective Association is formed, and love reigns supreme on Spanish Peaks Ranch. The story is typically Grey because of its themes—the transforming qualities of the West, western chivalry, defending private property—and because of its descriptions of cowboys. There is little difference in the personality of a cowboy who fights for "law and order" and one who rustles cattle. The same type of humor (usually in the form of practical jokes) characterizes both persons, and the same inclinations toward the fair sex are paramount. The difference, then, between violent men who are good and violent men who are bad, Grey indicates, was indeed minute.

This concept is pursued in Grey's novel, *Arizona Ames,* serialized in 1929 by *McCall's,* and published in 1932 as a book. Rich Ames, from the Tonto country, knows the ways of violence, but he never uses them for ill until he shoots three men, one of whom raped his sister. The deed necessitates Rich's flight from Arizona and dooms him to a life of wandering under the name of "Arizona Ames." Rich becomes the Don Quixote of the West as he roams from place to place helping needy people, mostly females. He shoots Crowe Grieve for mistreating his wife and being, in general, a rotten human being. When Rich goes to Utah, he protects a Mormon from the overbearing tactics of bad men. Finally he wanders into Colorado where he meets Ester Halstead, falls in love with her, and accordingly plans to give up his travelings.

Arizona Ames, said Grey, "was a typical character of his period. Every range from the Pan Handle to the Black Hills, and as far west as the Pecos, had its Ames."[11] He fits admirably the role of the cowboy: "He [the cowboy] came from the four corners of the United States, and beyond. At most he was a boy not yet out of his teens; but then life of the range, the toil and endurance demanded by cattle raising, the border saloon, the gambling-hell, the rustler, developed him at once into a man, and one that eventually made the West habitable" (98).

Black Cowboys

In addition to depicting the stereotype cowboy in his novels, Grey also discusses some of the thousands of black cowboys who journeyed throughout the western regions. A recent book said of the black cowboy: "Now they are forgotten, but once they rode all the trails, driving millions of cattle before them. . . . They numbered thousands, among them many of the best riders, ropers and wranglers."[12] Most books about the West, both fiction and nonfiction, neglected the black man's contributions to western settlement—indeed, even his presence. Grey wrote about black cowboys in several of his books but in three in particular.

In *Knights of the Range* (1939), Ride-em Jackson is a highly respected person. He is asked once to give testimony against a white man, a procedure practically nonexistent in that country at the time. His riding abilities are unmatched in New Mexico territory, and his fame in this respect has spread far and wide. On a bet with Russ Slaughter, Jackson breaks the toughest bronc in the area: "He appeared to wrap himself around the horse and to bend flat, almost to the ground. . . . On the instant, with a horrid scream the horse raised himself spasmodically with a cracking of hoofs. Like a burr Jackson's body appeared stuck upon him. . . . He had sunk his teeth in the nose of the horse, which made it impossible for the animal to get its head. And when they came up together the horse had his head high, turned back in a distorted way, with the little Negro, like a leech upon his neck" (186–87). Although the champion rider of the outfit, Ride-em Jackson, along with Brazos Keene, is also a great practical joker. On Holly Ripple's wedding day Jackson goes to her and says in all seriousness that Frayne has just gone after rustlers and has no time to marry her. She believes him until she sees the other cowboys snickering at her discomfort.

Raiders of Spanish Peaks (1938) features a black vaquero who is a part of a rustling outfit headed by Lester Allen, the man from whom John Lindsay bought Spanish Peaks. (Here is another instance of a rancher, respectable on the surface, conducting a huge illicit cattle business.) The black man, Sam Johnson, is finally induced to incriminate Allen in the rustling operations, and his testimony is the key to breaking the rustling ring.

A third Grey novel with a black cowboy as a major character is *West of the Pecos* (1937). Sambo Jackson, whose reputation is well known west of the Pecos River, has accompanied his former master, Colonel Templeton Lambeth, to the area from East Texas just after the Civil War. Sambo becomes the protector of the Colonel's daughter, Terrill, after the Colonel dies. (The Colonel wanted a boy when Terrill was born, so he gave her a boy's name, dressed her like a boy, and taught her to act like a boy.) Sambo is the only person in the town of Eagle's Nest who knows that Terrill Lambeth is really a girl. The main white character of the novel, Pecos Smith, soon learns to respect Sambo Jackson: "Pecos Smith had known Negro slaves as worthy as any white man, though he had the Southerner's contempt for most of the black trash. This man, Sambo, had the build of a vaquero, and Pecos remembered him. His boots and spurs gave further proof to Pecos."[13]

The chief theme of *West of the Pecos* deals with the nuances of cattle rustling and appropriations of mavericks. Many cowboys, including Pecos Smith, got their start as ranchers in this way, although an unwritten law of the range dictated that, before a man could take mavericks, he had to be a rancher. Thus, for a nonrancher to brand mavericks was clearly a case of rustling. At the end of the book Pecos Smith and Sambo Jackson break the rustling ring in the area. Pecos discovers that Terrill Lambeth is really a girl, marries her, and becomes a powerful and respected rancher.

Grey sold *West of the Pecos* to *American Magazine*, where it was serialized in 1931 but not before revisions were made. Originally, Grey had given the story two unrelated beginnings, one dealing with Colonel Lambeth's journey from East Texas and the other with Pecos Smith's branding of Mavericks. For a magazine serialization, the story's beginning lacked the necessary unity,[14] so the Colonels' trip was to a large extent edited from the final version.

There are several instances in Grey's books of black cowboys herding, singing, cooking to keep the cattle drives moving and the ranches working. Although Grey was primarily interested in the Indian's minority status, he by no means overlooked the contributions of the blacks to western development.

Mavericks

On the matter of dealing with mavericks, Grey elaborated fully in his novel, *The Maverick Queen* (1950). Kit Bandon of Wyoming's Wind River Mountain area buys maverick calves from rustlers, and her purchases provide the foundation for a growing dispute between cowboys and cattlemen that ultimately produces a range war. Into the midst of these growing difficulties comes Lincoln Bradway from Nebraska to investigate the mysterious death of his friend, Jimmy Weston. Before the book ends, it is clear that Jimmy was caught appropriating mavericks and hanged by cattlemen: "Lincoln had heard that the ranchers of Western Wyoming, hoping to induce rustlers to give their ranges a wide berth, had adopted the ruthless practice of hanging a cattle thief without formality."[15]

Lincoln's desire to destroy Kit's operation is tempered by his affection for Kit's niece, Lucy. This love affair infuriates Kit, who wants Lincoln for herself. She throws temper tantrums when she discovers that Lincoln is one man she cannot manipulate. Finally, however, Kit is captured by a group of cattlemen and unceremoniously hanged, thereby showing the terribly direct justice of the frontier and indicating that womanhood, respected as it was in the West, still had to maintain certain codes of conduct or suffer the consequences. When the book ends, Lincoln has turned Wyoming into the major character: "He [Lincoln] had come to avenge a crime and had found his true mate here in these hills. He knew that this love of Wyoming was permanent and ineradicable and that somewhere under the shadow of these peaks he would make his home." (155–56). Again, Grey allows setting to triumph over characterization, for *The Maverick Queen* depicts the cruelty of frontier days. If any proverb could effectively describe the theme of this novel, it would be, "Pride goeth before a fall." Kit Bandon is full of vanity and arrogance during the time she is the "maverick queen," and these very characteristics, as well as her deeds, lead her straight to the gallows.[16] (See chapter 9 for a discussion of *The Maverick Queen* as Grey originally wrote it.)

A Rustling Preventive

One way to limit rustling was to use a drift fence, a barbed wire structure built so that cattle could be controlled in their grazing. Although often illegal because it crossed open range or private property, it was a way for ranchers to keep a close watch on their cattle and provided an easy patrol area. Drift fences, however, were unpopular with cowboys because of the barbed wire. Moreover, people in areas where the cattle were prevented from wandering regarded drift fences as affronts to their honesty. Nonetheless, many ranchers resorted to drift fences to keep their cattle from straying and thus being rustled. Grey wrote of such an event in his novel *The Drift Fence* (1933).

The book describes the effects of suddenly thrusting a tenderfoot into the role of a foreman who has to supervise a wild group of cowboys. When Jim Traft from Missouri arrives in Arizona at his uncle's invitation to head the Diamond Ranch outfit in the Tonto region, the tenderfoot's first decision is to build a drift fence one hundred miles long to solve the rustling problem. Many cowboys balk at the idea, and only through perseverance and fistfights does Jim Traft have his

way. While constructing the fence, the cowboys, trying to force him
to give up the project, play all kinds of practical jokes on Traft.

Traft meets and falls in love with Molly Dunn of the Cibeque, an
area isolated by the drift fence. Traft's and Molly's initial hostility because of the drift fence is soon overcome, but trouble persists between
Traft and Molly's brother, "Slinger," a gunman. When they fight,
Slinger tries to "rooster" Traft by fighting on his back and swinging
his spurs at his antagonist. Traft wins the fight, however, and also
Slinger's respect. If there was anything that a true Westerner liked, it
was fortitude and bravery, especially in someone who was not a native
Westerner. After the event, Slinger helps the Diamond Ranch group,
and by the time winter stops the building, sixty of the planned one
hundred miles of the drift fence are constructed.

The Drift Fence, serialized in 1929 by American Magazine and published in 1933 as a book, regained for Grey some of his popularity
among readers of America because it gives excellent glimpses of what
cowboy life was really like. Perhaps the realism in this respect came
from Grey's own personal experiences in living with cowboys. He knew
their ways, and also their tricks, and he became fond of practical joking, the trademark of the American cowboy. Grey knew he had a winner with The Drift Fence, even while writing it. It took him only fifty-
seven days to write the original manuscript of 466 pages. He never
missed a day of working on it, rising each morning at five and working
for two hours. The early morning labor was a real revelation to him:
he felt it was "some stunt. If the novel is good, I sure have discovered
something."[17]

One of the obstacles in building the drift fence is a gang of outlaws
known as the "Hash Knife," and Grey writes of this group in a sequel
to The Drift Fence: The Hash Knife Outfit. The novel was so entitled
because these outlaws always leave their calling card after a job—a
picture of a hash knife, although its original title had been The Yellow
Jacket Feud. In the novel, the plot is generated by the competition over
ownership and operation of the Yellow Jacket Ranch. Jed Stone, a
leader of the Hash Knife outfit, has mellowed in his ways; he wants to
give up his wild life, but a member of his gang, Croak Malloy, will
not let him. Finally, after Stone shoots the scoundrel, he turns his
attention to a traditional western practice: the "saving" of Jim Traft's
sister, Gloriana, who has come to Arizona. Jed makes Gloriana believe
that all sorts of dreadful things are about to happen to her, causing her
to turn away from her characteristic petulance. Her experience helps

her accept a cowboy's offer of marriage. Thus another successful Zane Grey romance was placed before readers eager to read it.[18]

The Long Drive

Grey's study of the American cowboy extended far beyond the ranch and the range, for an important aspect of the cowboy's life was the long drive from the range to the rail head. Life on the trail was vigorous, requiring immense amounts of stamina; indeed, the work on the trail, rather than on the ranch or on the range, ultimately produced for most people the image of the cowboy. On the trail cowboys sang ballads, told tall tales, imagined fantasies of wealth and faraway places, and dreamed of home and sweethearts. Their life on the trail turned the cowboy into an American institution that endeared itself to millions of people. To an extent, all of Grey's cowboy novels featured the trail, but two were specifically about the long drive.

Although *Wilderness Trek* (1944) was set in Australia, its characters and events were typically American. The central figures of the novel, Sterling Hazelton and Red Krehl, are former Arizona cowboys who left the United States because of problems with love and law. In Australia, they agree to lead a huge herd of cattle across the continent, a feat that requires two years of as strenuous an existence as it is possible for man to have. On the trail, race hatred flares when Ashley Ormiston mistreats the aborigines; peril stalks the way as the group crosses several crocodile-infested rivers; unbearable heat and hordes of flies accompany the group; but there is, finally, the one thing that makes the trip worthwhile: love. This book, like so many other of Grey's novels, ends in a double wedding. (This was probably the longest book Grey ever wrote. It came to nearly a thousand pages in manuscript but was mercilessly whittled down on its way to the publisher.)

Grey first visited Australia in the mid-1920s to fish for swordfish, tuna, and anything else he could catch. Impressed with Australia's likeness to America in regard to cattle raising and the long drives, he thought for years of writing a novel with an Australian setting. He did not accomplish his goal until 1936, and the novel was not published by Harper's until 1944. A letter from Dolly predicted the book's future popularity: "It is really remarkable that you have achieved so much popularity in Australia—or perhaps it is not so remarkable at all. You are doing a great deal to put Australia on the map in a sporting way and I am glad they appreciate it. . . . I think the Australian cowboy idea might go over pretty well in this country."[19] Although Grey had earlier angered some New Zealanders and Australians for casting aspersions on their fishing methods, he continued to be a household word in those areas. One of his favored remembrances was seeing in New Zealand a ship named after one of his novels *Desert Gold.*

A book that put Grey briefly on the best-selling lists again was *The Trail Driver* (serialized by *McCall's* in 1931; published by Harper's in 1936), the story of a cattle drive that suffers numerous hardships from rustlers, electric storms, stampedes, floods, double-crossings, and Indian attacks. Only the strongest could survive these ordeals along the Chisholm Trail. In the words of one of the book's characters, Adam Brite, the cattle drives represent the "swing of Texas toward an Empire." The cattle industry becomes so significant that thousands of Easterners eagerly invest their money in the enterprise.[20] The movement, Brite believes, is "singular" and "tremendous," providing a way for Texans to restore themselves to economic solvency.

The Trail Driver is typical of Grey's writing for its romances, mistaken identities, and overheard conversations. It gives a vivid description of Dodge City, Kansas: "On the wide sidewalk a throng of booted, belted, spurred men wended their way up or down. The saloons roared. Black-sombreroed, pale-faced, tight-lipped men stood beside the wide portals of the gaming-dens. Beautiful wrecks of womanhood, girls with havoc in their faces and the look of birds of prey in their eyes, waited in bare-armed splendor to be accosted. Laughter without mirth ran down the walk. The stores were full. Cowboys in twos and threes and sixes trooped by, young, lithe, keen of eye, bold of aspect, gay and reckless."[21]

The Gunman

Grey also discusses the gunman in *The Trail Driver,* as he did in several other novels: "The gunman sought the dramatic, took advantage of the element of surprise, subjected no other to risk [except, of course, his opponent] than himself" (145). The western gunman is the strongest drawn character in all the Zane Grey novels, and characters like Lassiter of *Riders of the Purple Sage* and Jim Lacy of *Forlorn River* and *Nevada* are more believable than most of Grey's other characters. Competition as a way of life in the West was a historical fact, making it reasonable to expect a gunman's reputation to be constantly challenged. To keep himself alive, the gunman had to become ever more adept at his deadly art. Most gunmen were cowboys of whom their home communities were proud; this type of gunman killed only when he had to. On the other hand, fast-draw artists in the West were often sheriffs with an itch to kill instead of arrest, cowboys on the rampage, gamblers who shot to hide their cheating.[22] There were also gunmen whose status as either outlaw or peaceful citizen was uncertain, and gunmen who had repented of their deeds but had to suffer the consequences.

In *The Lone Star Ranger* (1915) Grey shows the stages of creating a gunman, and the novel is valuable for its psychological insights into the gunman.[23] It is also pessimistic, hinting broadly that Buck Duane, the central character, whose father was a gunman, really does not have a choice in the matter—that some chromosome factor dictates that he be a gunman.

When Cal Bain forces Buck to draw, Buck's victory in the shoot-out causes him to acquire an instant reputation. He hits the trail, for Texas Rangers are warring on gunmen at the time (1870s) and trying to eliminate the shoot-out as a way of settling arguments. Therefore, a gunman is regarded by the Rangers as a criminal, no matter how pure of heart he is. The gunman's life is a haunted and lonely one; he is always blamed for crimes whether he commits them or not; his victims constantly come back to haunt him; as he sits before campfires and as he tries to sleep at night, "Every one of his victims, singly and collectively, returned to him for ever, it seemed, in cold, passionless, accusing domination of these haunted hours. They did not accuse him of dishonor or cowardice or brutality or murder; they only accused him of death" (142). In time, he accepts the dictum: "A gunfighter has to kill a man to forget his last victim." Thus, his lot is one of unceasing situations in which he must kill or be killed.

Buck Duane is one of the lucky gunmen, for Captain McNelly of the Rangers, who has been chasing Duane, offers a pardon in return for Buck's help in capturing the elusive outlaw Cheseldine, an offer that Buck quickly accepts. He travels to the Texas area West of the Pecos where he comes in contact with Granger Longstreth, who has a beautiful daughter, Ray. Ultimately, Buck discovers that Longstreth is behind the outlaw operations, so he faces a dilemma: how to expose Longstreth (whom Buck suspects is Cheseldine) and love his daughter at the same time. This conflict is solved when Buck's and Ray's love for each other becomes so intense that Longstreth quits his illegal life and returns to his native Louisiana and Buck discovers that Floyd Dawson is actually Cheseldine.

After the outlaw leaders have been dispersed, either by train or by bullet, Duane's job is ended, but he decides to confront Poggin. Ray Longstreth remonstrates against him for still wanting gunplay, and Zane Grey explains why Buck wants to meet Poggin: "His father's blood, that dark and fierce strain, his mother's spirit, that strong and unquenchable spirit of the surviving pioneer—these had been in him; and the killings, one after another, the wild and haunted years, had made him, absolutely in spite of his will, the gunman. . . . Actual pride of his record! Actual vanity in his speed with a gun! Actual jealousy of any rival" (356–57). The two gunmen are roughly comparable in their talents. Poggin shoots Buck five times; but when Buck awakens, he learns that Poggin is killed.

Buck Duane's career as a ranger and seemingly as a gunman ends with his marriage to Ray Longstreth and their departure for Louisiana, for Buck wants to go where his reputation is not known; it was virtually impossible to find such an area in the West. The problem for Duane is how to escape the stigma of the past and lead an ordinary, peaceful life. In most instances, the man who tried to accomplish such a feat was doomed to disappointment.

An exception to this rule, however, was discussed by Grey in *Shadow on the Trail,* which was published in 1946, seven years after Grey's death. Grey was inspired to write the novel by the experiences of Sam Bass and his outlaws. One day in the 1870s in Mercer, Texas, Bass and his gang were ambushed while robbing the town's bank, and only one robber escaped. Grey wondered about former outlaws—about what they did and how they lived after they relinquished their careers of crime. He says in the book's foreword: "It is within the province of the creative writer to take upon himself the task of imagining and portraying what might have happened to one of these vanishing outlaws. And that is what I have tried to do in *Shadow on the Trail.*"[24]

The first objective of Wade Holden when the gang is ambushed is to elude the Texas Rangers, who are led by Captain Mahaffey, whose motto is "run the man down." Fortuitously, Holden finds in a prairie-schooner encampment a sympathetic female, Jacqueline Pencarrow, who hides him in her tent while Mahaffey is in the area. Then, predictably, the novel shifts forward several years to a setting in Arizona where Holden discovers the Pencarrow family. The father has tried ranching for some time, only to be intimidated by the area's bad men. Holden puts himself at Pencarrow's service, cleans out the outlaws and rustlers (earning a highly respected reputation as a gunman), and falls in love with Jacqueline. In time, the two are married, and happy years pass during which the Holdens become proud parents. Wade is just on the verge of forgetting his associations with outlaws, when Captain Mahaffey one day appears. But Mahaffey is impressed with Wade's present condition, for what a man becomes rather than what he has been is an important consideration in Mahaffey's thinking. Therefore, his visit turns out to be only social.

Shadow on the Trail shows conclusively that "violence is violence," whether it is committed by good men or bad, for Wade Holden does not give up violence but merely changes sides. The number of casualties he inflicts while on the side of "good" is as high, or higher, as when he belonged to the "bad." Grey's book does not live up to the promise that its beginning sets for it; the novel misses its chance at greatness by treating in an ordinary way themes of potentially intense poignancy. If Grey emphasized the attitude and thought of a reformed outlaw instead of allowing "business as usual," except in a different location and for a new clientele, the book would be more forceful than it is.[25]

Grey's life-long study of the American cowboy dealt mostly with chivalry, ownership of property, rustling, black cowboys, mavericks, the long drive, the gunman, cowboy humor, and the loner. In his "apologia" to the critics in the mid-1920s (discussed in chapter 8), Grey summarizes his feelings toward the cowboy: "The poor cowboy! Who is there to save him from oblivion? The cheap novel, the modern movie, have almost blotted him from history. But he was heroic. More than the frontiersman, the soldiers, the pioneers, the American cowboy opened the West for civilization. . . . Who could exaggerate the ordeal of the cowboy?"[26] Grey blended the cowboy's attributes into the cattle industry and thus described a fantastic era in American history. The cowboy took, however, a proprietary view of the western regions—an attitude that made inevitable trouble and war with the Indians. Two tribes of South Plains Indians in particular, the Kiowas and the Comanches, confronted the cowboy's advance, and Grey wrote two lengthy novels that deal with these encounters.

Cowboys versus Indians

In *Fighting Caravans* (originally titled *The Overland Freighter*[27] set in the 1870s and first published in 1928 by *Country Gentleman*), the characterization of the hero and the heroine is treated in a typically Grey manner, but the book is valuable for its geographical and historical descriptions. Clint "Buff" Belmet and May Bell, both mere babes, promise fidelity to each other as they travel West with their parents. Buff Belmet becomes an overland freight hauler after Indians kill his mother and father and kidnap his sweetheart, May Bell. Buff carries furs, pelts, and buffalo hides along the Old Trail, which runs from Kansas to New Mexico. He earlier sympathized with the Indians but now is determined to be an Indian killer after the slaying of his parents and the kidnapping of his true love. The Kiowa Indian chieftain, Satock, is a constant menace to the caravans, but the most dangerous Indians are the Comanches led by Nigger-Horse. Not even the wagon trains' cannons can stop the Comanches when they are on the rampage. (It was rare for a wagon train to possess a cannon.)

One gruesome episode after another occurs as Clint (Buff) drives his wagon trains between Kansas and New Mexico, and Buff's reputation as a freighter and Indian fighter spreads rapidly. He is hailed everywhere, but at heart he is a lonely man, lamenting the loss of May Bell. Through his travels, Buff meets such prominent frontiersmen as Dick Curtis and Kit Carson, as well as the most famous rancher in New Mexico territory, Lucien Maxwell of Taos. Maxwell, a friend of the Indians, sells beef to the United States Army—a most profitable enterprise during the Civil War. When Maxell urges Buff to stop being a hauler and to settle down because the West needs permanent citizens, Buff cannot do so because he has to find May. After a huge Indian offensive, in concert with white renegades led by Charley Bent (the Simon Girty of the Plains), he finally finds her. May has believed all these years that Buff was dead. Their reunion ends *Fighting Caravans* on a poignant note.

Related to *Fighting Caravans* because of its descriptions of cowboy-Indian confrontation, is another Grey novel, *The Lost Wagon Train* (1936). The main character, Stephen Latch, a Southerner, is attending college in the North when the Civil War erupts. When his failure to obtain a commission in the Confederate Army embitters him, he goes West where he plans to rob wagon trains. He forms a partnership with Satana, chief of the Kiowas. (The other Kiowa Chief, Satock, stopped his operations in 1863.) Satana and his men have plenty of rum to fortify themselves for the job at hand. After attacking the trains, the Indians kill everybody and roll the wagons over a cliff so they cannot be found. At first, Latch is conscience-stricken because of all the murders, but he turns his heart to steel. He has been wronged by the world, he feels, and he intends to strike back.

On the very first wagon train, Latch discovers that his old sweetheart, Cynthia Bowden, is a passenger, and he saves her from the Indians and later marries her. They live in Spider Web Canyon in New Mexico where Cynthia knows little of Latch's activities. Latch takes possession of a wide area that he calls "Latch's Field," on which he wants to build a ranch that will rival Maxwell's in hospitality. When he hears that his wife has died giving birth to a child, Latch leaves the place without visiting the scene of birth and without learning that he has a daughter. When he returns six years later, he find his little girl, Estelle, who has been cared for in his absence by friends.

Latch gives up his business of massacring the occupants of wagon trains, for his one objective now is to keep his beloved daughter from learning about his dreadful past. There are people, however, like Leighton, Latch's former partner, who hold Latch's past as a hammer over his head. A fierce climax occurs when Leighton captures Latch, takes him to the canyon where the ruined wagon trains are located, makes him sign over his ranch to Leighton, and tells him that Estelle is being brought to the scene to hear the truth about her father's past.

An observer of these events, "Slim Blue" (who is really the brother of Lester Cornwall, one of Latch's early comrades) is hidden in the underbrush and intends to save Latch from Leighton. Before this happens, however, Latch works free and rips Leighton apart with his knife. Blue then comes out into the open and views the ghastly scene: "Faces of rugged pioneers, scalped heads of women, nude bodies of children gazed mournfully . . . upon Blue [though, apparently, the massacres had occurred long ago]. . . . He had seen the work of Satana and Latch. Bloody devils! He ground his teeth in irrepressible rage. But the fierce Kiowa chief could be understood, for the white man had driven him into the waste places, robbed him of meat. But not so Latch! What a monster."[28] Even so, Blue marries Latch's daughter, Estelle, and moves to Boston with her so that Latch's secret will be kept from her. This is the only book Grey ever wrote in which going East from the West had a beneficial effect and in which a major villain is not punished for his crimes.

Grey wrote much of *The Lost Wagon Train* in early 1931 while on the way to Tahiti. He must have been in a bloody frame of mind, for *Collier's* changed the manuscript on the grounds that the massacre conspiracy between Latch and Satana was so utterly cruel that readers would be unpleasantly affected.[29] The book, however, incorporated all of the gruesome events.

Fighting Caravans and *The Lost Wagon Train* are historical studies, hinting broadly at the inevitability of conflict between red and white men. Grey again makes it clear that the white man was basically responsible for the confrontation. The books were valuable, too, for their descriptions of caravan trails, such as the different routes of the Old Trail: Mountain and Middle, along the Cimarron River to Santa Fe, and *Journado del Muerta* (Journey of Death) across the desert. Grey notes the effects of the Civil War and its aftermath on the southwestern regions as he describes the multitudes of Northerners and Southerners who poured into the area to start their lives anew. Such migrations produced a frenzied time, indeed. The books show, also, the once proud Native Americans reduced to a level of bestiality. Elsewhere in Grey's writing, he states that the freighter era was the first great movement of frontier history (the periods of the buffalo hunter and cattle industry being the next two) because it lays the foundation for the cowboy-Indian hostilities.

Other Indian Stories

Grey wrote several short stories dealing specifically with habits, customs, and activities of various Indians, but his best story was "The Great Slave," which is about a Crow named Siena to whom a "shooting stick" was a symbol of salvation. Siena uses the instrument at first to kill elk and moose for food and later to free his tribe from slavery. The story is ironic because the "shooting-iron," so valuable to Siena and his tribe, ultimately figures most prominently in destroying Indian power. Another short story that deals with racism, vengeance, and the terrific differences between slavery and freedom is "Yaqui." The Yaquis and the Mexicans are sworn foes, and neither receives mercy at the hands of the other.[30]

Still another short story is "Blue Feather," which concerns ancient groups of Indians known as the Nopahs (the name Grey gave to the Indians in his novel, *The Vanishing American*) and the Sheboyahs. Blue Feather, from the Nopahs, is sent into the Sheboyah camp to undermine their culture to make invasion possible and easy. He does not count on meeting the beautiful maiden, Nashta; he falls so deeply in love with her that he lies to his father, Nothis Tah, about the strength of the Sheboyahs, saying that their cliff dwellings are worthless. When Nothis Tah attacks and discovers Blue Feather's prevarications about Sheboyah strength, he wants to execute him. Love saves the day, however, when Nashta successfully begs for Blue Feather's life. Nothis Tah contents himself with setting aside a day on which a large number of "little people" (the Sheboyahs) will be thrown off cliffs. Thus is born a traditional celebration (for everybody, that is, but the Sheboyahs!) in honor of the Nopah victory over their enemies.

Grey had the greatest sympathy for the Indian, and he constantly lamented the government's mistreatment of them. Grey regarded the broken treaties and the reservation system as shameful—a dark blotch in United States history. Certainly, he did not condone the Indian's violence, but in apportioning blame for violence in general, Grey argued that the onus rested on the white man's shoulders. All the way from *Betty Zane,* written in 1903, to *The Lost Wagon Train,* published in 1936, Grey defended the rights of the American Indian.

Grey truly loved the American cowboy, both the historical ones and those contemporary to him. He deeply respected American Indians because he sincerely believed they had been wronged and because Indian blood flowed in his own veins. The two forces—cowboys and Indians— competed against each other, the cowboys forging an empire, the Indians fighting for survival. Grey became the leading chronicler of the hostilities engineered by the clashing objectives.

Grey's Modern Cowboys

Although Grey usually discussed only those cowboys who had passed into history, *The Code of the West* (1934) is a major novel about the effects of automobiles and other equipment, as well as modern thinking, on the American cowboy.[31] *The Code of the West* emphasizes, too, the cowboy in a setting of change—not an unusual thing for Grey to do, for he employs this theme in other novels such as *The Light of Western Stars.* The automobile changed the lives of most cowboys in the 1920s. Usually, cowboys drove cars as though they were breaking broncs. In general, the car was viewed with suspicion by cowboys and by Grey personally, for automobiles, which made noise, disrupted the normal flow of events for nature's creatures. Thus, the motor, an unnatural thing thrust into natural surroundings, was entirely out of place.

The novel struck a familiar chord among Grey readers because it condemns the "new morality" that crept into the American system after World War I. After Mary Stockwell, a teacher, arrives in the Tonto Basin in Arizona, her seventeen-year-old sister, Gloriana, joins her. Gloriana, a flapper type, is much interested in the liberation of the American woman. Even when Gloriana is at her rebellious worst, however, the reader knows instinctively that the West will ultimately conquer her. The West's openness, its naturalness, "the simplicity of its people," the "necessity for development of physical strength," and the code of cowboy Cal Thurman, work its magic on the spoiled young girl from the East.

When Cal Thurman forcibly takes Gloriana and marries her, he tells himself he does so to protect Gloriana from herself. If she is married, scoundrels like Bid Hatfield will stop making advances toward her, and she will be freed from much temptation. Cal's deed is the ultimate step in the code: it is easy to beat up a man under the code, perhaps even to kill, but to marry someone in tribute to the code is magnanimous indeed. As it turns out, however, Cal really loves Gloriana, and she really loves him. It is not love, though, that counts as far as the code is concerned; it is Cal's willingness to marry her to uphold the "code" that is important. He does not do so consciously; his is just the way of the true Westerner.

Grey was pleased when Dolly complimented *The Code of the West,* for he respected her judgment above all others. She wrote to him as she edited the novel: "I like the story very much indeed. It is in a lighter vein than your others, yet does not belittle its title: 'The Code of the West.' Possibly it's a truer picture of real conditions than many you've done."[32] A few days after this letter from Dolly, Grey heard from the editor of *The Country Gentleman,* which serialized *The Code of the West* for thirty-thousand dollars. The editor told Grey: "At last you seem to have broken through the reserve of that New York bunch who scratch each other's back and who look upon the country West of the Hudson as largely waste territories from a literary standpoint."[33] For a man who had fought editors and critics for most of his adult life, Grey found these words most soothing.

The western novels that made Zane Grey famous ranged in setting and subject from the deserts, mountains, and corrals to history, horseflesh, and humanity. Probably of all the types of western novels Grey wrote, it was writing the straight cowboy story that made him most comfortable. Within the category of cowboys and Indians, Grey used a formula (proprietary thoughts about the land, practical joking, especially against a "greenhorn," and inevitability of clashes with Indians) that could very quickly be spotted by his readers. The only author of the time who equaled and surpassed Grey's output (but not sales) was Frederick Faust (Max Brand). These two filled the pages of pulp magazines, each writing so voluminously that even their most ardent followers had trouble keeping up with their productions. As has been noted, Grey did not confine himself completely to stories of the West. He also attempted to write plays (usually in collaboration with someone); he produced a large amount of fiction about baseball; and he wrote several books and articles on fishing. He personified everything that a sporting-literary life could give to a man. Yet he suffered long, dreadful spells of depression as he went through his days of writing, traveling, and fishing. He talked at length sometimes in his diary about the brevity of life, and perhaps this preoccupation accounted for his occasional morbidity. Despite his personal feelings, however, he still managed to "grind out" the hundreds of thousands of words that delighted his readers.

Chapter Seven

Short Works and Fishing Stories

In late October 1922 Zane Grey told his wife that he planned to write ten short stories before Christmas.[1] This forecast was not unduly optimistic, for Grey's talents and his ability to write for sustained periods coincided with America's Golden Age of pulp magazines. It was a good time to write short stories. Most of Grey's short stories have, oddly enough, better characterization than his novels. Because he intensifies moods and personalities in his short pieces, some of Grey's best writing is in the form of the short story.

Baseball and Western Short Stories

Grey's love for baseball inspired several short stories and articles. "The Winning Ball," published in *The Popular Magazine* in 1930,[2] was about a "rabbit" ball that, after the first bounce, was likely to take a huge leap away from the defensive player. When one of Grey's baseball stories, *The Young Pitcher,* was chosen by the United States government for use in Philippine schools, Dolly remarked to Grey that the selection "is a landmark; one of the significant things that count."[3] *The Redheaded Outfield and Other Stories,* published in 1920, contains most of the significant Zane Grey baseball stories. Many, if not most, were reminiscences from Grey's early life when he played the game. Although the stories were written as entertainment, there were enough baseball-playing factory workers leaving their jobs for the freedom of the diamond at the time to allow Grey, perhaps inadvertently, to get in some social comment.

Most of Grey's short stories, however, like his novels, deal with the West. Thematic materials for his shorter works are essentially the same as in the novels: the life of a Texas lawman is described in "The Ranger"; the reform of wayward ways is delineated in "Canyon Walls"; brotherly love and sacrifice are featured in "Avalanche" and "Monty

Price's Nightingale"; repentance is the moving force of "The Secret of Quaking Asp Cabin"; and consolation is a theme in "Amber's Mirage." To a considerable extent, Grey's short stories were variants, therefore, of larger works for which he was already known.[4]

Grey discusses the Texas Rangers at length in some of his novels, so "The Ranger," a 1929 feature of *Ladies' Home Journal,* came as no surprise to his readers. Vaughn Medill of this story may be the prototype Texas Ranger and may fully accept the Rangers' time-honored dictum "run the man down," but when love and private enterprise offer the opportunity, he settles down to a peaceful life of farming and ranching. Throughout his writings, Grey praised private ownership of property and true love. Although the Rangers were highly dedicated, professional men, they still recognized that it is possible for men to leave their bad ways behind them and become positive social forces. Such an event occurs not only in Grey's novel *Shadow on the Trail* but also in his short story "Canyon Walls." In this story, Monty Bellew enjoys a happy married life for two years until the law catches up with him, but seeing what Monty has become rather than what he was persuades the sheriff to leave him alone. Grey hints that Monty's punishment for his past crimes is the constant dread of suddenly being deprived of his beloved wife and family—this fear is a greater penalty than anything the law could mete out to him.

Whereas Monty Bellew exemplifies a man's efforts to live down his past, Monty Price, a featured cowboy in *The Light of Western Stars,* is the central figure in "Monty Price's Nightingale" and epitomizes self-sacrifice. As a young cowboy, Monty Price is troublesome to his associates and is always cursed in "hearty cowboy fashion." When a forest fire breaks out, Monty saves a small child, Del Muncie, from the flames, but in carrying out his deed of heroism, Monty is horribly maimed. He becomes a lonely man because of his disfigurement and listens to the plaintive song of the nightingale as it whistles away the nighttime hours. The song gives outlet to the "passionate and irrepressible strain in his blood" and soothes him when he thinks of his physical appearance. The song also seems to bond two creatures of nature who have reached the heights of nobility.[5]

Grey uses the idea of sacrifice in another short story, "Avalanche," first published in 1928 by *The Country Gentleman.* The setting is the Tonto country, where every emotion seems to be magnified beyond those of ordinary mortals. Jake Dunton and his stepbrother Verde fight for the affections of Kitty Mains, and in time the two brothers become bitter enemies. When Jake trails Verde into Black Gulch Canyon, intent on killing him, an avalanche causes survival to be uppermost in Jake's mind. When Jake escapes the onslaught and Verde is seriously injured, to save Verde becomes Jake's consuming passion. Jake has to amputate Verde's leg to combat gangrene and then has to nurse the injured man for weeks before leaving the area where the avalanche happened. During this period, the question of which one would win Kitty Mains is thought of but rarely mentioned. When the two return to civilization, they discover that Kitty has been married for several weeks. Sacrifice and irony are the major themes of "Avalanche." This story was a popular one, and apparently it was one of Grey's favorites, as he frequently identified himself in his manuscripts as the author of "Avalanche" and other stories.

Sacrifice can often be related in its effects to repentance. Grey clarifies this point in one of his best short stories, "The Secret of Quaking Asp Cabin," printed in 1954 in *American Weekly*. The first-person narrator of the story gets lost from his camping ground in the Mogollons and wanders until he comes on a cabin in the midst of some asp trees. In the cabin is the imprint of a bloody hand on the fireplace, and several bullet holes are scattered around the walls. The narrator marks the place, and when he finds his way back to camp, he tries to get someone to tell him the story of the cabin.

Finally, a half-breed Apache tells him that the first occupants of the cabin were Richard Starke, his wife, Blue, and his younger brother, Len. One day Richard saw Blue and Len making love to each other; the two, who knew Richard had seen them, kept expecting him to do something, but he did not. Richard finally was shot, presumably by Len, and his right arm and shoulder as well as the top of his lung were blown away, but through sheer willpower and hate, he survived the ordeal. Len left as soon as it was apparent that Richard would survive, but Blue stayed at the cabin to wait on Richard for the rest of her days in atonement for her wicked deed. The two did not speak to each other for ten years, becoming studies in grotesqueness. Finally, Richard forgave his brother and, when he had done so, started to die, since only his hatred had kept him going. One day he sat down in his easy chair and spoke to Blue for the first time in a decade to tell her that he forgave her and that he had invited Len to return. As the hoofbeats of Len's horse were heard in the distance, Richard died. Such is the secret, the narrator discovers, of Quaking Asp Cabin.

The cabin is mentioned in other Grey works. For example, some members of the notorious Hash Knife outfit use it as a hideout on occasions. It is a symbol, however, not of outlawry but of betrayal, contrition, sacrifice, and forgiveness. Although the story is set in the western regions, its events and themes are universal in nature. In Grey's story forgiveness for injuries sustained, both physical and mental, is the most ennobling of all man's acts.

Grey as a Playwright

Mankind's ability to forgive is pursued by Grey in "Amber's Mirage," which is both a play and a short story. The tale is an allegorical explanation of the conflicts that arise from the love of both gold and women. Although the play, co-authored by Grey and Millicent Smith, was called *Amber's Mirage,*[6] its leading character is Ruby Low. Her husband, Luke, is a tall, comely person, who finds that even after marrying Ruby and fathering her daughter, he still must compete with Al Shade (her former lover, who was away searching for gold) and Joe Raston (the villain, who loaned money to Ruby's mother in return for her promise that he would ultimately have her daughter). Amber, the prospector, is old, gray, blind, long, lean, with a desert-lined face; and his mirage is "a city of amber an' gold risin' out of a lake where the water was gentle an' blue, an' shed the sunlight with a blindin' radiance". For all of its splendor, however, Amber's mirage is a "lonely empty city . . . like a city built for people who forget or lose their way". Thus, the fanatical love that a man can have for gold and what seeking it can do to his soul are explained.

The play grows in complexity as the three men—Luke, Al Shade, and Joe Raston—compete for Ruby Low. Because Al Shade returns with a load of gold and because Raston is already wealthy, it appears that Ruby will desert Luke because she loves money. The climax comes when Ruby discovers that her and Luke's baby is missing. The lesson of the story is revealed when she looks at Luke and laments the loss of "our baby." It turns out that shrewd old Amber "borrowed" the little girl for a time, knowing full well how his "kidnapping" would affect Ruby's and Luke's relations with each other. The play ends with the baby's return and with Al Shade's decision to leave the area.

Of the plays that Grey collaborated on, *Amber's Mirage* is probably the best, for it is a faster-moving, more complex effort than the other playwriting attempts of Grey. There is no evidence, however, that this play or any other play that Grey wrote or collaborated on was ever performed. A month after *Amber's Mirage* was copyrighted (April 1929) as a play, it appeared as a short story in *Ladies' Home Journal,* and in

that form the story received most of its attention. Even the most zealous supporters of Zane Grey were not too impressed with his "career"
as a playwright.

Grey also tried to succeed as a dramatist with a 1930 play, *Port of
Call,* again co-authored by Millicent Smith.[7] Grey, a frequent visitor
to the South Seas, took long fishing trips to New Zealand and Australia, and one of his favorite places was Tahiti. In *Port of Call,* which
is similar to *The Reef Girl* (a novel that Grey wrote about Tahiti and
the South Pacific but that was not published until 1977; it is discussed
in chapter 9), Grey shows that the natives are debased by the white
man's presence. Grey was impressed with the noble stature of the South
Sea Islanders, and almost without exception every character in the play
who speaks ill of them is a scoundrel. The story's main character is Guy
Rotherick, who intends to stop off at Papeete and live with his brother
Harvey, a resident of the Islands for several years. Aboard the S.S.
Tahiti, Guy meets and falls in love with a half-caste Tahitian, Frannie
Marlowe.

When Harvey meets Guy, he pleads that Guy leave, for Harvey,
who has become degenerate while living in the islands, says that he
wants to spare Guy these travails. A trinity of evil forces, says Harvey,
works on white men in the Islands: the tropical sun stops healthy activities and produces languor, indulgence in native women, and addic-
tions to liquor. To "save" Guy, Harvey convinces Frannie that she
should give up her amorous attachment to Guy. Harvey and Frannie
stage a big courting session for Guy, planning for him to discover them
and hoping that he will be infuriated enough to depart. Harvey's va-
hine (woman), Turea, cannot bear the monstrous sham that Harvey has
performed and tells the whole sordid story to Guy. In the final scene,
which shows Guy and Frannie sailing away on the S.S. *Tahiti,* they
attract some attention, and a passenger, Mr. Ovington, says to his wife:
"These Island natives are a primitive people, not very far removed from
the savage. It stands to reason that white inheritance can't combat that
in a generation. They're all alike. They're children. That's why they
are dangerous for a white man."

The significance of *Port of Call* is that Grey makes it clear that
Ovington's statement is inane. The play, on the whole, is an attack
against racism, for Grey brings into sharp focus the differences between
the "advanced" white culture and the "primitive" natives and shows
that in most instances, the natives are the happier of the two. Grey,
an admirer of Herman Melville, believed, with the author of *Omoo* and
Typee, that the white man in the islands caused a decline in native well-

being. Therefore, Grey opposed, as had Melville, the business of white traders and the work of Christian missionaries, for their appearance marked the beginning of native degradation. Other than emphasizing these ideological points, *Port of Call* is weak in sustaining interest. The long dialogues and the lack of action scenes cause the play to progress slowly. The problem (that of Harvey "saving" his brother, Guy) is not dramatic or crucial enough to be convincing.

Yet Grey persisted in writing plays. Another drama with Millicent Smith's collaboration, *Three Tight Lines,* is set in the late 1920s in New York and in the woods of upper Maine.[8] This "comedy in three acts" is bad, even for melodrama. It starts with three wives who lament their status as "fishing widows" and plan a surprise visit to their husbands' camp in Maine. The husbands forget to tell their wives that the camp cook is a last-minute substitution, a young lady named Mary Ann, and just before the wives appear on the scene, another woman, Hyacinth Hemming, shows up after falling into the lake. She borrows some dry clothes from Mary Ann, so the first thing the wives see when they enter the cabin is the forsaken attire that belongs to Hyacinth. After several pages of confrontations between wives and husbands, it develops that Hyacinth belongs to a bootlegging ring based in that part of the country and that Mary Ann is part of the special police force sent to capture her. Once this is accomplished and the misunderstandings are cleared up, peace and love are restored.

The great differences between *Three Tight Lines* and *Port of Call* is that the clichés and the superficiality in the former are not shown to be in poor taste as in the latter, for Grey does not "editorialize" in *Three Tight Lines* as he does in *Port of Call.* Both plays are poorly written, but at least there is *some* substance in *Port of Call. Three Tight Lines* has people in it whose views and practices would be condemned in any number of Grey's western novels; they are shallow, unthinking, for the most part idle people, who really do not contribute to the betterment of the world. Grey is intolerant of such people in most of his writings.

Fish Stories

Fortunately, Grey did not spend too much time with plays, and he did write a very large number of fishing stories. Approximately one hundred fishing articles, either by Grey or about him, appeared in leading sports journals like *Sports Afield, Field & Stream,* and *Outdoor America;* and many of the articles were later printed in collected form in one of the nine major fishing books that Grey authored: *Tales of Fishes* (1919), *Tales of Southern Rivers* (1924), *Tales of Fishing Virgin Seas* (1925), *Tales of the Angler's Eldorado* (1926), *Tales of Swordfish and Tuna* (1927), *Tales of Fresh Water Fishing* (1928), *Tales of Tahitian Waters* (1931), *An American Angler in Australia* (1937), and *Zane Grey's Adventures in Fishing* (1952), edited by Ed Zern. (There have been additional Grey fishing stories published since 1973; see chapter 9.)

Grey hunted some, but his first love was fishing. The quiet boyhood joys of fishing along the banks of the Muskingum and Licking Rivers turned into boisterous assaults on huge inhabitants of the sea. Ocean trips brought out the pensiveness in Grey. As he recorded in his diary, "The sea, from which all life sprung, has been equally with the desert my teacher and my religion." He related further that he never saw the sea until late in his college career, but he knew at once that it "would fulfill vague dreams."[9] His favorite coastal sites in the United States were Seabright (New Jersey) on the Atlantic, Long Key (Florida) on the Gulf of Mexico, and Avalon (California) on the Pacific. He also fished the waters off Nova Scotia, and there in 1924 he bought a sailing ship, *Fisherman I*, previously named *Marshall Foch*.[10]

Grey's first fishing book appeared in 1919 and was titled *Tales of Fishes*. A collection of articles, many of which already were published in *Field & Stream*, the book describes events and places from the Florida coast to the Indian Ocean. Grey enjoyed excellent reviews of *Tales of Fishes: The Boston Transcript* called it a volume "filled with matter that will arouse and hold the true fisherman's mind enthralled."[11] The *New York Times* said of the book: "Somehow the true atmosphere of the sea and its mystery has been caught and held throughout, and for all who love for real 'salt' there is a great treat awaiting."[12] Theodore Brooke, always a friendly reviewer of Grey's books, predicted that *Tales of Fishes* would become a classic "which all good followers of Isaac Walton will treasure";[13] and Robert Hobart Davis, a leading sportsman himself and editor of *Munsey Magazine*, chided Grey for not remembering to let Davis write an introduction to the book as promised.[14]

In *Tales of Southern Rivers*, a 1924 collection of stories and articles by Grey, two of the tales relate fishing experiences in the Gulf Stream and on the rivers of the Everglades. The third tale, "Down an Unknown Jungle River," is an account of adventures on the Santa Rosa River in the jungles of Mexico that Grey experienced in 1911. On this trip Grey and two companions elude tigers and wild hogs, and they stoically reconcile themselves to torment from giant ticks. Two short stories, "Tigre" and "The Rubber Hunter," were inspired by Grey's visit to the wilds of Mexico. The *Springfield* (Massachusetts) *Republican* lavished praise on the book: "Grey is noted for his descriptive powers. All his books carry this quality. But in this new book, he excels in this faculty and his knowledge of the equatorial wilderness and waters is spread before his reader in a way that is a treat for the lovers of outdoor life."[15]

Grey's fishing books give insights into his philosophy and attitudes perhaps better than any of his other writings, for the vastness and the loneliness of the open sea enthralled, troubled, and depressed him. Whenever he lamented the brevity of life, he was usually on a fishing trip or was planning one. He expresses all these moods in a 1925 fishing book, *Tales of Fishing Virgin Seas*. When Grey was off the Cocos Islands, he pondered the ferocity of sharks fighting over fish carcasses: "Such swift action, . . . such unparalleled instinct to kill and eat! But this was a tropic sea . . . where life is so intensely developed. . . . The beauty was there to see, but not the joy of life."[16] Grey worried because he had heard stories about sharks attacking and sinking boats. Despite his anxieties, Grey comforted himself with the belief that "Thought and intelligence have considerable power over the primitive in man. That is the hope of progress in this world" (31). The Cocos Islands made Grey know that "there are places too primitive for the good of man—too strangely calling to the past ages and their deep instincts" (31).

From the Cocos, *Fisherman I* sailed toward Marchenas and the Perlas Islands. Marchenas reminded Grey of the long ridges of the Arizona desert, and he became contemplative as a result: "The lure of the sea is some strange magic that makes men love what they fear. The solitude of the desert is more intimate than that of the sea. Death on the shifting barren sands seems less insupportable to the imagination than death out on the boundless ocean, in the awful windy emptiness. Man's bones yearn for the dust" (95–96). Grey believed that the fisherman grew, in time, to "regard all with tranquility, with the simplicity of the Indian" (121–22). Such a stage in one's life, Grey argues, is the attainment of wisdom.

Throughout these musings, which Grey carefully recorded in his diaries, he and his crew were busy catching and observing fish. Grey was enchanted to see for the first time a sperm whale. He was entranced, too, by the evidence of evolution that was about him. In his western novels, he spoke of evolutionary schemes, and the ocean confirmed these truths. He frequently mentioned in this book Charles Darwin's voyage on the *Beagle,* and the influence on him that Darwin's books had had. Grey exclaimed: "Always the ocean was yielding some superlative quality of beauty. Always the beauty! It seemed such a mystery to me. But perhaps Nature required beauty as well as other attributes in its schemes of evolution" (143).

Grey's most frequent reaction to the sights about him on this trip was to remark on the constant competition among the creatures of the sea. It was "survival of the fittest," the test to which all living things were subjected whether on the ocean or on the desert. He concluded that man, although having to conform to "natural selection," was equipped with a higher order of mental faculties than other animals. This gave man supremacy, at least to the extent that nature allowed any permanent alteration of its system. The smallness of man in relation to nature was a thought that Grey often expressed, for man was but an atom whirling around in a vast universe that he neither created nor controlled. The sea's splendor, its overpowering might, and its mystery reflected the eternal; man was the image of transiency. It was not the sea alone that produced such thoughts in Grey, but it greatly influenced them.

Grey sailed for the South Pacific, largely as a result of New Zealand's invitation to publicize its fishing waters, and he spent the last day of 1925 at sea aboard the British mail ship, SS *Makura*. He was in a serious mood as he wrote in his diary and later in *Tales of the Angler's Eldorado,* a 1926 production: "What was the old year to the sea, or the new year soon to dawn with its imagined promise, its bright face, its unquenchable hope?"[17] Perhaps preoccupation of one sort or another caused Grey on that New Year's eve to smash his thumb in a door, inflicting a long and painful, but not permanent, injury, and although Grey was often querulous, his accident made it worse:

I smashed my thumb in the door. It is a very painful injury. Today I could not hold a pencil. Besides I was not well from the hurry and worry of preparation . . . [of leaving]. . . . Was quite sick all day, with headache, cold, and fever from sore thumb. In the afternoon my left eye became greatly inflamed, so that at length I could not see out of it. Finally it closed completely. . . . Developed a congestion in my breast and it grew worse until midnight when it began to grow easier. . . . We are now in equatorial regions . . . and the climate is singularly enervating. No doubt it would be bad enough if I was perfectly well, which I am not. I couldn't walk five lengths of the deck without wanting to rest.[18]

In addition to these troubles, Grey found it difficult to adjust to the English custom of "meals six times a day" and to "dinner at bedtime."[19]

Things improved considerably for Grey in mid-January when the *Makura* paid calls to Tahiti and other South Pacific Islands. Grey reacted with interest to the things he saw. Papeete, for example, was the "eddying point for all the riffraff of the South Seas." Tahitian women presented a new race to Grey: "They had large melting melancholy eyes." But the tourists angered Grey: he wondered why they traveled all the way to Tahiti just to eat and drink. After leaving French-ruled Papeete, Grey went to Roratonga, which was under British control. Liquor was prohibited at Roratonga, and Grey, an abstainer, credited the fact with producing an advanced culture.

Finally the *Makura* arrived in New Zealand, where the name of "Maui" was bestowed on Grey in honor of the Great Fisherman legend of the Maoris (144). In addition to this honor, Grey was astonished at the friendliness proffered to him. He wrote to Dolly that the government wanted to extend everything to him free: "Yesterday I had the Prime Minister's car! You should have seen the people look."[20] His prominence in New Zealand caused his friend Davis to write to him: "Isn't it enough for you to be the world's best seller without being the world's greatest angler? Truly the Lord has been good to you."[21] It was a new world for Grey as he toured the farming enterprises and fished the waters of New Zealand, and the fishing he did caused him to exclaim: "How often fishing leads a man to find beauty otherwise never seen!" (173).

Grey's popularity, however, did not last, for he wrote several articles for newspapers criticizing the New Zealander's methods of fishing. He chided the fishermen for using a three-pronged hook, which he believed was elementary and cruel, and he also criticized other New Zealand fishing equipment, as when he told fishermen that placing the reel over a rod would simplify their job. The controversy finally became so intense that Grey refused to write any more articles for newspapers. However, the argument with New Zealanders did not keep Grey from returning every year from 1926 to 1929 to fish its rivers and streams. He was still a "household" word in the area, and he became an authority on New Zealand sheep farming. He wrote an article on this subject in 1927 for *Country Gentleman* titled "Sheep Raising in New Zealand."

The materials that Grey collected on his trips to New Zealand were sufficient for four books and scores of articles. In addition to *Tales of the Angler's Eldorado,* he wrote *Tales of Swordfish and Tuna* in 1927, *Tales of Tahitian Waters* in 1931, and *An American Angler in Australia* in 1937.[22] As a result of his fishing expeditions, Grey became one of the world's most renowned sportsmen. In 1929 he held eleven world fishing records; in 1936, six. He was the first man ever to use a rod and reel to land a one-thousand-pound fish.[23] A sailfish, *Isiophorus greyi*, was named after him.[24] He used the sea to gain knowledge of life and of its evolution.

Another collection of Grey's fishing stories was brought out in 1928, titled *Tales of Fresh Water Fishing*. Included in the volume is "A Day on the Delaware," the first article that Grey ever published. The major point of the article is his regret over losing a huge pike. Grey apparently never outlived disappointment at failing to catch fish, as Dolly wrote to Davis in 1929: "losing a fish assumes to him [Zane] the proportions of Greek tragedy!"[25] Other articles in this well-accepted book include "Crater Lake Trout" and "Trolling for Trout at Pelican Bay" (both published by *Country Gentleman* in 1920), "The Fighting Qualities of the Black Bass" (*Field & Stream*, 1912), and "The Lord of Lackawaxen Creek" (*Outing*, 1909). The prolonged popularity of such articles assured Grey a position as an authority on fishing and conservation. Although no evidence exists that Grey read the works of Henry David Thoreau, he was much like the New Englander in relating to the outdoors.

Despite his successes, Grey still suffered rounds of melancholy. To Dolly he wrote in March 1927: "I can't stand the truth. Realism is death to me. I cannot stand life as it is!"[26] A month later he said, "I have been and still am pretty badly discouraged. . . . I'm all right in the day time, but when I awake in the night, as I do every night, it is simply hell. I don't know what's wrong unless the exhaustion of the day makes me morbid at night. . . . It seems such an endless time since I left home and such an eternity until I get back."[27]

Significance of Fishing to Grey

In *Tales of Fresh Water Fishing* Grey names William Radcliffe, "An English author and Oxford man," as the person most influential on his fishing moods and methods. Radcliffe's *Fishing from the Earliest Times* was such a great book in Grey's opinion that he did not feel equal to reviewing it for American publication. Nonetheless, he says of the book (building at the same time a great case for the fisherman):

It [the book] is a treasure-mine of truth about the oldest sport and one of the earliest trades known to men. Fishing has history little suspected by the mass of men who love to follow it. My father used to punish me for running off to fish when I should have mowed the lawn or swept out his office. He declared the only good fishermen who had ever lived were Christ's four fishermen disciples. My father was sure I would come to some bad end because I loved to fish. But he was wrong. All the fathers of youthful Isaac Waltons or angling Rip Van Winkles should read this wonderful book and learn how fortunate they are in having such inspired sons. For fishing has a dignity, a simplicity, a ruggedness and honesty little dreamed of in this materialistic world. Its history is profoundly revealing and tremendously interesting to the angler, whether he be naturalist or not. But every fisherman, unconsciously or otherwise, is something of a naturalist.[28]

Grey concludes his praise of Radcliffe's book by asserting that it invests fishing with the "dignity of education, of culture, of an affinity with great minds of the past, with an important place in the history and progress of the world" (154).

Although Grey obtained some of his profoundest thoughts while fishing, the "universal boy" in him probably motivated his expeditions to a considerable extent. He had a keen sense of competition, and he was never really content with any of his accomplishments. Life to Grey, then, was movement from one high plane to another high plane in his "quest for the unattainable." Grey sometimes abstained from fishing for months, but he would hear that one of his records had been broken and off he would go to recapture his title. Sportsman Ed Zern, who edited *Zane Grey's Adventures in Fishing,* said: "If he [Grey] had landed a ten ton serpent on 39-thread line he would almost certainly have fretted over reports of a twenty-ton sea serpent sighted off the coast of Madagascar. What's more, he might have gone and caught it."[29] Fortunately for his readers, Grey usually wrote down his thoughts in diaries before he reached the areas of big fish. These reflections became the basis for the next novel or short story about the American West.

Not only the oceans and seas thrilled and invigorated Grey and inspired him to write; fresh water fishing delighted him as well. He frequently visited the Rogue River and the Umpqua River in Oregon. He stated once that "the happiest lot of any angler would be to live somewhere along the banks of the Rogue River, most beautiful stream of Oregon."[30] He bought a cabin at Winkle Bar on the Rogue and spent many quiet, happy hours of contemplation there.

Early in his career as a fisherman, Grey felt twinges of conscience about hurting his victim. In 1918 he rationalized the sport and at the same time offered an insight into his reasons for writing: "As a man, and a writer who is forever learning, fishing is . . . tempered by an understanding of the nature of primitive man, hidden in all of us, and by a keen reluctance to deal pain to any creature. The sea and the river and the mountain have almost taught me not to kill except for the urgent needs of life. . . . When I read a naturalist or a biologist, I am always ashamed of what I have called a sport. Yet one of the truths of evolution is that not to practice strife, not to use violence, not to fish or hunt, that is to say, not to fight, is to retrograde as a natural man."[31] Grey came to believe that catching fish was only incidental to the true purposes of his expeditions. To study the "infinite" sea and to exult over a "shaded and murmuring stream" was the real objective, and it provided him a sort of transcendental experience of unity with nature.

The sea and fresh water did not always put Grey into a philosophical frame of mind, for as indicated in his *Field & Stream* article, "Avalon, the Beautiful" (1918),[32] he was angered during World War I by Austrian and Japanese fishing activities around Catalina Island off California. Fishing interests from these two countries netted huge amounts of white sea bass, which were used for fertilizer. Moreover, the Austrians gathered kelp, from which potash, useful for war purposes, was made. Grey believed that the United States government should ban fishermen from these two countries, especially since the United States was at war against Austria at the time.[33]

Grey showed with this article ("Avalon, the Beautiful"), as well as others, that he did not fear controversy. He did not "glory" in it, but he addressed the issues when things really mattered to him. In the mid-1930s when he wrote some articles in *Sports Afield* favoring lever-action rifles,[34] he was criticized by supporters of bolt-action rifles, one critic saying that Grey was a "kitchen mechanic" who should stick to his fishing.[35] Grey closed his side of the argument by asserting that the real culprit attacking lever-action rifles was the United States Army, which believed that, if hunting was going on, it might as well be done with rifles similar to those used in the military. This instance was not the first one in which Grey blamed the government for supporting a practice he did not approve.

As a novelist, sportsman, and world traveler, Grey attained international fame. He was the spokesman for the great American West and for the world's fishermen. When he had obtained enough wealth through his writings to do generally as he pleased, his stature grew with every word he wrote. He may not have been the most eloquent or the most accomplished author in the world, but he was highly competent. Americans have long valued pragmatic rather than theoretical things, and perhaps this pragmatism, built into America since colonial times, turned Grey into a phenomenally successful author and sportsman. He was direct in his descriptions and accounts and was able to give his readers a keen sense of participation. He wrote to such an extent and to such a depth about American institutions that he almost became one himself. His readership of several millions proved him to be a literary force and a sports authority whose influence is still significant.

Chapter Eight
Zane Grey: Writer

Zane Grey's successful career as a writer was a case of the times and the man meeting each other at the most opportune moment, for Grey visited and roamed the West at probably the best of all possible periods. The West was still wild—with plenty of animal and climatic difficulties—but the hardships confronted by the first settlers had been overcome. Grey's relationship with the West came before the tourism that altered much of the area's natural beauty. Grey saw the Wild West when pioneer conditions no longer prevailed but before the modern era had begun, and this fact may have been instrumental in his constant romanticizing of the American West.

He brought with him to the West a deep respect for natural beauty. He loved naturalness so much that he would not allow leaves to be raked from the garden at his home in Altadena, California.[1] His regard for the natural state of things was ingrained into him early in life. His first twenty years were spent in essentially rural and small-town settings, and these influences worked steadily on him. Grey's love of nature came first in his order of priorities, then love of literature, and third, love of the West. These three attributes worked in combination to produce Grey's literary career.

Grey possessed a lively curiosity and an independent mind, both qualities apparent even in his youth when he wrote "Jim of the Cave" and when he disputed points of protocol with his teachers. These two characteristics, plus a desire to write, were vital to a literary career. Grey's writing talents were latent, and it took several years of vigorous effort to make him a success. The greatest influence on Grey was Dolly, but he also read technical books on writing and developed his own "rules for literary work."[2] These guidelines were so important to Grey that they deserve extensive quotation.

Grey's Literary Rules

The first part of his literary rules dealt with reading. A book should be read creatively, "that is, slowly, repeatedly, carefully, resolving al-

118

lusions, following suggestions, . . . until thoroughly imbued with the power and thought of the writer."[3] Every day, he believed, one should read selections of Shakespeare, Tennyson, Hugo, Tolstoi, Stevenson, James, and Wordsworth. Grey indicated the influences of certain authors when he wrote: "Hawthorne awakens in me a cold purity of sensation, a mystic soul-perception of beauty, of shadow, of spiritual life. How solitary and sweet must have been his thoughts! He must have been a watcher with a sympathetic heart, yet aloof and self sufficient. I can see compassion in his dark eye as he gazes upon the lives of people. Dearest souled of men, he searched for and found the fountain of wisdom. From him I learn of moral evil and moral good. Arnold's poetry lights the white flame in my heart. . . . His sadness, his melancholy, his dreams, are mine."[4] Wordsworth was valuable to Grey also; nice weather one day after a bad spell caused him to exclaim that he had just received a "Wordsworth uplift."[5]

The second part of Grey's literary rules urged him always to keep eyes and ears open for new ideas: "Look at things so keenly as to find unknown characteristics, unsuspected points of view, secret depths, the life & soul of natural facts."[6] A writer must constantly study nature, men, and women, said Grey, so that "every situation would yield significance for thought." This procedure enabled an author to develop "self-culture" in which he would always "live among beautiful thoughts."[7]

After these generalizations concerning his literary objectives, Grey turned his attention to particulars—to detailed and intricate methods of composition. On writing's basic unit, the sentence, he instructed himself (probably with the help of Clayton Hamilton and J. H. Gardiner):

Think what the sentence is to exist for—what is its central thought. Do not crowd in irrelevant thoughts. Do not change subjects if it can be helped. Be watchful of pronouns. Keep participles within the body of the sentence, and watch their subjects . . . adverbial adjuncts must adhere closely to the words they are intended to modify. Do not hang a relative clause upon another relative clause. Cut out intensive expression and superlatives that are unnecessary. Beware of "but," "it," and "there." Cut them out when possible. The skill with which a writer deals with the small connecting words, particles, and pronouns is the best evidence of the extent to which he has attained a mastery of the art of composition. Adapt sound to sense; as the hum of the bee. The hiss of the serpent. The whistling of the wind. Work for clearness, sequence, climax. Do away with conjuctions, if possible, except when the meaning changes. Do not suppress subject. Do not use second person. Do not use italics except in dialogue. A proper variety requires that periodic sentences should be used; have a care of these. Make the meaning plain, and give it all the force possible. This last important point in any given sentence is secured by attending chiefly to the position of the principal subject and the principal predicate, and by placing these words so that in reading they are naturally and easily emphatic. Be careful to have infinite variety of sentences; intersperse periodic sentences occasionally with those that are loose. Avoid sameness of stress and emphasis. Long and short sentences help variety. Be familiar with equivalents of the relatives. Think or write sentence over several ways before finally committing it. Brevity helps action and make strength and force.[8]

Grey violated these rules a number of times as he wrote his novels, short stories, and articles, but such entries in his diaries proved that, contrary to what some critics said, he did have a concern for the technical aspects of writing.

Rules for paragraphing also were important to Grey: "Write topic sentences at beginning, and endeavor to have succeeding sentence amplify and grow out of preceding. Parallel construction aids delicacy of effect. . . . The subject should be clearly determined in the writer's mind, if not stated in the paragraph."[9] Grey said, "Eternal vigilance is the price of a good style."[10] A writer should learn to phrase thoughts in his mind without putting them on paper and to become a ruthless self-critic. Also, fledgling writers, as well as fully accomplished ones, should study the masterpieces of literature because this was the best way to improve stylistic sensitivity.

Most critics agreed that Grey's strongest talent was in the power of description. Grey wrote in his diary that description should appeal to memory and reason: "A cunning writer will avail himself of images likely to be stored in the minds of his readers; with appeal to emotions, to the general experiences of mankind."[11] He believed, too, that, in viewing a scene, the mind should dwell on the impression first, allowing the observer to select the central idea. After the impression of the scene was formed, the writer could go ahead with the description, which should evolve from the simple to the complex. Original descriptions, Grey believed, come from "traits, epithets, and thought which people have used before" but that have been "fused anew" in the mind of the writer and used as a "new force."

Grey asserted that a writer had a responsibility to say what he thought was wrong with society. He did so in a number of novels, *The Day of the Beast* and *The Vanishing American* being particularly significant in this respect. As early as his 1905 diary entries, Grey formed these conclusions: "The author must so thoroughly understand human nature that he will know exactly what and how great a motive is necessary for a certain act of a certain person. . . . The great gift of a writer is sincerity. A writer must have strong and noble convictions about life."[12] In communication with Murphy, Grey expostulated on the importance of being natural: "As there is no possibility of me ever becoming sophisticated, I may as well be natural. . . . Isn't to be natural a great strength in writing? [Herbert] Spencer says the natural style, that in which he—the writer, writes as he thinks and feels, ought to be the aim of every literary aspirant!"[13]

Grey: A "Loner" in Literature

Zane Grey did have "strong and noble" convictions about life, and he attempted to incorporate them into his novels. His thoughts on strength and nobility, however, differed sharply from those held by most other writers of the day because he felt that a novelist should be something of a crusader and at the same time should delineate positive as well as negative forces at work in society. It was his philosophy and his difference from others that caused Grey to turn his back on most contemporary literature and to become a "loner," that person of the West he described in so many of his books.

Grey also objected to the coterie of naturalist writers who gained some prominence in the first part of the century. He believed that some of their work was worthwhile, but their pose as authorities on wildlife caused Grey some consternation. As he said in a letter to Murphy: "Stewart White I never met. I think his work, what I have read, good and reliable, but . . . [Ernest] Seton and [Jack] London are pure fakes, as far as animals go. What they write is as the President [presumably of the United States—probably Theodore Roosevelt] said—a closet product."[14]

In part, his unconventional relationship to current literature caused Grey to experience spells of moroseness as well as self-righteous defiance. A 1917 diary entry, for example, showed that he was at least conscious of his problem: "A hyena lying in ambush—that is my black spell!—I conquered one mood only to fall prey to the next. And there have been days of hell. Hopeless, black, morbid, sickening, exaggerated, mental disorder! I know my peril—that I must rise out of it, very soon for good and all, or surrender forever. It took a day—a whole endless horrible day of crouching in a chair, hating self and all, the sunshine, the sound of laughter, and then I wandered about like a lost soul, or a man who was conscious of imminent death. And I ached all over, my eyes blurred, my head throbbed, and there was pain in my heart. Today I began to mend and now there is hope."[15]

His tendencies toward depression did not really endanger his literary career; on the contrary, they probably ensured it. Such entries reflected Zane Grey, the overly sensitive man, rather than Zane Grey, the really depressed man. Grey worried about things: slow royalty checks, World War I, the well-being of his family, things costing more than he anticipated, critics, and, to a very great measure, success itself. He seemed to feel a bit frightened about being a "winner" in the literary field, and it is doubtful that he would ever have made such overdramatized inclusions in his diary if he had not been an author to begin with. Dolly noted his tendency toward self-pity when she upbraided him for condemning everything and everybody for the unsettled conditions of the time and for his turgid frame of mind.[16] To a degree, statements in letters and diaries that reflected moods of dejection were simply his ways of reconciling himself with the world in which he lived; they were not symptoms of a deep-rooted or permanent difficulty.

World War I troubled Grey, for the war was a bad time, he said, for a thinking man and fatal for an idealist.[17] Apparently he believed with eminent historian Carl Becker that the preceding century of historical research was worthless because it did not prevent World War I.[18] Like Becker, Grey felt that history should be primarily a social force. His feelings of helplessness in the midst of historic events was most intense. He said, "I feel like an atom whirling in a universe of winds."[19] The war caused him to quote three of his favorite authors: "Tennyson wrote 'Through all the ages an increasing purpose runs.' Perhaps! And maybe civilization is progressing. Stevenson wrote: 'sure not all in vain!' . . . I am low-spirited these days. Wordsworth wrote: 'The world is too much with us,' and 'where is the glory and the dream?' . . . of yesterday, he meant, the flower and the beauty and the life that has gone! Something dark and gloomy borders my spirit. I must work and move about, and cease brooding."[20]

Grey's anti-Germanism during the war and his obvious sympathy for the American soldier made his books the most popular ones with the masses and the doughboys. An executive of Harper's explained this popularity,"Your books were the first choice of the soldiers and . . .

. . . the spirit that was in them rather than the adventure was what made them strong in their belief that Zane Grey is the great American writer of his day."[21] Grey was delighted also to be told that, if he continued to live in the open, "loving nature, loneliness, etc., . . . I could die the greatest writer of America."[22] John Wannamaker, who once told Grey, "never lay down your pen," believed that President Warren Harding should send Grey to Russia to interpret America.[23] Grey's popularity was capped when Macy's Department Store in New York started selling a new colored paint, "zane gray." Harper's was so impressed with the idea that Grey's books were covered with dustjackets of this "color."

After the war Grey lamented the apparent indifference of the government toward veterans. Although Grey generally supported Republicans, he disagreed with the vetoes of veteran pension bills by Presidents Harding and Coolidge. He wrote several novels that dealt with the plight of World War I veterans, with *The Call of the Canyon* and *The Shepherd of Guadaloupe* being perhaps the most prominent. Other authors, of course, attacked this problem, but their way of doing so apparently did not please Grey. He objected to the new psychological trends of the day and to increasing emphasis on sex in such books.

How Grey felt about certain types of modern literature was shown by an exchange of letters between Dolly and R. H. Davis. Grey read John O'Hara's *Appointment at Samarra,* and on its back cover were lavish praises of it by reviewers, including Dorothy Canfield and Alexander Woolcott. Dolly said: "To me these laudings smelled of people who were afraid of being Victorian or not modern if they didn't swallow a particularly nauseous dose of medicine with a broad smile. The book is clever, it is true to certain phases of modern existence, it more or less comes within the experience which most of us are acquainted with, but I ask you, aren't certain things better left to the imagination? Should Mr. O'Hara be called 'courageous' for writing it? I somehow see him laughing at the adjective."[24]

Dolly admitted that she looked at O'Hara's book through her bias for her husband: "The man [Zane] has always lived in a land of make-believe, and has clothed all his own affairs in the shining garments of romance, and it is as if these were rent and torn and smirched."[25] In agreeing with Dolly about Zane's status in literature, Davis replied: "The trend in literature is along the O'Hara lines, a little dirtier, I imagine, and I trust better written. . . . Zane is a naturalist. Zane is a disciple of the horse and buggy days. . . . I prefer Zane's reserve, while deploring his lack of familiarity with the world, the flesh and the devil. We ought to be glad he's that way."[26]

Grey constantly worried about his literary standing because of the popularity of the kind of fiction he did not write. To the mid-1920s, he fretted over reviewers who sometimes were not at all kind to him. Dolly helped him with these difficulties by writing: "A lot of these second-rate reviewers and writers would give their immortal souls to do what you're doing. What if you're not a high-brow? If you were, thousands & thousands whom you are delighting & helping would never read you."[27] Despite such assurances, Grey continued his anxieties: "I am worried about my stories and the modern trend. Such books that are published now! I am afraid that pretty soon no one at all will read me. Do you ever feel that way?"[28] Less than a month before his death, however, Grey was autographing his books in a department store at the rate of five per minute, finally having to stop because of exhaustion.[29] Clearly, therefore, Grey never really ran the risk of the catastrophe that he feared so much, that of becoming an outdated author.

Grey's Contemporaries

Frederick Faust (Max Brand) was a contemporary of Grey's, and the two were easily the most authoritative novelists on the West. Brand produced a more "action type" story than Grey and was not as concerned with descriptions and the expressions of moods. When Grey died in 1939, he had sixty published books to his credit. Through 1944 the year of Faust's death, 128 books had appeared under his various pseudonyms. Yet Grey occupied the best-selling lists for nine years; Faust, never once. The great difference between the two authors, according to one opinion, was that Grey wrote about the West as he imagined it; Faust wrote about the West as he dreamed it. He felt that if he could not dream a story, he could not write it.[30]

Grey's affinity for history helped also to produce the differences between the two men. In 1893 historian Frederick Jackson Turner delivered his famous speech on the importance of the frontier to American history. He pointed out that, as of 1890, census figures indicated that the Western frontier was no longer open. Turner's thesis dealt with the idea that more democracy existed in the West than in the East; that if one wished to learn the origin of American democratic institutions, he would have to study the West. Both Grey and Faust wrote when the Turner thesis was popular among historians and was known just enough by the middle classes to generate some interest. Grey's work had a more historical ring to it than Faust's, and this quality, in conjunction with ideas already made prominent by Turner, made Grey the most significant western novelist of the time. Moreover, Grey always visited the places he wrote about, and his output was almost entirely western. Faust, on the other hand, lived in Italy for several years while writing his books; and his interests ranged beyond the western story.[31]

Another writer, who was contemporary to Grey whose creation became more famous than its creator was Edgar Rice Burroughs, author of the Tarzan series. Burroughs and Grey, along with Faust, caused something of a revolution in the movie industry,[32] which tried to film everything they created. The stories were set on different continents, but essentially the same types of emotions and incidents prevailed. Burroughs liked to end his books on a note that necessitated a sequel. Grey did this too, but not to the same extent.[33] Despite the care both men exercised in their work, their books were banned in at least one elementary school in California—Grey's for obscenities, and Burroughs's for portraying Tarzan and Jane in love with each other without benefit of marriage.

Still another contemporary of Grey's who wrote for the masses was James Oliver Curwood. What Grey was to the western, Curwood was, in large part, to the "northern." Like Grey, he lived among the people he described in his pages. Like Grey, also, Curwood realized one day that his hunting expeditions were actually helping to destroy the nature he loved, so he put away his rifles and guns to become, with Grey, one of America's most prominent conservationists. Curwood died before Grey (1927), but the two careers were concurrent enough for Grey and Curwood to be hailed as great authors.[34]

Most critics considered the Grey/Faust/Burroughs/Curwood "combine" an echelon below the Hemingway/Fitzgerald/Anderson/Lewis one. Grey and the authors like him were not debunkers and did not deal solely with what had gone wrong in America. They were not members of a "lost generation." Instead, they wanted to point out the essentially positive aspects of the country and show that its past indicated a brighter future than many of the most prominent contemporary writers were willing to accede. They showed both the weaknesses in the American system and many possible solutions to its problems. In the manner of the muckrakers, who were most influential between 1900 and 1910, Grey and his followers managed to bring public attention to many important social issues.

Grey's total output was phenomenal, especially considering that he wrote entirely in longhand and sometimes went for days without composing anything. His high volume was in large measure a product of sustained, feverish work periods. As a diary entry indicates, Grey had troubles with writing: "There is always an extreme difficulty in the taking up again the habit of writing. I wonder if this is because a relapse from literary work forms another habit. At any rate I am tortured before I can begin to write. This morning I had no desire to write, no call, no inspiration, no confidence, no joy. I had to force myself. But when I mastered the vacillation and dread, and had done a day's work—what a change of feelings. I had a rush of sweet sensations."[35] He had enough "sweet sensations" in his exceedingly busy life to write eighty-five books (twenty-five of which were published after his death; see chapter 9 for a list of even more of his works), scores of articles, several diaries, and an average of five letters—long, involved ones—a day.

His work could, at times, produce confidence in him: "I believe absolutely in myself, my singular place, my gifts, my force. . . . My zeal to work, my destiny . . . all I need is time—years to fulfill work. But dreaming so much I let the years slip by. Yet in 10 years I have written 19 books, none of which are equal to my ability. I have never spent myself. I am capable of great work."[36] Such exultant promises were tempered, however, by pessimism: "It is a terrible time. The seething revolution of the age affects me adversely, and forces me to think there is no use to write on. But I am compelled to."[37] The act of writing, then, caused Grey's mood to fluctuate between optimism and gloomy reflection.

Often his state of mind, at least to the mid-1920s, depended on how critics viewed him at any given moment. They frequently tended either to ignore his work altogether or brutally to assault it. Both approaches were intensely unsettling to Grey. When he was attacked by reviewers, he usually aired his feelings in private to Dolly and in his diaries. A review of one of his novels (which he did not name) "was so bitter, so hateful, so amazingly unjust and false that it made me ill."[38] Several reviewers felt that Grey's books were not true to life and that the characters he created were not realistic. Grey's popularity remained a mystery to them, when a check with the middle- and lower-classes of rural and small-town America would have provided their answer. The reviewers reached the limit of Grey's endurance when they began hinting and then broadly asserting that the huge fish Grey caught were largely fiction. Grey was so angered that he wrote that such tactics "will eventually drive me to defend my reputation."[39]

Defense against the Critics

He did defend his reputation in a lengthy treatise, written in the mid-1920s but never published: "My Answer to the Critics." He had taken the critics too seriously in the first part of his career, he said, and had thus always been too humble toward them. In his quest to write permanent literature, he had wanted a "great audience. I chose to win that through romance, adventure, and love of the wild and beautiful in Nature. The West appealed tremendously to my imagination. I recognized it as one of the greatest fields for an American novelist. . . . I hoped and I prayed that the critics would judge me not from the result but from the nature of my effort."[40]

He noted his familiarity with the literary works of Wordsworth, Tennyson, Arnold, Ruskin, Stevenson, Jeffries, Hudson, Defoe, and Bunyan and with the Bible. He was not "anti-intellectual," as some critics said, because he was a graduate of a school that rivaled Harvard—the University of Pennsylvania, a school that "not so long ago . . . honored me with a degree of letters."[41] Grey was born and raised in Ohio, as was Sherwood Anderson, the man to whom most contemporary realistic critics gave first place in the ranks of American novelists. Grey said that he was familiar with the type of people Anderson talked about and he knew Anderson was wrong: "Mr. Anderson may be a very great writer. But if so, why did he not use his gifts toward the betterment of the world? Why not write of the struggle of men and women toward the light? He is a destroyer, not a builder."[42]

On the charge that he created unbelievable characters, Grey said that he had known a hundred cowboys like Venters (*Riders of the Purple Sage*), and dozens of Western women who were as "sweet and innocent, and ignorant of life" as Bess Erne (*Riders of the Purple Sage*), Lucy Bostil (*Wildfire*), and Fay Larkin (*The Rainbow Trail*). Grey thought it singular that only the eastern newspapers and periodicals printed adverse criticism of his work, for "Seldom does a critic West of the Mississippi accuse me of falsifying character. Never of action or setting. Western people know I am absolutely true to the setting of my romances."[43]

Grey reached the height of his impassioned plea for fairness from the critics when he wrote: "Who reads my books? Ask your janitor, your plumber, the salesgirl in the department store, the librarians, the firemen and the engineers, the carpenters, your lawyers, your doctors, the preachers who snatch a few hours for fiction out of their crowded lives, the school girls and boys, the teachers, the trained nurses, the farmers, the convicts in jail, the baseball players, the actors—John Barrymore,

if you like—the motion-picture people, and the millions who support
the screen. Ask anybody, ask New Englanders. I have an amazing public in Boston. Ask anybody but your brother critics. They do not
know."[44]

After spending himself so emotionally on the question of critics,
Grey said he would never be bothered by them again; and he was not.
He ignored the barbs, continued writing his books and stories at a
fantastic rate, and stayed high in the ranks of popular writers. During
his lifetime, *Riders of the Purple Sage, The Light of Western Stars,* and
Wildfire were favorites of the public.[45]

Impact of Grey's Books

Grey reached the height of his popularity in the United States between 1914 and 1928. That period was marked by war and then by
social change in the 1920s. It was an affluent time when the average
citizen was sports-minded, fun-loving, and movie-going. He was also
"addicted" to his newspaper, especially the newly developing "Sunday
sections." There was a growth in culture for the masses, a "democra-
tization" of entertainment. Grey and his works fit very well into this
picture. He could be used by the escapist for relief from the never-
ending boredom of assembly lines, and for those of the 1920s who
wished to learn something about the generation of their fathers, Grey
offered the opportunity. The bulk of Grey's audience, however, was the
unsophisticated masses who still remembered enough of the rapidly
passing rural scenes of America to wish they were back there. Grey
enabled them to return vicariously to such settings, using the West for
the purpose, and his reader was likely to identify quickly with the
settings that Grey created. Those who revolted against the modern
trends of industrialism and liberalized thinking turned to Grey. There
was not just one single reason, therefore, for people to read Grey's
books. The multiple uses of his work assured him a lasting place in
American literature.

Grey's contribution to the western novel in American literature was
his greatest accomplishment. No other writer in the genre has yet ap-
proached his output and his sustained popularity. He wrote in a more
descriptive and philosophical style than do most contemporary writers
on the West. A western novelist, Tom Curry, explains it this way:
"The . . . magnetism which draws and compels people to read his
[Grey's] works . . . is elusive, and difficult to define; also it cannot be

taught in any fashion. Technique may be, but the ability of a creative writer to hold his public is apparently inborn, some magic the author brews with the words he puts down, the fashion in which he delivers his thoughts, carrying his readers along in a grand sweep to the end."[46] Grey was a writer for the masses—those millions throughout the world who have long been fascinated with the American West and the role it has played in American cultural history. To many minds, the West today still possesses the romantic qualities of a century ago, and this thought surely has helped Zane Grey's works to remain prominent.

In a less noticeable but equally important way, Grey's contributions to the conservation movement in the United States are significant. In dozens of articles he lamented wasteful practices—whether those of sportsmen or big business. In numerous novels he railed against factions that were apparently bent on scourging the land of its timber and other resources for economic gain and against various governmental policies toward herds of wild animals. Despite all of this, Grey's view was a positive one; when he criticized his country, it was more out of love for it than repulsion.

His books that have remained the most prominent and popular through the years include *Riders of the Purple Sage, Wildfire, The U.P. Trail, The Light of Western Stars, Heritage of the Desert, To the Last Man, Nevada, The Vanishing American, Western Union,* and *The Maverick Queen.* Perhaps their popularity is due to their movie versions, which are still shown periodically on television. They also are faster paced than some of his other writings (and thus fit most quickly into changed reading habits that demand a lot of action) and have personalities within them (such as in *The Vanishing American*) that can be identified and sympathized with.

Zane Grey should be judged on the quality of his total output and of his best books rather than on the weaknesses of some of his lesser books. The picture that evolves of Grey reveals him to be a chronicler of events of the Old West, who had enough analytical power to give his work a historical aspect. His main strength was description; his main weakness was characterization. The picture of Grey shows, too, a concerned citizen disturbed over the abrupt changes occasioned by war. He became a social commentator—one who never equaled people like Upton Sinclair in this respect but who nevertheless affected certain individuals, particularly important conservationists. Finally, this picture of Grey shows him as a man of great sensitivity and ability, with an active, almost naive, curiosity about the life around him. Possessed with an indefatigable energy, Grey believed that a rugged, outdoor life would increase a man's longevity. (Grey was five feet eight inches tall and kept his weight at around one hundred fifty pounds.) He even installed a fishing rod attached to heavy weights on the porch of his home at Altadena so he could stay in condition for the next fishing expedition. Shortly after exercising with the rod, Grey suffered a fatal heart attack on the morning of 23 October 1939. He was sixty-seven years old.

His death attracted worldwide attention, with so many tributes to him that a Harper's executive wrote to Dolly, "I had no idea that some of the reviewers loved him and so many admired his work."[47] Dolly wrote to a friend that Grey's death was sudden and unexpected: "It seems to me that he is just away on one of those adventurous trips he loved so well—and perhaps he is."[48] Though critics often scorned Grey for his characterizations, they almost universally agreed that he was a good storyteller and that tales of adventure were his forte.

Chapter Nine

Latter-Day Grey

Zane Grey published for his time but did not always write for it. Because he was the "common man's writer," he had to meet certain requirements of morality and good taste. Occasionally, however, he wrote what would have been for his era rather risqué material, which had to be edited to suit reading tastes. Only in the 1980s have some of these "unexpurgated" Zane Grey works come to the surface. (Such discoveries raise a perhaps unanswerable question: If Grey knew that his "exotic" materials would be edited out, why did he write them in the first place? He could have done it simply to keep his editors alert; he had been around enough cowboys to become quite a practical joker himself.)

The Unexpurgated Zane Grey

In 1981 Zane Grey's son Loren republished *The Maverick Queen* as Grey had written it in the 1920s. (The book was not first published until 1950.) In the new edition, it becomes apparent that Kit Bandon is a prostitute who has her way with many a young cowboy just into town from several weeks on the trail. Also, in this version there is much more swearing than in the first. The book is adorned with *by Gods*, *hells*, and *damns*. These words were studiously excluded from the first publication of *The Maverick Queen*.

The same was true of the other 1981 republication of a Zane Grey novel, *30,000 on the Hoof* (first published in 1940). In the book, Lucinda Baker comes out West to meet Logan Huett and to be his wife. In the second publication, when Lucinda arrives on the stagecoach, she wears tight jeans that reveal just about every curve in her body. Cowboys hoot and whistle at the sight of her, to the amusement of Logan, her fiancé. Earlier reading audiences probably would have been offended by the number of references to Lucinda's body, Logan's descriptions of her as "hot-blooded," and his bid "to make love to her."

It may well have been that *30,000 on the Hoof* was Grey's first real move into "steamy fiction." According to his son, Loren, "In the case of *30,000,* it was so different from anything he had ever written that he had great difficulty getting the flow of his material going in the early part of the book. So, in the first three or four chapters the sentences were short and choppy, and read poorly. . . . After he actually got Logan and Lucinda settled in Sycamore Canyon, he seemed to get back into that marvelous flow of words of which only he was capable."[1]

One of Logan's bitter enemies in *30,000 on the Hoof* is an Indian named Matazel. One day while Logan is away, Matazel intrudes into the Huett household. Lucinda is alone, and Matazel's clear intention is rape. In the first published version of the novel, Matazel is scared away. In the 1981 edition, however, it is clear that Matazel rapes Lucinda and that a child, Abe, is born from the incident. Throughout the second half of the book, Grey gives unmistakable clues that Abe is Matazel's son, primarily through physical descriptions such as gray eyes and a prominent nose. Thus, the reader knows what Logan never finds out—that Abe is another man's son.

The most profound changes were made in Grey's enduring Indian novel, *The Vanishing American.* In his preface to the 1982 edition, Loren Grey cites a lengthy correspondence Zane Grey had regarding the "missionary element" in the novel. As is well known, Grey criticized, even condemned, various missionary practices toward the Indians. (Some of these practices are described in chapter 4.) He wrote to William Briggs and Henry Hoyns at Harper's on May 25, 1925, that "my personal Arizona men warned me that it was actually not safe for me to go on the reservation. There are hirelings, and even some missionaries, who might shoot me from some canyon wall."[2] (Grey also showed in this letter that he was quite capable of boasting of his accomplishments: "Now as to the business side of your letters. I am very sorry indeed that conditions are bad. But I beg to call to your attention this fact: that it is the reading public and the book business that have slumped. Not I! My work grows better. I know, because I am doing it. And I shall see to it that I do not fall down.")[3]

When the book was first published in December 1925, the main character, Nophaie, dies of exertion and heartbreak because he cannot marry his sweetheart, Marian Warner. When Grey wrote the novel, however, it had a happier ending; he allowed Nophaie and Marian to wed each other. It was not until 1982 that this version was allowed to be printed.

Loren Grey said in his preface to the 1982 edition of *The Vanishing American:* "In that day (1920s) it was acceptable for a white man to marry an Indian woman, but not the other way around. The Indian was still regarded as not equal to the white man, and thus an Indian male could not consort with a white female." Certainly the 1982 edition brought Grey's themes into line with the social mores of the 1980s, and in this respect, it may be argued that in the Indian question, as on so many other matters as well, Zane Grey was far ahead of his time.

These "uncensored" Grey materials might have been too racy for his own time, but the additions that have been made to these books are rather tame by late twentieth-century standards. On the other hand, these new editions are more honest than the ones that were originally published, and more true to the ideals and objectives of Zane Grey himself. Zane Grey was *human,* an attribute that some of his more fervent followers today do not seem to appreciate. He certainly was capable of creating a character with all the strengths and weaknesses of human beings everywhere, not just the sugar-coated Easterner turned macho man Westerner who, in many instances, was totally unrealistic. Zane Grey has been criticized because of flaws (or lack of them) in the various characters he created; he gave them qualities that no mere human being could have. These three novels, *The Maverick Queen, 30,000 on the Hoof,* and *The Vanishing American,* presented in the 1980s in their original forms, show clearly that description was not the only aptitude that Zane Grey possessed as a novelist. Apparently, these were the only three novels for which "strong" versions originally existed. There is no evidence that any of his other novels have this "distinction."

Latter Day Grey: The Western Short Stories

First and foremost, Zane Grey was a writer of the American West. It is true that he won worldwide acclaim for his fishing expeditions, but they paled by comparison with his explications of the Old West in United States history. Even today, from the middle-aged urban dweller to the fictional Colonel Sherman Potter on *M*A*S*H,* Zane Grey sets the pattern for Wild West lore.

Since 1973, Zane Grey, Inc., has published twenty Grey works[4] that were left over from the prodigious author's output. Many of these are short stories or novelettes and are included in anthologies of well-known Zane Grey stories. For example, "The Saga of the Ice Cream Kid," was a part of *Amber's Mirage and Other Stories,* published by Pocket Books in 1983; the following year Santa Barbara Press printed the story in its *The Wolf Tracker and Other Stories*. The story of the "Ice Cream Kid" was found among the personal effects of Grey's son Romer when Romer died in 1976.

The Kid is stranded on the desert, where the unmercifully hot sun causes the Kid's eyes to swell shut and his tongue to become black and dry. "Death dogged his footsteps and his past life kept paradin' before him."[5] Ultimately, however, the Kid recovers and becomes addicted to eating huge dishes of ice cream everytime he goes to town, probably because of the memory of his ordeals in the desert. This ability of the desert to magnify human characteristics was discussed in many of Grey's books, where the desert usually causes either great goodness or great evil to be manifested in man.

Included in the Pocket Books anthology is another desert short story, printed in 1983. Its title is "Fantoms of Peace." Its plot is corny and coincidental. Dwire has ruined a woman's life. Hartwell's daughter's life has been ruined. The two men go into the desert to live lives of reflective sadness. They meet each other, become partners, and share their lives on the desert, and finally learn that Dwire's wife is Hartwell's daughter.

As in so many Grey works, however, one must look beyond characterization in "Fantoms of Peace" and note Grey's descriptions of the desert. Again, place in Grey's philosophy becomes more important than character. "It was a terrible ordeal for Dwire to stand there [in the desert] alone and realize that he was only a man facing eternity; but that was what gave him strength to endure. Somehow he was a part of it all, some atom in the vastness, somehow necessary to an inscrutable purpose, something indestructible in that desolate world of ruin, and death and decay. . . . In that endless, silent hell of desert there was a spirit, and Dwire felt hovering near him fantoms of peace" (218–19).

On numerous occasions, Grey compared the desert to the sea, arguing that both places would prove or disprove the mettle of a man. They were ultimate testing grounds for a person's character; a man would find out very quickly on either the sea or the desert about survival of the fittest. Grey's desert short stories did not examine the Darwinian theme of natural selection as much as his desert novels did, and the reason for the difference is rather obvious. In a short story, action is essential; in a novel, philosophical development sometimes becomes important. Regardless of the emphasis of his treatment, it remains clear that Grey stood in awe of the great deserts as the most formidable landmarks on earth, and he seemed to be obsessed with attributes given to man through the desert.

In 1979 Black published *The Camp Robber and Other Stories.* As with "Fantoms of Peace," "The Camp Robber" was highly coincidental. Lex Wingfield's wife has died and his daughter has been raised by another man. Only years later are father and daughter reunited. Another story in this collection is "On Location," which contains all the Hollywood stereotypes. The star, Bryce Pelham, is in a snit because his double has not shown up for the dangerous parts. Wesley Reigh, a cattleman, is substituted. Pelham insinuates an affair between Reigh and the beautiful co-star, Vera Van Dever. He also wants to reshoot the entire picture because Wes has turned his face toward the camera in one of the takes. At the end, Wesley and Bryce have a go at each other. Wes wins not only the fight but the pretty stunt woman, Betty Wyatt, as well. With the exception of Reigh and Wyatt, "On Location" is full of superficial characters. Apparently Grey wanted to vent his own feelings toward flippant and shallow people. His treatment of Hollywood types, however, did not stop the movie moguls from filming much of what he wrote. The movies and Zane Grey were a natural combination.

"John Silver's Revenge" is included in the Black edition of *The Camp Robber and Other Stories,* and it has a theme similar to that found in "The Secret of Quaking Asp Cabin." Jane runs off with Jim Warner, leaving behind her husband, John Silver. Years later Warner deserts Jane, and Jane comes back to Silver with Lily, her terminally ill daughter. Jane then tells John that Lily is *his* daughter, not Jim Warner's. The story ends with Lily rallying and telling everyone that John Silver is her father. Melodramatic? Corny? To be sure, but this is the kind of story the reading public and, more important, the heads of movie studios wanted in the 1920s and 1930s. (It might well be argued that the reading public and movie audiences of the 1980s are really that way, too. Note the tremendous continuing success of Walt Disney movies, and best-selling efforts like James Herriott's *All Things Bright and Beautiful.* Who is to say that the public would not accept romantic and sentimental novels if innovative editors published them in great quantities?)

Pocket Books published a collection of Zane Grey stories in 1983 that includes "The Flight of Fargo Jones." This highly visual story is about Fargo Jones, who is unjustly accused of cattle rustling. After his arrest, Jones slugs the sheriff, escapes from jail, and goes up into the mountains. Weeks later, Sheriff Smith catches up with Jones, only to tell him that the real rustlers have been caught and that he is a free man.

"Lightning" follows a theme that was dear to Grey's heart: love of good horseflesh. Lee and Cuth Stewart are "tall, lean Mormons, as bronzed as desert Navajos, cool, silent, gray-eyes, still faced." For months they trail a wild stallion they dub "Lightning" for the large monetary reward to be given to the person who catches the horse. Finally the Stewarts are successful, but they are so enthralled by "Lightning's" magnificence that they keep him. Another latter-day Grey short story is "Lost in the Never Never." Its theme is similar to *Wilderness Trek,* a novel Grey wrote about cattle drives in Australia.

Since it was not unusual for Grey to write 100,000 words a month,[6] it is a fairly good guess that he wrote many of these short stories in a single sitting. Grey always took a lapboard and Morris chair with him wherever he traveled, and no matter how busy he was with fishing, hunting, or advising on movie sets, it was rare for many days to go by without a substantial writing effort.

The Western Novels

It is, of course, the novels for which Zane Grey is primarily remembered. Some critics have called his 1912 classic *Riders of the Purple Sage* the best western ever written.[7] The sequel to *Riders—The Rainbow Trail*—was almost as popular. Regardless of Grey's weaknesses in characterization, even the harshest critics praised his abilities to depict action and his colorful descriptions of the Old West.

One recently published Grey novel (actually a novelette), *The Tenderfoot,* was originally an unpublished part of the full-scale novel, *The Dude Ranger.* In 1977, Belmont-Tower Publications (now defunct) excerpted *The Tenderfoot.* The background in *The Tenderfoot* is editorially described, and then at certain points in the manuscript, action and dialogue occur.

The procedure followed by the editors of *The Tenderfoot* is similar to the treatment given recently to Ernest Hemingway's *The Garden of Eden.* The respective results are certainly not "pure Grey" or "pure Hemingway" but an amalgam of the authors' works and editorial intrusions. This is not a good literary p ocedure; it is designed more to capitalize on an author's name and make profits than to give the reading public a legitimate product. All famous authors leave fragments behind. The question is, then, should these fragments be pieced together to obtain yet another "writing" by a famous author? Regardless of the outcome, the procedure justifiably raises suspicions among an author's following.

Also in 1977, Belmont-Tower brought out Grey's *The Westerner,* a novel that might just as well never have been published. Katherine Hempstead from the East checks into a Reno divorce hotel. She is there to end her mother's affair with a fortune hunter. Also at the hotel is Phil Cameron, "the Westerner," trying to dissuade his mother from divorcing his father. Katherine and Phil concoct a scheme by which to bring their mothers to their senses. They live together, drink raucously, and create scenes in public. Their strategy works, for their mothers ultimately return to their respective spouses.

If *The Westerner* (originally given a better title, *Loose Bridles*) has a theme it is the transition from old values to the age of modernism. The book has considerably more profanities than Grey's readers were accustomed to. Whenever it has any focus, it is on Katherine Hempstead, and not "the Westerner." The dialogue is stilted, to say the least: "Turn 'round you! . . . Western men don't talk that way to women. Out heah we'd call you a low-down city skunk";[8] "Come now, let's hie ourselves to lunch" (82). And the descriptions did not fare much better than the dialogue: "She kissed his twitching mouth, which was suspiciously carmine in hue" (111).

The book was lavishly illustrated with drawings of the Old West that had nothing to do with characters or plots. *The Westerner* ultimately sold some 25,000 copies,[9] a formidably low figure for a Zane Grey work.

Coming off somewhat better than *The Tenderfoot* and *The Westerner* was *The Rustlers of Pecos County,* published in 1980 by Ian Henry in Essex, England. This novel is more "vintage" Zane Grey than the others published after 1973. It concerns two lawmen torn between duty and love. Diane Sampson's father is the man Ranger Vaughn Steele is after. His partner, Russ Sittell, loves Sally Langdon, Diane's cousin. Both Steele and Sittell are put on notice that if they kill any of the girls' kinsmen, they will lose Diane and Sally's love. This conflict propels the novel and, despite its stilted dialogue, gives it purpose. In the end, all is resolved and a Zane Grey happy ending is accomplished.

Although Grey's western novels that were published in their original forms long after his death may provide a new sense of realism about the author, such cannot be said of those works originally published in the 1970s and 1980s. His writing for these latter novels (if indeed it is his writing), with the exception of *The Rustlers of Pecos County,* is decidedly inferior to his earlier productions. It seems that everything he wrote that was published during his lifetime is better than anything he wrote that has come out since his death. It may well be that Grey himself recognized among his works what was "good" or "bad" and made his own priorities. Possibly, he never intended for some of the things he wrote to be published. Nevertheless, it is undeniable that "bad" Zane Grey today is infinitely better than the so-called adult Westerns that are unmercifully thrust on the reading public.

Fishing and Other Stories

Zane Grey's fame as a world-class fisherman remains undiminished. Writing was Grey's first love; fishing his second.[10] He became a familiar figure to people in Australia and New Zealand in the 1920s and 1930s as his ship plied their waters looking for big fish. He was fascinated by sharks and awed by their beautiful ferocity, speed, and power. He wrote many articles about sharks and went against the conventional wisdom of his day that sharks will not attack until provoked.[11]

In 1976 Belmont-Tower published Zane Grey's *Shark: The Killer of the Deep*. He had, Grey said, documented 300 tragedies and disasters related to sharks, a fact that "will be a revelation to those distinguished scientists in the United States who do not believe a shark will attack a human being."[12] Even though sharks were deadly, Grey still believed in giving them a sporting chance. He went after them with bait and regular hooks. In Australia, he claimed, people shot sharks with high-powered rifles, and in New Zealand they harpooned them. Grey's disapproval of both practices produced much criticism of him in the down-under.[13]

In *Shark*, Grey gives minute details of various types of the big fish. He caught the world's largest tiger shark off the coast of Australia in 1935.[14] He was impressed with the great fighting powers of the mako shark, noting the sheer exhaustion that the fisherman usually experienced bringing one in. The Rhineodon Typus, he said, was the largest shark of all but, fortunately, was exclusively vegetarian.

Grey was an expert on fish and fishing techniques, never tiring of the "incessant roar of the surf," and the "ever haunting presence of the sea" (40). He seemed, in his westerns and fishing books, to fulfill every man's dream of ruggedness and adventure. Zane Grey truly loved the sea and its environs. The sea embodied restlessness and ultimate truths about the evolutionary process. Grey thought the sea was probably the greatest natural power on earth, and he held to the philosophy of the early Greek thinker Thales that all of life sprang from water and would eventually return to water.

A 1978 book of Grey's, *Tales from a Fisherman's Log*, definitely inspired themes of vicarious experiences. "The harder a thing is to do," he declared, "the more fascination it exerts."[15] He spoke knowingly, even lovingly, in this book about the fine art of trout fishing and the joys of the Tongariro River in New Zealand. This book quickly became a collector's item among the world's fishermen.[16]

Although Grey wrote several short stories and plays dealing with the South Pacific—its waters and people—he penned only one full-length work of fiction about it. This was *The Reef Girl,* for many years unpublished because it did not fit the "Zane Grey image." Even after its publication in 1977 by Harper's, the book did not fare too well among Grey readers, an unfortunate circumstance because it contained some of Grey's best writing and most provocative themes.

Consider for example, the following passage from *The Reef Girl:* "Faaone glided stealthily to him, naked, fragrant as the frangipani in her hair. . . . Faaone crawled out on the reef, nude and golden in the sunlight, to wave something white—her last garment."[17]

The original title of *The Reef Girl* was "Faaone," and the story dealt with a number of romantic themes, primarily man from the West meets beautiful Tahitian girl and falls in love with her. This novel was Grey's "most modern" in terms of sexuality.[18] In 1939, however, when the manuscript was submitted for publication, the editors rejected it largely because Donald Perth, the protagonist, and Faaone live together without benefit of marriage. (Edgar Rice Burroughs, with Tarzan and Jane, experienced the same problems.)

Also, Grey showed his continuing disdain of corrupt missionaries coming to the South Seas with life-styles worse than those of the natives they proposed to convert to Christianity. As was well known, Grey had stirred up a hornet's nest a few years before when he described missionaries in an unfriendly light in *The Vanishing American.*

The Reef Girl was unacceptable in 1939 because of its sexual undertones, the likelihood that another controversy with organized religion would ensue, and because it was not "pure" Zane Grey. The great American West was first in Grey's affections for places; what was not so well known about him was that his second favorite place in the world was Tahiti. It was therefore more natural for Grey to write a novel about the South Pacific than most of his fans realized. Not until the late 1970s did editors consent to the idea that *The Reef Girl's* time had come. It was the most autobiographical of all Zane Grey's novels[19] and was the twenty-fifth of his books to be published since his death in 1939.[20]

It was the desert and the sea, with an accent perhaps on the latter, that dictated some of Zane Grey's most memorable moods. He could be lifted to the heights by either of these two great natural phenomena, but they also could throw him into the deepest depths of despair. The waves of the sea were as restless as the shifting sands of desert, and Grey's own personality took on this restlessness, primarily in the form of unsatisfiability. Whatever he did, whatever success he might have, he was not satisfied with it. This inability to be content with his accomplishments propelled Grey into moods of both elation and dejection, and it was almost certain that whenever Grey was in these moods, he was in the vicinity of either the desert or the sea.

The sea also taught Grey lessons in mortality. The sea had always been here and always would be; man was the transient, whose involvement with the sea was an injection of the temporary into the eternal. There was no ultimate fulfillment with the sea, no ultimate consummation, as with a man's life. Grey's life and activities were like the sea: restless, stormy, calm, serene, white-capping, and depressed. The sea prompted Grey to be introspective and to wax eloquent in philosophical thought. No wonder some of his best writings had to do with the sea.

Continuing Fascination with Zane Grey

At one time Zane Grey's works, after the Bible and McGuffey's Readers, were the third best-selling books in U.S. literary history. As late as 1973 they were still selling a million copies a year around the world. Today, in the late 1980s, Zane Grey sales have dropped to about a half million copies a year. Even with that lower number, considering that Zane Grey died fifty years ago, his sales statistics are phenomenal.

Riders of the Purple Sage sold 260,000 copies from 1982 to 1988. *Black Mesa,* originally called *Bitter Seeps,* a book initially rejected by Harper's because the hero was in love with a married woman, sold 475,000 copies from 1950 to 1978.[21]

Despite these dramatic statistics, the truth is that Zane Grey readership, although keeping pace with each of today's western novelists except Louis L'Amour, is declining in the television-dominated 1980s. The number of western movies has also declined. One reason for the decline in Grey readership is the discontinuance of the W. J. Black program in 1983. The cost of printing rose to the point that Black would have to charge $9.95 for each hardcover copy in the Zane Grey series, making it impossible to compete with the paperback market and to keep a steady supply of Grey's novels stocked in the nation's libraries. Nonetheless, the Black program sold some twelve million Zane Grey hardcovers while it existed, "no mean feat in itself."[22]

Who reads Zane Grey? "People over forty," is the usual answer to that question—people who can remember the United States in a somewhat rural setting in the immediate post–World War II era and yearn for some good "old-timey" western movies to be made again. As one writer put it, "One good remake of a Zane Grey movie would do wonders to bring in readers."[23]

It is not just that people are not reading Zane Grey today as much as they used to: many people—at least according to widespread opinion—are either not reading westerns or not reading *period*. Young people today, as the perception goes, are more interested in science fiction than westerns.

Nonetheless, "every bookstore carries Zane Grey new paperbacks. Someone is buying them. Zane Grey hard covers rapidly disappear from used book stores."[24] Grey fits well into the nostalgia moods that Americans experience from time to time. It seems clear that millions of Americans *do* look for sentimental, romantic quality in their reading matter, along with a yearning for simpler times and escapist values.[25] These people are prime candidates for a Zane Grey readership.

At least one English teacher has braved the storm of "sub-literary" ridicule offered by the more staid members of her profession and has begun to put Zane Grey on her reading list. Lisa Brown of Baxter, Tennessee, "sparked something . . . because undercover [Grey] fans were everywhere."[26] One was a happy father, "delighted that, in an age of computer chips and rock videos, here was something he could share with his son and do it in the name of education."[27]

The titles that Brown's students liked most were *Wanderer of the Wasteland* and its sequel, *Stairs of Sand*. Other "hits" were *Riders of the Purple Sage*, *The Light of Western Stars*, *Nevada*, and *Robber's Roost*. The Zane Grey project in Brown's class was quite successful: out of seventy students, only four continued to show a distinct dislike for Zane Grey. Brown thought it significant that those four "went mad" about Kurt

Vonnegut. Brown's "Zane Grey excursion" taught her that Grey is not an "intrusion in an American literature class," but that to some extent, "he belongs there."[28] She, along with many other Zane Grey fans, argues that once a student is introduced to Grey, he very quickly becomes an "addict."

In addition to slowly adding Grey to the syllabi of some English courses throughout the country, there also seems to be a growth of interest in Grey as evidenced by the number of reviews, magazines, fan clubs, and books about him in the past fifteen years. G. M. Farley of Hagerstown, Maryland, has been instrumental in creating and distributing news and articles, and in getting the Zane Grey Society together for annual meetings.

Interestingly enough, many of the most ardent Zane Grey fans today are fundamentalist ministers. Yet Grey was a confirmed evolutionist, quite familiar, and in general agreement with, the works of Charles Darwin. In some of the *Zane Grey Reviews,* and various books, these Grey followers say that toward the end of his life Grey began to back away from evolution and to express sentiments of creationism. These articles and reviews, however, cite no evidence for their claims and thus must be taken as wishful thinking rather than sound research. It is one thing to be a zealous follower of the works of Zane Grey; it is another to make something of him that he was not.

Grey's definition of God and his theology always remained an amalgam of Christianity and pantheism. To him it was plain common sense to talk about "natural selection" in the universe and "survival of the fittest." He never denied the existence of God, but in *Man of the Forest* and other books he argued persuasively that God comes in many forms and inscrutable ways and that He is not at all easily explained. Certainly, Grey abhorred religious fanaticism as he indicated with book after book on Mormonism as an institution and his continuing attacks against malevolent missionaries. He regarded the sea, desert, and mountain as the essence of God and nature.

In addition to latter-day followers trying to figure out his theology, there have been a few, rather amateurish, efforts at psychoanalyzing him. (It is true that a full-scale psychological biography or novel about Zane Grey is long overdue.)

In the mistitled *Undiscovered Zane Grey Fishing Stories,* George Reiger writes in effect in his preface that Grey was a social climber. He wanted to be known as three years younger than he actually was, so he could have the reputation of being Owen Wister's junior when each became prominent for their western novels. Grey, according to Reiger, also wanted to be the friend of presidents, and the highlight of his career supposedly came when he dined once with President Herbert Hoover, himself an avid fisherman.

Elsewhere in the same preface, Reiger describes Grey as "aloof and a loner." Again, as with the fundamentalist ministers, one cannot have Grey both ways. Either he was a social climber, caterwauling to all manners of people, or he was a loner, generally going about his business in his own way. It is true that Grey was a complicated person, with a mixture of respect and disdain for other human beings. He certainly wrote for the common man; he rarely thought in terms of the "upper crust" when he penned his stories. It would be ironic, to say the least, to find out that Zane Grey, the great literary commoner of our time, actually had his heart set on getting into the social registers. Generally, in his books, he had nothing but scorn for social climbers.

Perhaps a thing that motivated Grey was that by his own standards, he could never receive any peace, contentment, or satisfaction with the things he did. He was both elated and depressed every time he finished a manuscript. He was glad to be done with it so he could go on to other things, but after being with a manuscript for weeks or months, suddenly it was no longer there, and it was like losing a good friend. One does not have to be a writer or a psychologist to understand this phenomenon.

There is probably a difference between perfectionism and the inability to be satisfied. Grey was not a perfectionist; if he had been he would not have put forward any of his manuscripts for publication. He constantly talked of how he tried to improve his technique. Thus, he must have felt that with the passage of time he was getting better, and this pleased him. But the passage of time also reduced the opportunities for the greatness of writing he strove for, and this depressed him. The valleys and peaks of his life gave him such an intensity with his own preoccupations that people could conclude that he was either a snob not wanting the company of "ordinary" people, or that he was a writer and advocate of the "man on the street." Neither extreme is correct about Zane Grey. He was almost always in the middle in reference to blue blood and common, ordinary citizens.

Since 1973 there have been twenty-five new publications of Zane Grey works, either as he wrote them originally, as with *The Maverick*

Queen, The Vanishing American, and *30,000 on the Hoof,* or completely new, as with *The Tenderfoot, The Westerner,* and *Rustlers of Pecos County,* or included in anthologies, as with "The Ice Cream Kid," "Fargo Jones," and "On Location." In addition to these newly published writings by the author, works about him have proliferated.

Since 1973 about a dozen books, portions of books, booklets, and dissertations dealing with the works of Zane Grey have been published. Significantly, most of these latter-day Grey authors are academics; perhaps this scholarly interest in Grey is an example of "culture lag" in reverse. Instead of the general public absorbing ideas more slowly than they occur, here is a case of academia finally hitting on a thought that the general public has known for years: Zane Grey is worthy of their time and attention. Ironically, academic interest in Zane Grey has grown in direct proportion to the lessening of sales of his books.

What then can one make of Zane Grey in the closing years of the twentieth century? First, his books are still immensely popular throughout the world, as seen by sales and library borrowings. The overall sales of his books in the world are approaching one hundred million; his works have been translated into twenty languages, including Russian and Hebrew, and about 130 movies have been made of his westerns.[29]

Second, it seems clear that Zane Grey was "one of a kind"; he was a primitive genius to literature in the way Grandma Moses was to art and George Gershwin to music. As his son Loren says, "He created something totally unique and our understanding and love for the spirit of the American West would never have been the same without him."[30]

Interest in Zane Grey today goes beyond his literary productions. Scholars are showing an increased concern with his personal life as they try to figure out Grey's psychology and theology, and the inconsistencies between what he wrote about and his own private activities. His writings were usually of a high moralistic tone, yet in real life the rumors persisted that Grey had numerous amorous affairs. There seems to be a humanizing effort of Grey today, a search for the wholeness of the man. (Even the remake of the movie *The Jazz Singer* has Neil Diamond singing in a theater called the "Zaney Grey.") When the man himself becomes known, then his writings will possibly acquire the academic respectability they deserve.

Finally, Zane Grey today is a refuge from the computer–television–traffic jam–supermarket world with which most Americans have to contend. Grey can take us back to a time about which we can easily be nostalgic. Most important, though, he can give us pleasure, and make us feel good about things. Those characteristics of nostalgic pleasure and a profound sense of déjà vu are not to be taken lightly in the contemporary world.

Notes and References

Chapter One

1. This poem was found in a small collection of Zane Grey papers that for years were displayed in a Zanesville, Ohio, bank under the direction of Norris Schneider. The papers, along with this poem, are now on exhibit at the Zane Grey Museum, near Zanesville.

2. Charles McKnight, *Our Western Border* (Cincinnati: J. C. McCurdy, 1876). Grey's favorite character in this book was "Captain Jack of the Juniata." Even a cursory glance at the book shows its great influence on Grey in writing the Ohio River trilogy.

3. From "The Living Past," an unpublished autobiography that tells the story of Grey's life through college days. All quotations in this chapter not otherwise indicated are from *"The Living Past,"* Grey Collection, Zane Grey, Inc.

4. *Betty Zane* (1903; New York: Grosset & Dunlap, 1915), 291.

5. Frank Gruber, author of the official biography of Grey, said that the patient was none other than Dolly, Grey's future wife (*Zane Grey* [Cleveland: World Publishers, 1970]).

6. Daniel Murphy writing to Grey, 27 December 1907, Grey Collection, University of Texas.

7. R. R. Brown writing to Charles Francis Press, 1 February 1904, Grey Collection, University of Texas.

8. Fannie Burns writing to L. M. Gray, 20 January 1904, Grey Collection, University of Texas.

9. C. M. L. Wiseman writing to Grey, 1 February 1904, Grey Collection, University of Texas.

10. *Spirit of the Border* (1906; New York: Grosset & Dunlap, n.d.), 95; further page references cited in the text.

11. Eugene H. Roseboom and Francis P. Weisenberger, *A History of Ohio* (Columbus: Ohio State University Press, 1953), 40–41, discuss this and other frontier events.

12. Eleanor Early, "He Made the West Famous," *True West* 16 (April 1969):20. See also Norris Schneider, *Zane Grey, "The Man Whose Books Made the West Famous"* (Zanesville, Ohio: self-published, 1967), and *Zane Grey, The Man and His Work* (a compilation) (New York: Harper & Brothers, 1928).

13. *The Last Trail* (1906; New York: Triangle Books, 1938), 194.

14. Zane Grey's diary, 1 October 1905, Grey Collection, Zane Grey, Inc.

Chapter Two

1. For additional information on the "cattalo," see Lowell H. Harrison, "The Incredible Cattalo," *American History Illustrated* 2 (January 1968), 32–35. One of Jones's rivals in producing "cattalo" was Charles Goodnight, a rancher in the Texas Panhandle. Goodnight accused Jones of breeding the "cattalo" on paper but not on the ground. Goodnight said of Jones: "Jones has been quite a hunter, and has been over a great deal of the Northwest. In that country they have great wind storms, known as 'chinook' winds. They are warm and harmless, but the Colonel seems to have got in one of those storms and imbibed [*sic*] immense quantities of hot air. It has been escaping from him ever since—mostly from the wrong end." J. Evetts Haley, *Charles Goodnight, Cowman and Plainsman* (Norman: University of Oklahoma Press, 1949), 453.

2. Robert Easton and MacKenzie Brown, *Lord of Beasts, The Life of Buffalo Jones* (London: 1964), 146–47.

3. Zane Grey, *The Last of the Plainsmen* (New York: Outing Publishing Company, 1908), 18.

4. "My Own Life," cited in Zane Grey, *Zane Grey, The Man and His Work* (New York: Harper & Brothers, 1928), 4.

5. Ibid., 4.

6. Ibid., 5.

7. Grey writing to Daniel Murphy, undated, Markham Collection, Wagner College.

8. *History of Finney County, Kansas* (Garden City, Kansas: Finney County Historical Society, 1950), 1, 114.

9. "The Man Who Influenced Me Most," *American Magazine* (August 1929), 52–55, 130–36.

10. Ibid., 53.

11. Ibid., 54.

12. Ibid., 136.

13. The prototype for August Naab was Jim Emett, the man who most influenced Grey on Grey's western trip. Emett's oldest son, who had no use for either Jones or Grey, was named Snap.

14. Silvermane actually existed. Grey, along with Jones and Jim Emett, tried several times to capture the animal. "The Man Who Influenced Me Most" (136) tells the difference between Jones and Emett in reference to wild animals. Jones mastered them through making them fear him; Emett, through making them love him. Grey preferred Emett's method to that of Jones.

15. *Heritage of the Desert* (New York: Grosset & Dunlap, 1940), 183.

16. Grey writing to Daniel Beard, 6 June 1910, Beard Collection, Library of Congress.

17. "My Own Life," 18.

18. "What the Desert Means to Me," *American Magazine* 98 (November 1927), 7.

19. Zane Grey's diary, 19 January 1919, 29 May 1919, Grey Collection, Zane Grey, Inc. Unless otherwise noted, further citations of Grey's letters and diaries are from material at Zane Grey, Inc.

20. *Wanderer of the Wasteland* (New York: Harper, 1923), 143; further page references cited in the text.

21. The transition from manuscript to printed page caused Grey some anguish. Harper's wanted him to shorten *Wanderer of the Wasteland* by three thousand words. Grey ultimately complied with the request, but not before expressing a rather strong opinion. He asked Harper's: "What do you suppose Conrad would say to such proposition, or Tarkington?" He reminded the publishers that they rejected his first five efforts, all of which were ultimate successes. Grey writing to Dolly Grey, 6 July 1922; Zane Grey's diary, 22 October 1923.

22. Burton Rascoe, Review of *Wanderer of the Wasteland, New York Tribune,* 21 January 1923, 19. Also "New York's Awe at the Best Seller," *Literary Digest* 76 (10 March 1923), 30–31.

23. T. K. Whipple, "American Sagas," *Zane Grey, The Man and His Works,* 25.

24. *Stairs of Sand* (New York: Grosset & Dunlap, 1928), 253.

25. Loren Baritz, *City on a Hill* (New York: Wiley, 1964), 261–66.

26. Discussions of this fascinating tribe of Indians are in Henry Bamford Parkes, *A History of Mexico,* 3d ed. (Boston: Houghton Mifflin, 1966), 79, 296. See also Howard F. Cline, *Mexico, Revolution to Evolution, 1940–1960* (New York: Oxford University Press, 1963), 73, and Charles G. Cumberland, *Mexico, the Struggle for Modernity* (New York: Oxford University Press, 1968), 200.

27. *Desert Gold* (New York: Grosset & Dunlap, 1915), 273.

28. Grey writing to Murphy, 21 July 1912, Markham Collection, Wagner College.

29. *Majesty's Rancho* (New York: Grosset & Dunlap, 1938), 109.

30. *The Call of the Canyon* (New York: Grosset & Dunlap, 1924), 234; further page references cited in the text.

31. L. H. Robbins, Review of *The Call of the Canyon,* cited in *Zane Grey, the Man and His Works,* 52.

32. Ibid., 54.

33. This book was first called *The Shores of Lethe,* various versions of which were written well before American involvement in World War I. On 29 November 1921 Grey wrote in his diary that he wanted the book to embody everything that was wrong with modern times. Later he changed the title to *Return of the Beast,* and still later to *The Day of the Beast.* He rewrote the book at least five times. When it was finally published, Dolly wrote to Grey, 27 June 1922: "You cannot expect 'Day of the Beast' to be liked . . .

It will hurt you with some of your readers & you will get a lot of protestations. But they'll swing back to you again. This book shows versatility at least."
    34. "Writer of the Range," *MD* 13 (February 1969), 202.
    35. *The Man and His Works*, 6.

Chapter Three

    1. Grey writing to Daniel Murphy, June 2, no year, Markham Collection, Wagner College.
    2. *Riders of the Purple Sage* (New York: Grosset & Dunlap, 1912), 132; further page references cited in the text.
    3. "Popular Novels and Short Stories," *Review of Reviews* (June 1912), 762.
    4. Review of *Riders of the Purple Sage, Nation* 94 (15 February 1912), 161.
    5. "A God [*sic*] Novel," *New York Times* 17:82 (18 February 1912).
    6. Romer Grey (Zane's brother) writing to Grey, 12 March 1913.
    7. "More to Come," *New Yorker* (19 July 1950), 17–18.
    8. Grey visited the area in 1913 and said of it: "Sound, movement, life seemed to have no fitness here. Ruin was there and desolation and decay. The meaning of the ages was flung at me. A man became nothing." Grey, "Nonnezoshe, The Rainbow Bridge," *Recreation* 2:52 (New Series, February 1915), 63–67. Joe Lee, a Mormon cowboy, helped John Wetherill guide Grey to the area. Lee was a character (Lake) in *The Rainbow Trail* and died during the influenza epidemic of 1918. Grey lamented his passing: "He was a fine bighearted Mormon cowboy and one whom I had great admiration for. I can see the lonely cabin on the bleak desert where he must have fought this Spanish influenza, as he fought everything, like a man. He was alone. He did not give up until overpowered by death. Alas! the sadness, the tragedy of it . . . I hear the coyotes, the mournful wind sweeping the sand, the silence of the waste places! Another of my men of the open, gone to the great unknown." Zane Grey's diary, 17 December 1918.
    9. Dolly Grey writing to Grey, 18 August 1915.
    10. (New York: Modern Library, 1900), 508.
    11. *Man of the Forest* (New York: Grosset & Dunlap, 1948), 126.
    12. *Under the Tonto Rim* (New York: Grosset & Dunlap, 1954), 80.
    13. Several critics faulted Grey for using unreal dialect in his novels. The only unreal thing, however, about *Under the Tonto Rim* is that the usual western drawl is missing. Why he chose to employ "straight language" in this novel is unknown. Some typical quaint sayings of the West that Grey used in other novels were to show anger: "Don't that make you so mad you want to spit all over yourself?"; to show intelligence: "He must of swallowed a dictionary onct"; to denote a hopeless situation: "It's Katy-bar-the-door"; to express amazement: "By the great Horn-Spoon"; to show darkness: "It's darkern' the milltail of Hades"; and to show hospitality to horse-riding visitors:

"Get down and come in." Critics who insisted that these and similar expressions used by Grey were unreal merely proved their lack of familiarity with the western regions.

14. Henry Hoyns writing to Grey, 12 December 1925.

15. *The Deer Stalker* (New York: Grosset & Dunlap, 1953), 16.

16. *Stranger from the Tonto* (New York: Grosset & Dunlap, 1956), 213.

17. Zane Grey's diary, 20 December 1911.

18. A typed copy of this play is in the Grey Collection, Library of Congress.

19. Grey writing to Dolly Grey, undated.

20. Grey wrote a mountain novel, set in the Tonto, about another "discovery"—the production of "white mule," or illegal whiskey. He wrote much of the novel in 1926 while on an expedition to New Zealand and the South Seas. The book concerned the "Lilly-Hathaway feud" over sorghum rustling and "rights" to the output of "white mule." The work's title was changed and published in 1958 as *Arizona Clan*.

21. Grey writing to Robert Hobart Davis, 6 March 1915, Davis Papers, New York Public Library.

22. *The Border Legion* (New York: Grosset & Dunlap, 1944), 242.

23. *Thunder Mountain* (1935; Boston: G. K. Hall, 1982), 145; further page references cited in text.

24. *30,000 on the Hoof* (New York: Grosset & Dunlap, 1940), 254–55; further page references cited in the text.

25. Grey writing to Romer Grey (Zane's son), 18 March 1937. Grey Collection, Zane Grey, Inc.

26. Dolly Grey writing to Grey, 2 June 1937. Grey Collection, Zane Grey, Inc.

27. Grey writing to Henry Hoyns, 2 October 1939, Grey Collection, Harper's.

28. Grey mentions Jones in *Tales of Lonely Trails* (New York: Harper, 1922), 240–41.

29. *The Shepherd of Guadaloupe* (New York: Grosset & Dunlap, 1930), 91; further page references cited in the text.

30. Ruby Johnson writing to Grey, undated.

31. Edith Berry writing to Grey, undated.

32. Zane Grey's diary, 11 January 1920.

Chapter Four

1. Grey's handwritten tribute, not only to Doyle, but to Ripley Hitchcock (to whom he dedicated *The U.P. Trail*), is in the Grey Collection, Library of Congress.

2. In a historical novel, the events are the major consideration. The characters are guided by these events and are therefore subordinate to them.

3. Outline of *The U.P. Trail,* Grey Collection, Library of Congress.

4. Slingerland typifies all those who hated the "shining steel band of progress connecting East and West." In this respect, he agrees with Nathaniel Hawthorne, who wrote in 1844: "There is the whistle of the locomotive— . . . No wonder that it gives such a startling shriek, since it brings the noisy world into the midst of our slumbrous peace." See Leo Marx, *The Machine in the Garden* (New York: Oxford University Press, 1967), 13–14.

5. *The U.P. Trail* (New York: Grosset & Dunlap, 1946), 106.

6. Zane Grey's diary, 15 February 1918.

7. Grey writing to Ripley Hitchcock, 20 February 1918.

8. Grey writing to Anna Andre, 16 February 1918.

9. Zane Grey's diary, 3 April 1917.

10. Zane Grey's diary, 29 December 1918.

11. The original manuscript of *The Desert of Wheat* is in the Grey Collection, Library of Congress.

12. *The Desert of Wheat* (New York: Grosset & Dunlap, 1947), 323; further page references cited in the text.

13. Original manuscript, *The Desert of Wheat*, Library of Congress.

14. Theodore Brooke, Review of *The Desert of Wheat*, *Harper's Magazine* (February 1919), 825.

15. Zane Grey's diary, 23 November 1921.

16. Dolly Grey writing to Grey, 17 March 1920.

17. Jean Karr, *Zane Grey, Man of the West: A Biography* (New York: Grosset & Dunlap, 1949), 204.

18. Grey writing to Dolly Grey, 27 February 1924.

19. This feud was the basis for Dane Coolidge's *The Men Killers*. Coolidge was a frequent critic of Grey, saying that the West he created was not realistic. For additional information on the Graham-Tewksbury feud, see Joe B. Frantz and Julian E. Choate, Jr., *The American Cowboy* (Norman: University of Oklahoma Press, 1955), 111–14.

20. *To the Last Man* (New York: Grosset & Dunlap, 1950), 230; further page references cited in the text.

21. Theodore Brooke, Review of *To the Last Man*, "The Bookshelf," *Harper's Magazine* (February 1922).

22. *The Thundering Herd* (New York: Grosset & Dunlap, 1953), 373.

23. Zane Grey's diary, 4–5 June 1923.

24. Zane Grey, undated note to *Boy's Magazine*, Zane Grey, Inc.

25. Grey writing to Dolly Grey, 8 July 1923.

26. William H. Briggs writing to Zane Grey, 16 May 1925.

27. Grey did research for his book on a Navajo reservation. There is no Nopah tribe of Indians.

28. *The Vanishing American* (New York: Grosset & Dunlap, 1953), 150; further page references cited in the text.

29. Zane Grey's diary, 24 June 1922.

30. Burton W. Carrie writing to William H. Briggs, 22 August 1923, Zane Grey, Inc.

31. Grey writing to Dolly Grey, 21 June 1924.

32. Grey writing to Dolly Grey, 16 March 1924.

33. Grey writing to Dolly Grey, 17 August 1924.

34. Grey writing to William H. Briggs, 23 May 1924.

35. Ibid.

36. Grey writing to Lucien Hubbard, 31 July 1924.

37. *Western Union* (New York: Grosset & Dunlap, 1941), 7–8; further page references cited in the text.

38. It is 726 feet high, 660 feet long at the base, and 1,224 feet long at the top. It created Lake Mead, the largest artificial body of water in the world.

39. Grey writing to Romer Grey, 20 July 1934.

40. *Boulder Dam* (New York: Grosset & Dunlap, 1964), 177.

41. Much of the plot for *Boulder Dam* was inspired by the existence of the white-slave traffic in and around Las Vegas while the dam was being constructed. The leading female character, Anne Vandergrift, reads an advertisement for a job in a Los Angeles newspaper, goes to Las Vegas, and is threatened by a white-slave operation. At the time Grey wrote *Boulder Dam,* he was intently reading Albert Londres, *The Road to Buenos Ayres* (1928), which dealt with white-slave traffic. Romer Grey writing to Evan Thomas, 27 June 1962, Grey Collection, Harper's.

Chapter Five

1. Grey writing to Dolly Grey, 13 February 1917.

2. Clayton Hamilton, *Manual of Fiction* (Garden City: Doubleday, 1924), 3–20.

3. Grey writing to Dolly Grey, 19 March 1922.

4. Grey writing to Dolly Grey, 7 August 1922.

5. Another story, "Lightning," could be put into this category. Lightning did not possess fidelity to man, as Jenet and Wildfire did. "Lightning" is discussed in chapter 9.

6. *Nevada* (New York: Harper, 1928), 362.

7. Grey's first year of being on the best-selling lists was 1915, with *The Lone Star Ranger.* The last time was 1924, with *The Call of the Canyon.* His nine books on the list put him on a par with Booth Tarkington. Only Mary Robert Rinehart, with eleven best sellers, and Sinclair Lewis, with ten, exceeded Grey. See Alice Payne Hackett, *70 Years of Best-Sellers, 1895–1965* (New York: Bowker, 1967), 7.

8. Grey writing to Henry Hoyns, 8 November 1927.

9. Grey writing to Dolly Grey, 19 August 1929.

10. *The Zane Grey Collector*, 2:2:9; Hackett 87, gives the number sold at 2,087,837.

11. Grey writing to Dolly Grey, 29 January 1924.

12. *Wild Horse Mesa* (New York: Grosset & Dunlap, 1952), 29.

13. *Valley of Wild Horses* (New York: Pocket Books, 1959), 123.

14. *The Last of the Plainsmen*, 137.

15. In 1930 Arizona passed a law regulating the hunting of wild animals. Because Grey believed that his novels had done more than anything else to make Arizona a popular tourist state, he felt that he should be exempt from the new hunting law. When the state government refused to make an exception of Grey, he left the state and never returned. He continued to write stories and novels, however, with Arizona settings. See Candace Kant, *Zane Grey's Arizona* (Flagstaff: Northland Press, 1986), for additional possible reasons why Grey never went back to his favorite state.

16. *Horse Heaven Hill* (Black, 1959), 63.

17. Grey originally set *Horse Heaven Hill* in the 1920s. The book was not published until 1959, however, twenty years after Grey died. To maintain the "Zane Grey image," the time was set back by the publishers to the 1880s and 90s weakening the book in comparison with most of the other Grey works. Besides, Grey set many of his most successful novels in the 1920s: *The Call of the Canyon*, *The Shepherd of Guadaloupe*, and *The Desert of Wheat*, to name three. These certainly did not hurt his image.

18. Grey writing to Romer Grey, 2 April 1937.

19. As early as 1904, Grey took Dolly's advice and started carrying a notebook around with him—in the manner of Robert Louis Stevenson, whom Grey greatly admired—in which to record his thoughts. Dolly told Grey to "take the commonest objects and write one or two little themes every day. They needn't be more than a few words, but make everyone of those few words count for a great deal. Learn to say just what you mean in the most concise way possible." Dolly Grey writing to Grey, 8 June 1904.

20. J. A. Wiborn, "Tribute to Grey," [1924?], Grey Collection, Zane Grey, Inc.

21. Zane Grey's diary, 23 November 1920.

Chapter 6

1. John D. Hicks, *A Short History of American Democracy* (Boston: Houghton Mifflin, 1946), 506.

2. *Knights of the Range* (New York: Grosset & Dunlap, 1936), 244; further page references cited in the text.

3. William Chenery writing to Dolly Grey, 22 December 1932.

4. Harry Burton writing to Dolly Grey, 6 March 1933.

5. At first, Brazos Keene was called "Pecos Smith," but the name was changed in deference to another of Grey's novels, *West of the Pecos.*

6. Grey writing to Henry Hoyns, 2 October 1939, Grey Collection, Harper's.

7. Dolly Grey writing to Grey, 30 June 1933.

8. Dolly Grey writing to Grey, 13 March 1933.

9. The original manuscript of *Raiders of Spanish Peaks* is in the Grey Collection, Library of Congress.

10. *Raiders of Spanish Peaks* (New York: Grosset & Dunlap, 1938), 59.

11. *Arizona Ames* (New York: Grosset & Dunlap, 1933); further page references cited in the text.

12. Philip Durham and Everett L. Jones, *The Negro Cowboys* (New York: Dodd, Mead & Co., 1965), 1.

13. *West of the Pecos* (New York: Grosset & Dunlap, 1937), 97.

14. Perhaps the lack of unity was indicated by all the absentminded drawings and "doodles" on the back of several pages of the manuscript of *West of the Pecos.* The original copy is in the Grey Collection, Library of Congress.

15. *The Maverick Queen* (New York: Grosset & Dunlap, 1950), 4; further page references cited in the text.

16. Many reviews of Grey's books were ludicrous in that the reviewers adopted a high-blown "western" jargon that was misleading. *The Maverick Queen* was reviewed by *Time* on 19 June 1950. The review took a minor incident (the shoot-out between Lincoln Bradway and "Gun Haskel") and treated it as the major event. The review also implied that "Gun Haskel" was the leading character in the novel.

17. Grey writing to Dolly Grey, 27 September 1928.

18. Still another novel about the operation of a ranch was *The Dude Ranger,* serialized by *McCall's* in 1930. It was, of course, about an Easterner taking over a ranch and rather hurriedly "learning the ropes."

19. Dolly Grey writing to Grey 17 June 1936.

20. Doing so, however, turned attention away from the South, rendered economically prostrate by the Civil War. With investors preferring cattle to cotton, the postwar reclamation of the South was hindered. See William A. Harris, *Presidential Reconstruction in Mississippi* (Baton Rouge, Louisiana: State University Press, 1967), 162.

21. *The Trail Driver* (New York: Grosset & Dunlap, 1936), 300; further page references cited in the text.

22. *The Lone Star Ranger* (New York: Grosset & Dunlap, 1943), 55, 99; further page references cited in the text.

23. This book was one of Grey's more successful creations. Through 1951, its domestic sales came to 835,750 copies.

24. *Shadow on the Trail* (New York: Grosset & Dunlap, 1946), i.

25. Another Grey manuscript, *The Fugitive Trail,* not published until

1957, deals with the Cain-Abel thesis in which a man takes the blame for his brother's crime and eludes Texas Rangers for several years. The plot is very thin, and the characters are wooden. The book caused one English reader to inquire if it had been ghosted; it had been meticulously edited.

26. "My Answer to the Critics," no date, Zane Grey, Inc.

27. The original manuscript of *Fighting Caravans* is in the Grey Collection, Library of Congress.

28. *The Lost Wagon Train* (New York: Grosset & Dunlap, 1936), 374.

29. William Chenery writing to Dolly Grey, 2 July 1931.

30. The Yaquis are discussed in Grey's novel, *Desert Gold.* See pp. 443–45.

31. Grey wrote another, less popular, book about western cowboys in modern settings. *Wyoming* was first called *The Young Runaway* and was serialized in 1932 in *Pictorial Review.* Its theme is the familiar one of an Easterner finding happiness in the West.

32. Dolly Grey writing to Grey, 12 February 1923.

33. John E. Pickett writing to Grey, 27 February 1923.

Chapter Seven

1. Grey writing to Dolly Grey, 22 October 1922.

2. 16:2:217–24.

3. Other short stories of Grey's not discussed in the text included "From Missouri," "Tigre," "The Horse Thief" (first called "The Outlaws of Palouse"), "The Rubber Hunter," and "Strange Partners of Twofold Bay." The last story was printed first in 1955 by *The American Weekly.* Another story, "The Adventures of Finspot" (San Bernadino, Calif.: D. J. Books, 1974), for children, is about a small fish who learns the lessons of survival among predatory fishes. The importance of parental supervision of children is an undercurrent of this story.

4. See chapter 9 for a continuation of this practice in the latter-day works of Zane Grey.

5. "Monty Price's Nightingale" was published by *Popular Magazine,* (7 May 1915), 111–19.

6. The typewritten manuscript of "Amber's Mirage" is in the Grey Collection, Library of Congress.

7. The typewritten manuscript of this play is in the Grey Collection, Library of Congress.

8. The typewritten manuscript of this play is in the Grey Collection, Library of Congress.

9. Zane Grey's diary, 5 June, no year.

10. Later, Grey owned other, more sophisticated fishing boats. One was the *Gladiator.* In 1943, the ship *Zane Grey* was christened.

11. Review of *Tales of Fishes, Boston Transcript,* 3 September 1919, 8.

12. Review of *Tales of Fishes, New York Times,* 26 October 1919.

13. Theodore Brooke, Review of *Tales of Fishes, Harper's Magazine,* 831 (August 1919).

14. R. H. Davis writing to Grey, 3 September 1919, Davis Collection.

15. Review of *Tales of Southern Rivers, Springfield Republican,* 23 November 1924, 5a.

16. *Tales of Fishing Virgin Seas* (New York: Grosset & Dunlap, 1925), 24–25; further page references cited in the text.

17. *Tales of the Angler's Eldorado* (London: Wilson & Horton, 1971), 4.

18. Zane Grey's diary, 1–5 January 1926.

19. Grey writing to Dolly Grey, 31 December 1925.

20. Grey writing to Dolly Grey, 19 January 1926.

21. R. H. Davis writing to Grey, 23 November 1926, Davis Collection.

22. Grey visited Australia for the last time in 1938. In planning for the trip, he was intensely excited: "I can get a lot of magnificent material, some of it for fiction, and particularly I can round out the motion picture that I want to use on my lecture trip. . . . I know that trip will be hard work, but I am simply crazy to do it. . . . I will get a tremendous kick out of appearing before these audiences and of autographing books in big stores." Grey writing to Hoyns, 10 October 1938, Grey Collection, Harper's.

23. One reader of Grey's fishing books was Ernest Hemingway, who once turned down an offer from Grey for a joint fishing extravaganza, believing, apparently, that Grey wanted to ride to fame on his reputation. Hemingway's biographer, Carlos Baker, calls this thought "the silliest of surmises." See Carlos Baker, *Ernest Hemingway, A Life Story* (New York: Scribners, 1969), 271.

In the first part of 1930 Grey fished for eighty-three days in Tahiti without a strike. On the eighty-fourth day he caught, with rod and reel, a giant Tahitian marlin that weighed 1,040 pounds. Although Grey tried desperately to get the creature ashore, the fish was ravaged by sharks. Some Grey fans today credit Grey's experience with inspiring Hemingway's *The Old Man and the Sea.* See Zane Grey, *Tales of Tahitian Waters* (1931), and *The Zane Grey Collector,* 3:1:12–13.

24. An instructive article on Grey's life as a sportsman is Robert H. Boyle's "The Man Who Lived Two Lives in One," in *Sports Illustrated* (April 1968), 70–82.

25. Dolly Grey writing to R. H. Davis, 23 August 1929, Davis Collection.

26. Grey writing to Dolly Grey, 16 March 1927.

27. Grey writing to Dolly Grey, 12 April 1927.

28. *Tales of Fresh Water Fishing* (New York: Harper, 1928), 152–53; further page references cited in the text.

29. *The Zane Grey Collector,* 3:1:3.

30. *Tales of Fresh Water Fishing,* 10.

31. Zane Grey, "Bonefish," *Field & Stream* (August 1918), 297–302,

32. See Zane Grey, "Avalon, The Beautiful," *Field and Stream* (May, 1918).

33. Ibid.

34. See *Sports Afield* (July 1933, January and August 1934, May and June 1935).

35. See *Sports Afield* (January 1962).

Chapter Eight

1. Margaret McOmie, "Zane Grey's House as Exquisite Natural Beauty," *Better Homes and Gardens* (March 1928), 28.

2. Ibid.

3. Zane Grey's diary, 1 October 1905.

4. Zane Grey's diary, 8 August 1910.

5. Zane Grey's diary, 20 May 1917.

6. Zane Grey's diary, 1 October 1905.

7. Ibid.

8. Ibid.

9. Ibid.

10. Ibid.

11. Ibid.

12. Ibid.

13. Grey writing to Daniel Murphy, undated, Markham Collection.

14. Grey writing to Murphy, undated, Markham Collection.

15. Zane Grey's diary, 30 April 1917.

16. Dolly Grey writing to Grey, 12 March 1920.

17. Zane Grey's diary, 23 April 1917.

18. See Charlotte Watkins Smith, *Carl Becker: On History and the Climate of Opinion* (Ithaca, N.Y.: Cornell University Press, 1955).

19. Zane Grey's diary, 7 April 1917.

20. Zane Grey's diary, 5 April 1917.

21. Thomas Wells writing to Grey, 23 April 1919.

22. Grey writing to Dolly Grey, 8 July 1918.

23. Grey writing to Dolly Grey, 14 February 1922.

24. Dolly Grey writing to Robert H. Davis, 4 January 1935, Davis Collection.

25. Dolly Grey writing to Davis, 4 January 1935, Davis Collection.

26. Robert H. Davis writing to Dolly Grey, 3 June 1935, Davis Collection.

27. Dolly Grey writing to Grey, 18 May 1922.

28. Grey writing to Dolly Grey, 27 November 1928.

29. Grey writing to Henry Hoyns, 2 October 1939, Grey Collection, Harper's.

30. William Clark writing to the author, 13 November 1969. See Wil-

liam Clark, "Faust and Grey: A Study," *The Zane Grey Collector,* 2:4:3. See also Robert Easton, *Max Brand: The Big Westerner* (Norman: University of Oklahoma Press, 1970).

31. He was, for example, the creator of the *Dr. Kildare* series.

32. There are several lists showing the movies that were made of Grey's works. The best seems to be that of G. M. Farley in *The Zane Grey Collector,* 4:4, with additions by Dale E. Case. Those novels that have been filmed at least four times include *Riders of the Purple Sage, The Light of Western Stars, The Lone Star Ranger,* and *The Mysterious Rider.* Filmed at least three times were *Heritage of the Desert, The Border Legion, Desert Gold, Nevada, The Last Trail, The Rainbow Trail, Sunset Pass, Under the Tonto Rim,* and *Wild Horse Mesa.* Jack Holt, Tim Holt, Randolph Scott, John Wayne, Robert Young, James Mason, Buster Crabbe, Dean Jagger, Scott Brady, Richard Arlen, Bebe Daniels, Lillian Leighton, Ann Sheridan, Wallace Beery, and Maureen O'Sullivan were a few of the many stars in movies made from Zane Grey's books. Well over a hundred movies were based on Grey's writings.

33. See G. M. Farley, "E.R.B. and Zane Grey," *The Zane Grey Collector,* 2:3:3.

34. See Ivan A. Conger, "James Oliver Curwood, Son of the Forest," *The Zane Grey Collector,* 3:1:7.

35. Zane Grey's diary, 24 January 1920.

36. Zane Grey's diary, 25 October 1917.

37. Zane Grey's diary, 11 October 1932.

38. Zane Grey's diary, June 1921.

39. Grey writing to Dolly Grey, 29 August 19??.

40. Zane Grey, "My Answer to the Critics," unpublished essay, Zane Grey, Inc.

41. Ibid.

42. Ibid.

43. Ibid.

44. Ibid.

45. Through 1951, *Riders of the Purple Sage* had domestic sales totaling 1,035,750; *The Light of Western Stars,* 995,600; and *Wildfire* 926,250.

46. Tom Curry, "Zane Grey," *The Zane Grey Collector,* 5:18:10.

47. Henry Hoyns writing to Dolly Grey, 18 November 1939, Grey Collection, Harper's.

48. Dolly Grey writing to Daniel Beard, 25 November 1939. Beard Papers, Library of Congress.

Chapter Nine

1. Loren Grey writing to the author, 26 February 1988.

2. Quoted in *The Vanishing American* (New York: Pocket Books, 1982), vii.

3. Ibid.

4. Loren Grey, *Zane Grey, A Photographic Odyssey* (Dallas: Taylor Publishing Co. 1985), vii.

5. *Amber's Mirage and Other Stories* (New York: Pocket Books, 1983), 171; further page references cited in the text.

6. Carol Gay, *Zane Grey, Story Teller* (Columbus: State Library of Ohio, 1979), 6.

7. Ann Ronald, *Zane Grey* (Boise, Idaho: Boise State University, 1975), 17.

8. *The Westerner* (New York: Belmont-Tower, 1977), 103; further page references cited in text.

9. Loren Grey writing to the author, 26 February 1988.

10. This is a somewhat disputed claim. Some critics argued that Grey turned out his literary accomplishments to afford his insatiable appetite for fishing.

11. Peter Benchley, author of *Jaws,* famous for his works on sharks in the 1970s, agreed with Grey that sharks do not need any particular provocation before attacking. Although Benchley is familiar with Zane Grey, he did not use any of Grey's books in his own research on sharks. Peter Benchley writing to the author, 17 February 1988.

12. *Shark: The Killer of the Deep* (New York: Belmont-Tower, 1976), 180; further page references cited in the text.

13. See chapter 7 for the controversy Grey got involved in for opposing three-pronged hooks.

14. Grey marveled over Australia's largest city: "There are few places in the world where big game fish can be caught within easy sight of one of the busiest shipping centers in the world. Sydney Harbor is one such place" (177).

15. *Tales from a Fisherman's Log* (London: Hodder & Stoughton, 1978), 11.

16. The last of Zane Grey's nonfiction stories of rivers and fish appeared in a volume edited by George Reiger, and titled *The Undiscovered Zane Grey Fishing Stories,* (Piscataway, N.J.: Winchester Press, 1983). Unfortunately, this book seems to be more an effort to "cash in" on Grey's name than to explicate any of his works. Only about half the volume actually concerns fishing stories, while the remainder is taken up with a lengthy preface and two long stories that have nothing to do with fishing. "Trails over the Glass Mountains" and the well-known "Monty Price's Nightingale" are good works, but it takes some imagination to call them "fishing stories."

17. Joseph Lawrence Wheeler, "Zane Grey's Impact on American Life and Letters: A Study in the Popular Novel," Ph.D. diss., George Peabody University, 1975, 91.

18. Ibid., 234.

19. Ibid., 235.

20. Loren Grey, Preface to *The Reef Girl* (New York: Harpers, 1977), viii.

21. Loren Grey writing to the author, 26 February 1988.

22. Ibid.

23. James H. Vickers writing to the author, 21 February 1988.

24. Ibid.

25. Ibid. Cena Richeson writing to the author, 29 January 1988.

26. Lisa Brown, "Zane Grey in the Classroom," *The Zane Grey Reporter,* 1:2 (1986), 11–12.

27. Ibid.

28. Ibid.

29. Charles G. Pfeiffer, "Cowboys, Indians, and God: The Theology of Zane Grey's Western Novels," unpublished essay.

30. Loren Grey writing to the author, 26 February 1988.

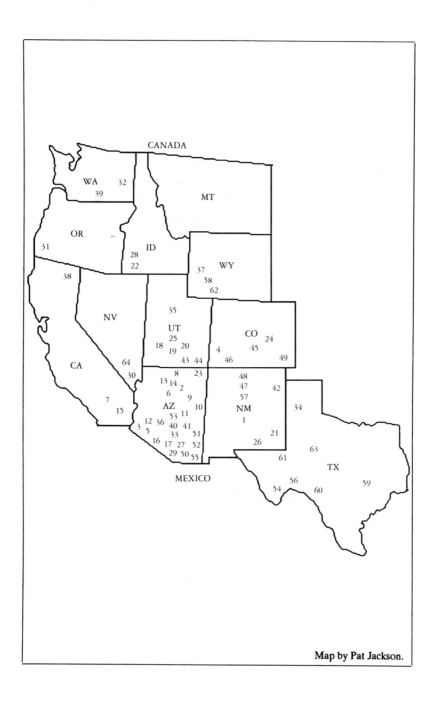

CANADA

WA   32
  39

MT

OR
31
        ID
      28
      22

38

      NV   35

              UT
              25
          18   19 20
                43 44   4
                              CO   24
                                   45
CA   64   46   49
        30   8   23
              13 14   48
              6   2   47   42
        7   9   57
        15   AZ   10   NM   34
                  53 11   1
          12 36 40 41
      3 5   33   51   21
        16 17 27 52   26
              29 50 55   61   63
                                              TX
      MEXICO   54   56
                            60   59

Map by Pat Jackson.

Selected Bibliography

An asterisk (*) in front of an entry indicates a publication since 1973. Numbers in the map correspond to numbers after some novels listed under Books in the Primary Works. They show the main setting of the novel.

PRIMARY WORKS

Books

*Amber's Mirage and Other Stories. New York: Pocket Books, 1983.
An American Angler in Australia. New York: Harper, 1937.
Arizona Ames. New York: Harper, 1932. (45, Arizona)
Arizona Clan. New York: Harper, 1932. (16, Arizona)
Betty Zane. New York: Charles Francis Press, 1903.
Black Mesa. New York: Harper, 1955. (1, New Mexico)
Blue Feather and Other Stories. New York: Harper, 1961. (46, Colorado)
The Border Legion. New York: Harper, 1916. (22, Idaho)
Boulder Dam. New York: Harper, 1963. (30, Nevada)
The Call of the Canyon. New York: Harper, 1924. (9, Arizona)
*The Camp Robber and Other Stories. Roslyn, N.Y.: Walter J. Black, 1979.
Captives of the Desert. New York: Harper, 1952. (2, Arizona)
The Code of the West. New York: Harper, 1934. (51, Arizona)
The Day of the Beast. New York: Harper, 1922.
The Deer Stalker. New York: Harper, 1949. (23, Arizona)
Desert Gold. New York: Harper, 1913. (3, Arizona)
The Desert of Wheat. New York: Harper, 1919. (32, Washington)
Don. New York: Harper, 1928.
The Drift Fence. New York: Harper, 1933. (52, Arizona)
The Dude Ranger. New York: Harper, 1951. (53, Arizona)
Fighting Caravans. New York: Harper, 1929. (47, New Mexico)
Forlorn River. New York: Harper, 1927. (38, California)
The Fugitive Trail. New York: Harper, 1957. (54, Texas)
The Hash Knife Outfit. New York: Harper, 1933. (55, Arizona)
The Heritage of the Desert. New York: Harper, 1910. (10, Arizona)

Horse Heaven Hill. New York: Harper, 1959. (39, Washington)
Ken Ward in the Jungle. New York: Harper, 1959.
Knights of the Range. New York: Harper, 1939. (48, New Mexico)
The Last of the Plainsmen. New York: Outing Publishers, 1908. (11, Arizona)
The Last Trail. New York: A. L. Burt, 1906.
The Light of Western Stars. New York: Harper, 1914. (12, Arizona)
The Lone Star Ranger. New York: Harper, 1915. (56, Texas)
Lost Pueblo. New York: Harper, 1954. (4, Colorado)
The Lost Wagon Train. New York: Harper, 1936. (57, New Mexico)
Majesty's Rancho. New York: Harper, 1942. (5, Arizona)
Man of the Forest. New York: Harper, 1920. (17, Arizona)
The Maverick Queen. New York: Harper, 1950. (58, Wyoming)
The Mysterious Rider. New York: Harper, 1921. (24, Colorado)
Nevada. New York: Harper, 1928. (40, Arizona)
Raiders of Spanish Peaks. New York: Harper, 1938. (49, Colorado)
The Rainbow Trail. New York: Harper, 1915. (25, Utah)
The Ranger and Other Stories. New York: Harper, 1961.
*The Ranger and Other Stories. New York: Pocket Books, 1985.
The Redheaded Outfield and Other Stories. New York: Harper, 1920.
*The Reef Girl. New York: Harper, 1977.
Riders of the Purple Sage. New York: Harper, 1912. (18, Utah)
Robber's Roost. New York: Harper, 1932. (19, Utah)
Rogue River Feud. New York: Harper, 1948. (31, Oregon)
Roping Lions in the Grand Canyon. New York: Harper, 1924. (6, Arizona)
*The Rustlers of Pecos County. Hornchurch, England: Ian Henry Publications, 1980. (63, Texas)
*The Secret of Quaking Asp Cabin. New York: Pocket Books, 1983.
Shadow on the Trail. New York: Harper, 1946. (50, Arizona)
*Shark: The Killer of the Deep. New York: Belmont-Tower Books, 1976.
The Shepherd of Guadaloupe. New York: Harper, 1930. (26, New Mexico)
The Short Stop. New York: Harper, 1909.
Spirit of the Border. New York: A. L. Burt Co., 1906.
Stairs of Sand. New York: Harper, 1943. (7, California)
Stranger from the Tonto. New York: Harper, 1950. (20, Utah)
Sunset Pass. New York: Harper, 1931. (21, New Mexico)
*Tales from a Fisherman's Log. London: Hodder & Stoughton, 1978.
Tales of Fishes. New York: Harper, 1919.
Tales of Fishing Virgin Seas. New York: Harper, 1925.
Tales of Fresh Water Fishing. New York: Harper, 1928.
Tales of Lonely Trails. New York: Harper, 1922. (8, Arizona)
Tales of Southern Rivers. New York: Harper, 1924.
Tales of Swordfish and Tuna. New York: Harper, 1927.
Tales of Tahitian Waters. New York: Harper, 1931.

Tales of the Angler's Eldorado. New York: Harper, 1926.
Tappan's Burro and Other Stories. New York: Harper, 1923. (41, Arizona)
30,000 on the Hoof. New York: Harper, 1940. (27, Arizona)
The Thundering Herd. New York: Harper, 1918. (34, Texas)
Thunder Mountain. New York: Harper, 1935. (28, Idaho)
To the Last Man. New York: Harper, 1922. (33, Arizona)
The Trail Driver. New York: Harper, 1936. (59, Texas)
Twin Sombreros. New York: Harper, 1941. (60, Texas)
Under the Tonto Rim. New York: Harper, 1926. (29, Arizona)
The U.P. Trail. New York: Harper, 1918. (35, Utah)
Valley of Wild Horses. New York: Harper, 1947. (42, New Mexico)
The Vanishing American. New York: Harper, 1925. (36, Arizona)
The Vanishing American. Foreword by Loren Grey. New York: Pocket Books, 1982.
Wanderer of the Wasteland. New York: Harper, 1923. (15, California)
The Westerner. Edited by Loren Grey. New York: Belmont-Tower Books, 1977. (64, Nevada)
Western Union. New York: Harper, 1939. (37, Wyoming)
West of the Pecos. New York: Harper, 1937. (61, Texas)
The Wilderness Trek. New York: Harper, 1944.
Wildfire. New York: Harper, 1917. (43, Utah)
Wild Horse Mesa. New York: Harper, 1928. (44, Utah)
The Wolf Tracker. New York: Harper, 1930.
The Wolf Tracker and Other Stories. New Introduction by Loren Grey. Santa Barbara, Calif.: Santa Barbara Press, 1984.
Wyoming. New York: Harper, 1953. (62, Wyoming)
The Young Forester. New York: Harper, 1910. (13, Arizona)
The Young Lion Hunter. New York: Harper, 1911. (14, Arizona)
The Young Pitcher. New York: Harper, 1911.
Zane Grey Omnibus. New York: Harper, 1943.
Zane Grey's Adventures in Fishing. Edited by Ed Zern. New York: Harper, 1952.
Zane Grey's Book of Camps and Trails. New York: Harper, 1931.

Manuscripts

Daniel Beard Collection, Library of Congress, Washington, D.C.
Robert Hobart Davis Collection, New York Public Library.
Zane Grey Collection, Harper & Row, New York.
Zane Grey Collection, Library of Congress, Washington, D.C.
Zane Grey Collection, University of Texas, Austin
Zane Grey Collection, Zane Grey, Inc., Woodland Hills, California.
Edwin Markham Collection, Wagner College, Staten Island, New York.

Articles in Periodicals

This is a highly selective list of articles, designed primarily to show the different categories of subjects in Grey's articles.

"Big Game Fishing in New Zealand Seas," *Science America* 129 (August 1928): 116–18.

"Breaking Through, The Story of My Own Life," *American Magazine* 98 (July 1924): 11–13.

"Down into the Desert," *Ladies' Home Journal* 41 (January 1924): 8–9.

"Record Fight with a Swordfish," *Country Life* 38 (August 1920): 33–37.

"The Man Who Influenced Me Most," *American Magazine* 102 (August 1926): 52–55.

"What The Desert Means to Me," *American Magazine* 98 (November 1924): 5–8.

SECONDARY WORKS

*Cawelti, John. *Adventure, Mystery, and Romance. Formula Stories as Art and Popular Culture*. Chicago: University of Chicago Press, 1976. Contains some useful discussions of western novels, but is incomplete in its bibliography for not stating that there were already several good books written on Zane Grey.

Durham, Philip, and Everett Jones. *The Negro Cowboys*. New York: Dodd, Mead & Co., 1965. Valuable for its insights into an often neglected phase of western history, a phase that Grey discussed more than most western novelists of his time.

Easton, Robert. *Max Brand, the Big Westerner*. Norman: University of Oklahoma Press, 1970. Excellent biography of Brand, one of Grey's contemporaries as a western novelist.

Easton, Robert, and MacKenzie Brown. *Lord of Beasts, The Life of Buffalo Jones*. Tucson: University of Arizona Press, 1961. Study of the highly interesting Buffalo Jones; several pages devoted to Zane Grey.

*Farley, G. M. *Zane Grey: A Documented Portrait*. Tuscaloosa, Ala.: Portals Press, 1986. Written by a man who has spent much of his life following Zane Grey's life and career; especially valuable for its complete listing of everything Grey ever wrote and of the movies that were made from his works.

*Gay, Carol. *Zane Grey: Story Teller*. Columbus: State Library of Ohio, 1979. This booklet is a part of the "Ohio Author" series; a largely superficial account of Grey's life as an author that primarily uses already-used sources; not a very significant treatise in reference to studies on Zane Grey.

Goble, Danny G. "Zane Grey's West: An Intellectual Reaction." Master's thesis, University of Oklahoma, 1969. Useful study of Grey's impact on American literature.

*Grey, Loren. *Zane Grey, A Photographic Odyssey.* Dallas: Taylor Publishing Co., 1985. Most notable for its marvelous photographs—some quite rare—of Zane Grey and his family. Loren, Zane's son, accompanied his father on many fishing trips, and writes knowingly and personally about his father in this well-done book.

Gruber, Frank. *Zane Grey.* Cleveland: World Publishers, 1970. An overwritten account of Grey's life that is somewhat better than Jean Karr's earlier biography because Gruber had access to materials that Karr did not; loosely organized and does not sufficiently heed the motives behind Grey's writings.

Haley, J. Evetts. *Charles Goodnight, Cowman, and Plainsman.* Norman: University of Oklahoma Press, 1936. A well-written, informative account of one of Buffalo Jones's competitors in the production of cattalo.

*Kant, Candace. *Zane Grey's Arizona.* Flagstaff, Ariz.: Northland Press, 1984. A well-reasoned book that gives various explanations why Zane Grey left Arizona, never to return; a valuable addition to Zane Grey studies.

Karr, Jean. *Zane Grey, Man of the West.* New York: Grosset & Dunlap, 1949. Poorly written book that discusses mostly the trips that Grey took but not very many of his books.

McKnight, Charles. *Our Western Border.* Cincinnati: J. C. McCurdy, 1876. Highly important to Grey in his early writing career; contains several hair-raising episodes of life along the early Virginia frontier. Grey said he knew this book by heart.

*Pfeiffer, Charles G. "Cowboys, Indians, and God: The Theology of Zane Grey's Western Novels." Unpublished essay. Professor Pfeiffer is undoubtedly the greatest authority in the United States on the geographical aspects of Zane Grey's novels. His treatise on Grey's novels' theology is thought-provoking.

*Reiger, Barbara, and George Reiger. *The Zane Grey Cookbook.* Englewood Cliffs, N.J.: Prentice-Hall, 1976. A compilation of recipes for the outdoors that may or may not have been favored by Zane Grey.

*Reiger, George, ed. *The Undiscovered Zane Grey Fishing Stories.* Piscataway, N.J.: Wincester Press, 1983. The stories in this book were not particularly "undiscovered"; the thrust of the book seems to be to capitalize on Zane Grey's name rather than tell his followers anything new about him.

*Ronald, Ann. *Zane Grey.* Boise, Idaho: Boise State University, 1975. This booklet on Grey is somewhat better than the one by Carol Gay, but it is still so cursory that it is of minimal value.

Schneider, Norris F. *Zane Grey, "The Man Whose Books Made the West Famous."* Zanesville, Ohio: By the author, 1967. Informative booklet about Grey by a man who spent many years studying Grey's career.

Scott, Kenneth W. "The Heritage of the Desert: Zane Grey Discovers the West." *Markham Review* 2 (February 1970): 10–15. Well-written article on the novel that was Grey's first major success.

*Wheeler, Joseph Lawrence. *Zane Grey's Impact on American Life and Letters: A Study in the Popular Novel.* Ph.D. dissertation, George Peabody College for Teachers, 1975. An extremely valuable source for any Zane Grey scholar; Professor Wheeler discusses Grey and his work from a literary and sociological vantage point.

Zane Grey, The Man and His Works. A compilation. New York: Harper & Brothers, 1928. A valuable collection of articles either by Grey or about him.

Index